Maturing Masculinities

Maturing Masculinities

AGING, CHRONIC ILLNESS, AND VIAGRA IN MEXICO

EMILY A. WENTZELL

Duke University Press   Durham and London   2013

Printed in the United States of America on acid-free paper ∞
Designed by Courtney Leigh Baker and typeset in Warnock Pro by
Westchester Publishing Services.

Library of Congress Cataloging-in-Publication Data.
Wentzell, Emily A., 1980–
Maturing masculinities : aging, chronic illness,
and Viagra in Mexico / Emily A. Wentzell.
pages cm
Includes bibliographical references and index.
ISBN 978-0-8223-5491-8 (cloth : alk. paper)
ISBN 978-0-8223-5506-9 (pbk. : alk. paper)
1. Masculinity—Mexico.   2. Machismo—Mexico.
3. Impotence—Mexico.   4. Sildenafil—Mexico.   I. Title.
BF692.5W46 2013
305.310972—dc23
2013010158

To My Parents,

LYNN PURITZ-FINE AND STEVE WENTZELL.

THANK YOU FOR YOUR UNFLAGGING LOVE AND SUPPORT.

Contents

Acknowledgments

If the urology patients at the Cuernavaca IMSS hospital had not been so generous in sharing their stories and trusting me to tell them, this book would not exist. I am profoundly grateful to them, as well as to the urology department doctors and staff for adopting me as part of their unit; supporting my research; and sharing their work, lives, and delicious breakfasts with me. Although they are identified pseudonymously here, I have no doubt that they will recognize the parts of this work that they made possible. I have many other people to thank for their support of my fieldwork for this book, including the private-practice physicians, pharmacists, and drug representatives who shared their time and experiences with me; and Ivonne Szasz for providing excellent advice and institutional affiliation at the Colegio de México.

I thank Jorge Salmerón Castro, the director of the IMSS Unidad de Investigación Epidemiológica y en Servicios de Salud (UIESS), for providing crucial access to the field site, aid with the hospital bureaucracy, office space, and unflagging support for my research. That Dr. Salmerón was willing to do all this for an unknown American speaking such a different disciplinary language is a testament to his generosity in supporting junior researchers and his immense kindness. I also thank the UIESS staff for their companionship and help. Some local friends are largely responsible for keeping me sane during fieldwork: I thank my wonderful roommates Dulce Palomo Rojas and Ricardo Mendoza Fragoso; my movie, spa, and health research partner Yvonne Flores Leonard; and my fellow anthropological sex researchers Eva Alcantara and Sarah Luna.

I am deeply indebted to many other people and institutions that made this research possible. This includes financial support from the Wenner-Gren Foundation, Fulbright IIE, and the American Association of University Women, as well as several University of Michigan programs. This project began as my PhD dissertation, and I am grateful to the committee of professors who advised me and continually inspire me by combining intellectual vigor and daring with good humor and kindness: Holly Peters-Golden, Gayle Rubin, and Alexandra Stern. I owe my doctoral advisor, Marcia Inhorn, now a collaborator, mentor, and true friend, a major debt of gratitude for her ongoing academic and personal support. I thank my current colleagues at the University of Iowa for their support, especially Laurie Graham, Erica Prussing, and Ellen Lewin, for their helpful insights into the revision process. I am also deeply grateful to Ken Wissoker for embracing this project; to Leigh Barnwell, Elizabeth Ault, and other Duke University Press staff members for shepherding this book through production; and to the anonymous manuscript reviewers for their close readings and immensely helpful suggestions.

Finally, I cannot thank my friends and family enough for their support and kindness over the many years through which this project developed from idea to dissertation to book. Not all parents would be proud of their children crossing national borders to ask strange men about their erections. Mine are. Mom and Dad, thank you for unfailingly supporting everything I do, having faith in me, and raising me to find joy in understanding other people's lives. I am similarly grateful to my wonderful grandparents and to my parents' partners. For equal parts diversion, intellectual stimulation, and emotional support in graduate school and beyond I thank Sara Cooley, Lizzie Falconi, Kelly Fayard, Cameron Gokee, Kate Graber, Karen Hebert, Matt Kroot, Emily McKee, Robin Nelson, Rick Nance, Khori Newlander, Lauryn Parks, Jess Robbins, Drew Rodriguez, Jessi Smith Rolston, and Megan Styles. I also thank the friends who were there before I became an anthropologist (when I was just a person who liked to talk to strangers), especially Ali McDowell Cook & Jim Cook, Erin Maguire Daley & Dennis Daley, John Izzo, and Susannah Yovino. Without Mikaela Rogozen-Soltar, I would have probably gone crazy several times over, I would not have had nearly as much fun over the past decade, and there would also be some really ugly prose in this book. Mikaela, thank you for being a wonderful roommate, amazing friend, and patient yet critical editor. Last but not least, I am especially grateful to my cable for going out and bringing Adam Yack into my life. Adam, thank you for loving and encouraging me in my writing and everything else, for enriching my life in countless ways, and for the incredibly comfortable chair that I'm sitting in to write this.

Introduction

CHANGING BODIES AND MASCULINITIES
IN POST-VIAGRA MEXICO

Johnny's Story

Johnny said that he thought increasingly about death with the approach of his scheduled penectomy, an operation to amputate his cancerous penis.[1] A wiry, sixty-eight-year-old man, Johnny wore a USA baseball cap to honor the country where he had worked for many years and caught the sexually transmitted infection that caused his cancer. Full of nervous energy, Johnny moved around frenetically as we talked in the break room of the urology department in a hospital in Cuernavaca, Mexico. He stood up, sat down, and endlessly rearranged his medical documents, pausing only when he was overcome by pain from an earlier, unsuccessful removal of a penile tumor. Blotting tears with a crumpled tissue he said again and again, "Without my penis, I feel that now I'm not going to be a man." He told me that with luck, he would never wake up from the anesthesia.

Johnny's inability to work, as a result of the chronic pain from his illness and prior surgery, compounded his depression. He said he had nothing to do but sit around thinking about the upcoming loss of his penis and his prior way of life, in which sex had figured so prominently. When telling me the story of his past, Johnny focused on his achievements at work and in his sex life. These were key practices through which Johnny understood himself as a man. In fact, his work and sexual successes were interrelated, since he believed that his high-status position as the head chef at a midwestern airport hotel had made him attractive to women.

---

1   All names are pseudonyms. "Johnny" has an Americanized pseudonym because he asked me to call him by the nickname he was given in the United States.

He told me, "If I could work, I could get this out of my mind." But he was too sick to work, so he had returned to Mexico, where he spent his days arguing with his wife about whether he was a bad husband and reminiscing about the different kinds of women he had slept with in the United States. He often dreamily repeated a litany of past partners: "*gringuitas* [white women], blondes, brunettes, Japanese women, even a Polish woman . . ." Without sex and professional status to define him, Johnny feared that he would lose his identity after his operation. He wondered, "I who liked women so much, what will I do? How will I have relations?" In Spanish, the verb *to have relations* can imply sexual and/or nonsexual social relationships, and it was clear that Johnny also felt the latter to be in jeopardy. His greatest fear was that his male friends would find out and say, "Jiménez doesn't have a penis." If this knowledge became public, Johnny feared that he simply would not be able to relate to anyone "as a man."

Yet when I visited Johnny in his hospital room a few days after his surgery, his mood had completely changed. The man I had known as tearful and depressed had become cheerful and optimistic. He said he was feeling energetic and was focusing on his future rather than his operation. He had decided to tell his friends that he had simply undergone a prostate operation and would keep the news of the penectomy to himself. More importantly, he believed that he would soon feel healthy. Talking over his wife's and the nurses' protestations, he told me that he could soon return to the United States to work. He exclaimed, "Now I'm not thinking of dying; I'm thinking of traveling!" Despite his continuing ill health and his grim marital circumstances, Johnny was reworking his way of being a man so that it no longer depended on having a penis.

Aims of This Book

This book explores the social dynamics that make such radical attitude changes regarding the importance of penetrative sex to masculinity possible. Based primarily on interviews with over 250 male urology patients at a government-run hospital, I aim to shed light on the ways that older, urban Mexican men today are using sex, social interaction, and medical treatment to forge new ways of being men over time. Correcting the early omission of masculinity from gender studies, a growing body of research has shown that both masculinities and femininities are context-contingent performances, not natural essences. It is now time to work toward understanding how specific forms of masculinity emerge—on both cultural and individual levels (Inhorn and Wentzell 2011). Building on the insight that masculinities can be understood as "what men say and do *to be men*" (Gutmann 1996, 17; italics in original), this book provides a model for understanding how men's ways of being men change as they deal with altered bodies and social worlds. To do so, it focuses on a particularly understudied aspect of such emergence: the ways in which men's ideas and practices of masculinity change as they age, in relationship to cultural notions of health and the life course (c.f. Carpenter and DeLamater 2012; Hearn 2007; Tarrant 2010).

Studies of masculinity have frequently focused on Latin America, where local masculinities have long been self-consciously discussed, especially in terms of *machismo*. Popularized by the Mexican poet Octavio Paz in the 1950s, this concept dictates that as the progeny of conquistador-*indigena* rape, Latin American men are constitutionally predisposed to be aggressive, virility obsessed, and emotionally closed (Paz [1961] 1985). Masculinity studies based in this region have addressed men's practices of and divergences from stereotypical *machismo* (c.f. Amuchástegui and Szasz 2007; Carillo 2002; Gutmann 1996; McKee Irwin 2003; Prieur 1996) and have traced the ways that such beliefs about gender inflect men's daily lives. For example, various scholars have assessed the linked changes in gender and health practices that can occur with work migration (González-López 2005; Hirsch and Meneses Navarro 2009; Walter, Bourgois, and Loinaz 2004) and have just begun to examine the ways that Mexican men use reproductive and sexual health practices to assert particular forms of masculinity (Gutmann 2007; Huerta Rojas 2007). Yet the vast majority of ethnographic work on Mexican masculinities has focused on young or middle-aged men, and very few studies have examined the ways that Mexican men's understandings of masculinity change over their life courses (Núñez Noriega 2007; Varley and Blasco 2000). This book investigates such change, focusing on the ways that cultural ideals of the manly life course, together with individual bodily and social experiences of aging and sexual health intervention, shape older, working-class men's changing ways of being men.

To accomplish this, I examine men's responses to a simple but very socially symbolic physical change: decrease or cessation of erectile function. As Johnny's extreme case shows, changing sexual function casts the instability of masculinity into sharp relief. In Mexican and many other cultures, both having a penis and using it to penetrate others are important ways of asserting manhood. In Mexico in particular, unceasing ability to sexually penetrate has been a central way for men to continually assert their masculinity relative to those who are penetrated (Melhuus 1998). Despite changing gender norms in Mexican culture, penetrative sex remains a key signifier of manliness. Decreased erectile function, along with the aging, illness, and emotional distress that can cause it, are thus likely to require changes in a man's way of being a man. The global popularity of the medical notion that this decrease can be defined as the biological pathology known as erectile dysfunction (ED) offers men a new way to understand and treat this potentially socially disruptive change. Investigating how men define and react to decreased erectile function can reveal how they develop new forms of masculinity to reconcile their desired ways of being men with new social needs, physical constraints, and medical possibilities.

In this book, I analyze men's descriptions of the combined effects of aging, illness, structural constraints, and social difficulties on their erectile function and trace the practices through which they report incorporating all these factors into new ways of being men. I investigate how some Mexican men use ED treatment to act out forms of manhood partly constituted by sexual penetration, whereas many others reject such treatment, incorporating changing sexual function into new types of masculinity defined by other practices. I examine how a man's ability to attain firm erections can be central to his manhood at certain times but become insignificant as circumstances change and other markers of manhood come to the fore. Finally, I investigate how men's changing bodies and life experiences encourage them to relate differently over time to the common local stereotype that as Mexican men, they must be naturally sex obsessed.

The Concept of Erectile Dysfunction

Less-than-ideal penile erections have been attributed to varying causes throughout history and across cultures, ranging from aging to psychological distress to witchcraft (McLaren 2007; Wentzell 2008). Many healing systems have produced aphrodisiacs and potency enhancers meant to increase sexual desire or function (Ratsch 1997). Yet over the past two decades, the development of medical technologies for enhancing penile erection have spurred a worldwide "medicalization of impotence" that offers men new ways to understand and mediate changes over time in their sexual function (Tiefer 1994, 363). Since the widely publicized 1998 introduction of Viagra (sildenafil), a drug that enhances penile erection by creating chemical changes that increase penile blood flow and retention (Melman and Gingell 2005), it has become common to regard erectile difficulty as ED. The annual global sales of Viagra and other ED drugs, such as Cialis (tadalafil) and Levitra (vardenafil), are approximately \$5 billion, and these drugs are available worldwide through health-care providers or online pharmacies (Wilson 2011). Worldwide, men experiencing decreased erectile function now have the option of understanding and treating it as a medical problem.   — Seen as medical condition

Whether people adopt this perspective both depends on and influences their social context. Whether it makes sense to define changing sexual function as natural or pathological depends on one's beliefs about how men and male sexuality should be and about what constitutes bodily health. The presence of ED is thus in the eye of the beholder. The condition is clinically defined as follows: "the persistent inability to achieve or maintain an erection sufficient for satisfactory sexual performance" (Lizza and Rosen 1999). However, what firmness and frequency of erections men and their sexual partners understand as "sufficient" and which changes they think render their sex lives and relationships "unsatisfactory" depend on their expectations regarding what men of particular ages and social status should do with their bodies. In cultures where successful manhood is associated with frequent penetrative sex, ED drugs may thus function as "masculinity pills," alleviating the social ill of being unable to embody a key signifier of manliness (Loe 2006, 31). Yet in other cultural contexts, performing penetrative sex despite illness or older age may run counter to the accepted norms for the ways that men's lives, relationships, and sexuality should change over time (Rasmussen 2009; van der Geest 2001).

However, social scientists have noted that the availability of ED drugs may alter these cultural expectations. Critics argue that the drugs encourage restrictive norms for male embodiment, naturalizing phallocentric sexuality, obscuring individual or cross-cultural differences in sexual standards and desires, and contributing to the pathologization of aging (Katz and Marshall 2002; Mamo and Fishman 2001; Tiefer 2006). Indeed, biomedical research and treatment practices, as well as popular media coverage in many sites, tend to begin from the assumption that men would find any decrease in erectile frequency or firmness unsatisfactory (Baglia 2005; Wentzell and Salmerón 2009a). This perspective contributes to the medicalization of sexuality and erectile difficulty, meaning that the very presence of ED drugs can encourage people to understand changing erectile function as a medical problem.

The global popularity of ED drugs suggests that many men around the world are now adopting this view. Yet social scientists have found that even men living in cultures where decreased erectile function is commonly diagnosed as ED may reject this notion or seek nondrug methods for having sex despite erectile difficulty, such as expanding their nonpenetrative sexual activity (Oliffe 2005; Potts et al. 2006). Furthermore, men may be ambivalent about how to define and treat decreased erectile function. For example, some men who have tried ED drugs have also reported disliking the "mechanized" feel of drug-mediated erections (Potts et al. 2004). Overall, men make decisions about how to interpret or treat erectile function change within site-specific confluences of health-care accessibility; drug regulation; the local economy; and cultural ideas about sex, health, and masculinity. These same factors shape their ideals for— and the practices through which they enact—manhood more generally. Thus, examining men's responses to erectile difficulty offers an ideal starting point for tracing their development of individual ways of being men based on the social, physical, and structural limitations and possibilities they experience.

Erectile Dysfunction Treatment in Mexico

The ubiquity of discussion about ED in Mexico, along with the high level of debate about who Mexican men are and should be, made my decision to research male sexuality in Mexico seem logical to both my acquaintances and the study participants. When I began to explain my project, most assumed I was studying the area because of the *machismo*. Likewise, although my research focus often elicited chuckles, people remarked that it made sense because of Viagra, which they joked was enabling old men to "stay young." However, the same study participants who saw Mexico as a natural zone of *machismo* also critiqued and contested this traditional ideal of Mexican masculinity and usually rejected ED treatment for their own decreasing erectile function. Even those participants who used ED drugs generally sought to incorporate them into what they viewed as nonmacho forms of masculinity. Furthermore, despite the heavy marketing and press coverage that cast decreasing erectile function as a straightforward biological pathology, most of the participants saw it as a complex consequence of social, emotional, and physical factors. This book examines how and why these men developed these multifaceted understandings of erectile function change within a cultural context that would seem to facilitate its medicalization.

Following its 1998 introduction in Mexico, Viagra quickly became well known and widely available over the counter. Mexico is the developing world's largest market for the drug, with 2010 sales totaling $55 million (Wilson 2011). Sildenafil was quickly added to the list of drugs that government hospitals, including my field site, must provide cost free to eligible patients, and Viagra was dispensed free of charge to older Mexico City men in a government attempt to raise morale among the aged (CNN 2008). Although Viagra is the most recognizable ED drug brand, Cialis and Levitra are also widely available and heavily marketed in Mexico. In February 2008, a Cialis sales representative told me that the previous month, her drug was not only the most popular ED medicine in Cuernavaca but also the best-selling drug of *any* kind at the largest local pharmacy chain.

Medication for ED is expensive compared to the most commonly prescribed drugs in Mexico, priced to be accessible to the middle class but expensive for working-class patients. In Cuernavaca at the time of my research, a three pack of Viagra cost approximately 120 pesos ($9 USD). This was roughly equivalent to the price of two movie tickets or lunch at an upscale chain restaurant. In a context of marked economic inequality, a middle-class worker's lunch might cost the same as the daily wage for a working-class laborer. In 2008, the minimum daily wage in Cuernavaca was 49.5 pesos; in 2007, almost one third of *Instituto Mexicano del Seguro Social* (IMSS) eligible workers earned twice the minimum wage, meaning that a pack of Viagra purchased out of pocket would cost almost a full day's labor (CNN Expansión 2007). This illustrates why many IMSS patients relied on drugs supplied free of cost from the IMSS system and supplemented with inexpensive generic drugs sold at popular discount pharmacy chains. These chains do not stock a generic version of the ED drugs because these medications are still under patent.

Existing potency aides have also been repackaged as ED drug substitutes in response to the medicalization of erectile difficulty, and new herbal treatments also capitalize on the popularity of ED drugs. Both *naturista* (naturopathic) stores and pharmacies sell herbal male potency enhancers such as "Powersex" and "Himcaps," which often use English names in apparent attempts to cast themselves as foreign-produced cures

FIGURE 1.
Ads for herbal potency enhancers in a pharmacy window.
Photo taken by the author.

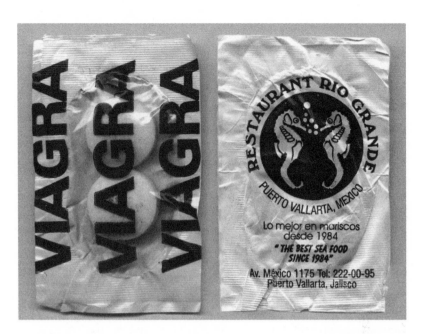

FIGURE 2.
"Viagra" mints.

similar to ED pharmaceuticals. Pharmacy employees told me that such herbal treatments were popular because they cost less and seemed to have less potential for harmful side effects than the ED drugs. "M-force," the most heavily marketed herbal supplement for ED treatment, is advertised frequently on Mexican network television. These ads feature a tuxedoed spokesman with chiseled features, clearly cast to embody virility. Whenever ED comes up in conversation, people of all ages impersonate his throaty voice and penetrating stare, repeating his face-saving catchphrase: "It's not for the man who can't. It's for the man who wants more."

Overall, ED pharmaceuticals are highly visible in Mexico today. ED treatments are advertised on television, in print media, in doctors' office brochures, and even on bus-stop walls. In taxis, I heard radio sexologists explain the ways that psychological problems could make it difficult for men to attain erections, and it seemed that every pharmacy was plastered with colorful ads for herbal and drug ED treatments. The first time I turned on my television in Cuernavaca, I saw a comedy show sketch in which a middle-aged man, sleeping with his maid, exclaimed, "You're so hot, I don't even need to use pills!" Similarly, at a seafood restaurant in the resort town of Puerto Vallarta, my complimentary after-dinner mints were printed with both the restaurant's name and the label *Viagra*. The owner explained that this joke played on seafood's reputation as an aphrodisiac. The name *Viagra* is also frequently attached to foods thought to have reinvigorating properties, such as fruit and vegetable smoothies advertised as "Viagra smoothies," or dishes touted as aphrodisiacs, such as sea urchin "Viagra soup."

The popularity of ED treatments resonates with cultural expectations that Mexican men will seek to perform macho sexuality even when faced with decreasing erectile function, along with population-level health and demographic trends that have created a large pool of men likely to experience this bodily change. Life expectancy has risen dramatically in Mexico over the past century thanks to improved primary health care, basic nutrition, and sanitation, but today's longer-lived citizens suffer from high levels of chronic disease associated with the downsides of industrialization, such as leading sedentary lives and consuming processed foods (INEGI 2009; McMurray and Smith 2001). Heart disease and type 2 diabetes are epidemics in Mexico and rank among the greatest national causes of death and morbidity (Dirección General de Información y Evaluación del Desempeño 2003; King, Aubert, and Herman 1998). These chronic diseases, along with their highly prevalent precursors (e.g., obesity), also hamper erectile function. Consequently, medical studies have shown that decreased erectile function is prevalent among older Mexican men (Barroso-Aguirre, Ugarte y Romano, and Pimentel-Nieto 2001).

Yet rather than simply adopting the notion that decreased erectile function should be defined and treated as ED, men decide how to understand this experience in relationship to ongoing cultural debates regarding the nature of Mexican masculinity. These discussions—whether in the realm of national politics, soap operas, or marital arguments I overheard in the hospital waiting room—tend to both critique and reproduce the assumption that Mexican men are machos. Debates regarding the accuracy and the desirability of various views of Mexican manhood figure prominently in the narratives presented in this book; the study participants and Mexican cultural commentators often simultaneously naturalize *machismo* and frame it as a "backward" trait that hinders the nation's progress toward modernization.

Changes in cultural ideals regarding marriage, love, and gender also shape these debates. Both historically and today, most adult Mexicans marry (INEGI 2009), but relatively recently widespread ideals of companionate marriage have replaced or augmented previous ideals of marriage as the performance of separate but complementary duties (Hirsch 2003; Jiménez Guzman 2003; Núñez Noriega 2007). With this emphasis on affective bonds between family members, and in the context of more readily available contraception and women's increasing economic participation and educational attainment, actual and desired family sizes have shrunk (INEGI 2009). Although most Mexicans self-identify as Roman Catholics, participants in this and other anthropological studies reported that they did not often feel the need to conform to church doctrine regarding gender and sexuality and saw common practices such as contraception and premarital sex as compatible with their faith (Amuchástegui and Aggleton 2007; De la Peña and Toledo 1991). Participants' understandings of ideal or appropriate sexual practice tended to vary widely, in ways related as much to media, friends' ideas about sex, and ongoing social debates as to religion. Most saw penetrative penile-vaginal sex as "real" sex and held widely divergent views about other sexual practices, such as oral, anal, or manual sex. These were, however, well-known practices. Although up-to-date statistics are not available, two decades ago a survey of adults in Mexico City found that 44 percent saw oral sex and 41.2 percent regarded anal sex as "acceptable" (De la Peña and Toledo 1991).

Overall, recent ethnographic studies reveal that Mexican men and women from many walks of life say that marital relationships and duties must become more equal and sexually fulfilling for both partners (Amuchástegui and Szasz 2007; Ramirez 2009). However, this discourse on the value of more egalitarian, companionate marriages usually translates not into calls for radical equality, but for increased task sharing and communication between men and women who are still understood to have separate and sometimes hierarchical roles (Carillo 2002). In this context, men's responses to decreases in erectile function, and their decisions about whether or not to consider it ED and treat it medically, are useful for understanding how people draw from cultural context and personal experiences when physical and social changes require them to forge new ways of being men.

Cuernavaca and the Hospital Field Site

This study is based in the Cuernavaca of 2007–2008, then a metropolitan area of almost 800,000 people (INEGI 2007). Located 85 kilometers south of Mexico City, Cuernavaca is a former elite vacation site and an agricultural area turned into a bustling urban center. Since the 1985 Mexico City earthquake sent refugees to settle in the city, Cuernavaca has been a key site for population resettlement in central Mexico. Growing quickly, it has now absorbed many formerly rural municipalities. Walmart super-centers sit at both the north and south edges of town, and busy streets are lined with strip malls and fast-food restaurants as well as more tradi-tional food carts, street vendors, and markets. The area's rapid urbaniza-tion and the population's frequent discussions of the benefits and pitfalls of modernization made it an excellent site for studying reactions to new medical technologies in the context of ongoing debates about gender.

Within Cuernavaca, I decided to base my research at a medical site. Men's sexual activities, like most of the practices through which they act "like men" in various ways, happen outside the clinic. Yet because of the stigma and the secrecy surrounding sexual difficulty, and social con-straints on discussing sexuality in many social settings, it is rarely polite or possible to broach the topic of changing sexual function. In Mexico, it is often considered improper to discuss sexual difficulties or transgres-sions, leading to the proliferation of "open secrets" about sex. In his work on same-sex sexuality in Guadalajara, the sociologist Héctor Carillo calls this phenomenon "sexual silence," noting that Mexican families may nor-malize and tacitly accept potentially stigmatizing sexual differences by simply not discussing them (2002, 139). Conversely, even intimate medi-cal issues are generally viewed as appropriate topics for conversation in urban central Mexico (Finkler 1991). Thus, although the social scientific critiques of the medicalization of sexual function discussed previously inform my research, this medicalization also made it possible. The clini-cal setting was a unique space in which people were likely to be eager to talk about sexual health concerns that could not be discussed in most other arenas.

Of the array of ED treatment sites in Cuernavaca, I chose to base my research in the urology department of the regional hospital of one of the main government social assistance organizations: the IMSS. The IMSS hospital is a modern high-rise on a busy street near a commercial district, a Coca-Cola bottling plant, and residential areas. It was an attractive research base for several reasons. Compared to other medical sites in the fragmented world of Mexican health care, it attracted a relatively diverse patient population, making it useful for comparative analysis across demographics. Even more importantly, many of the IMSS urology patients were older men, meaning that a high proportion of the patients were likely to have experienced decreased erectile function. Finally, as a general medical site, it provided access to not only ED treatment users but also the difficult-to-identify population of men who had experienced but had chosen not to medically treat erectile function change.

Founded in 1943 with the consolidation of state and national legislative and constitutional mandates, the IMSS system is the largest branch of the Mexican national social security system, providing a set of services ranging from pensions to child care to health care (Gutiérrez Arriola 2002). However, the IMSS's progressive aims of providing a range of social rights to citizens are not always borne out in practice. Because inclusion is based on formal employment, the system excludes the least financially secure Mexicans, the approximately 29 percent of workers employed in the informal economy (INEGI 2010).[2] Even those who can access the IMSS system are unlikely to have their needs fully met, in part because of its chronic underfunding and a failure to restructure health services in response to increased population life expectancy and the related rise of chronic illnesses (Moreno, Tamez, and Ortiz 2009). My hospital study site, a regional center that offered both primary care and referral-based specialty services such as surgery and chemotherapy, offered technologically advanced care but often lacked basic resources (e.g., blank paper). This hampered treatment and led to frequent logistical difficulties, frustrating both doctors and patients. As this book will show, this state of affairs also profoundly influenced the responses of IMSS patients to decreased erectile function.

Although financial constraints influenced the quality of IMSS health care, they also encouraged the study participants to use it. Although a significant minority of the participants worked at white-collar jobs in the clerical and education sectors, most worked as tradesmen, factory workers, or drivers. The long waits and scarce resources at the IMSS hospital sent most potential patients with the means to afford private care elsewhere. So even though the IMSS-eligible population includes the working, middle, and upper classes, most IMSS hospital patients belong to the working class. Many of the older participants were retired, although nearly all reported working as long as they could. These retirees, often

2 Patchwork systems have addressed certain elements of this gap for several decades. In 2003, with the aim of eventually providing universal health-care access, the Mexican national government began to offer health care to citizens not covered by an existing social security administration through a program called *Seguro Popular*.

surviving on no or extremely low pensions, generally participated in the informal economy by vending or doing day labor. The difficulty of getting by financially in Mexico was a constant theme in the interviews, as even men employed in secure jobs struggled to make ends meet. Despite this financial uncertainty, many of the older participants who had received little education and had performed manual labor had been granted IMSS privileges as dependents of their children, who they had sent to school and now held white-collar jobs. Although money was tight all around, many of the informants had created upwardly mobile families. Thus, the image of daily life that the participants gave was that of perseverance, often grounded in family obligations or bonds, through a difficult, dangerous, and stressful world. This book thus presents the experiences of a specific group of people—mostly older, working-class men and women, raised either in the growing city of Cuernavaca or the once-rural areas it has absorbed, who are likely to have very different ideas about sex, health, and gender than wealthier, younger, or more rural conationals. Although the study participants made frequent generalizations about what it is to be a Mexican or a Mexican man that this book discusses at length, it is crucial to note that demographically different people might not agree with their characterizations.

This book also describes people's experiences at a very specific point in Mexican and world history. In addition to the previously mentioned changing gender expectations and demographic shifts toward smaller families and increased women's education that facilitate them, Mexico has undergone a series of political, social, and economic upheavals. Although Mexico is still an overwhelmingly Roman Catholic country, conversion to Protestantism, particularly evangelical forms, is changing the nation's religious landscape. Since the 1970s, this movement has been growing by about 6 percent annually in Morelos, the state in which Cuernavaca is located (Dow 2005). The ways that some of the study participants used Protestant conversion to rework their ways of being men will be discussed in chapter 2. However, the visibility of conversion in Cuernavaca has increased dramatically since the 2007–2008 fieldwork discussed here, which is evidenced by the recent completion of Cuernavaca's first mega church, a six-thousand-seat auditorium housing a congregation that outgrew its location in the city center. The 2010 Mexican census estimates that almost 13 percent of the population of Morelos is now Protestant (INEGI 2010).

During my recent visits to Cuernavaca, many new Protestants have linked their conversion to the epidemic of drug violence and related crime that swept the nation after the fieldwork for this book had been completed, with some characterizing these as signs of the end times. During fieldwork for this book, Cuernavaca residents described *other* cities as dangerous, often recounting the muggings they had experienced or heard about in nearby Mexico City. However, most considered Cuernavaca, a tourist town known for its perfect climate, to be peaceful and relatively safe. Although narcotics-related violence had dramatically increased in northern regions in response to the 2006 federal crackdown on drug trafficking, at the time of my fieldwork, many people repeated the rumor that narcos had sent their wives and children to live in Cuernavaca because of its beauty and tranquility and thus had declared the area off-limits for violence. This notion of the city as a safe zone was shattered by an early incident of spectacular drug-related violence in 2010, when four mutilated bodies were hung off a bridge near a popular, upscale mall (El Economista .mx 2010). After repeated, sensational violence, Cuernavaca residents now describe their city as fundamentally insecure, and it has also become the base of antiviolence protests (Torres 2011).

The fieldwork for this project also took place just prior to the 2008 beginning of the current global economic crisis. Although economic inequality and instability were hallmarks of study participants' lives in 2007–2008, the economic situation has since worsened, with decreased investment and increasing violence reducing construction and tourism in Cuernavaca, thus eliminating many building and service industry jobs. The study participants' experiences presented here reflect a time before these crises.

The Urology Department

The hospital where this study was based was divided into a family medicine clinic and departments covering a range of specialties, including urology. Each specialty was composed of a morning and an afternoon staff consisting of several doctors, a nurse, and a clerical assistant; as a result of low IMSS salaries, most of the doctors also worked in private practices after their hospital shifts. I conducted research daily during the urology department's morning shift, when two doctors saw patients in the twin consulting rooms, and two others performed surgeries. The doctors were all men (although many female doctors worked in other hospital departments) and were relatively young, ranging from their late thirties to early fifties. The support staff consisted of women in their late forties, who usually cooked breakfast to share; the urology staff was a close-knit and jovial group who started each morning by eating together in the small prep room that also served as a break room.

After breakfast, I wiped down the break room table, which we joked then became "my office." The doctors would then begin to see patients from the growing crowd outside. Patients referred to any specialty service suffered long waits for appointments, and on their assigned days, they had to arrive early in the morning and often wait for hours to be seen. Scheduling at the IMSS hospital was an inexact and wholly paper-based procedure. The medical departments had no computers, so the clerks carried paper files from a central archive, which were sometimes mislaid. There was often confusion about which patient a doctor should be seeing. The assistant sat at a desk in front of the consulting rooms, placating the patients as best she could, but patients and their family members were often on edge by the time they saw the doctor.

Long waits were not the only factor that made patients uncomfortable. In one of the consulting rooms, the patients were examined under soccer star Ronaldinho's challenging glare. Someone had used a promotional poster from the FIFA '08 soccer video game to block the view through the glass wall that separated the break and consultation rooms, and I often wondered whether men like Johnny, removing their pants and laying on the table for invasive and reportedly embarrassing prostate, bladder, and kidney exams, felt unmanned by the soccer hero's caption, "Can you handle FIFA '08?" Tensions surrounding masculinity were more overt in the case of rectal exams, which I saw a few patients angrily refuse out of fear that "that is homosexual." In general, though, problems between doctors and patients stemmed from the high patient load and the lack of resources that hampered medical care.

IMSS physicians saw large numbers of patients, with sometimes as many as thirty scheduled in a six-hour shift. This volume meant that despite the doctors' best intentions, most simply had no time to discuss anything but patients' most pressing health problems. Although the urologists had close relationships with some of the long-term patients, doctor-patient interactions on the whole were rushed, and their conversation was brusque. Patients often reported feeling that the doctors had not taken the time to get to know them personally or fully understand

FIGURE 3.
The view from a consulting room exam table. Photo taken by the author.

their problems. They frequently made comments that revealed that they
had not received full explanations of the procedures they were to undergo.
In an extreme example, Johnny and his wife did not know whether his
testicles had been amputated along with his penis. He told me that they
would have to "wait until the bandage comes off to see if I still have my
buddies." Differences of class and status seemed to exacerbate this lack of
communication, since less-educated or lower-income patients often reported feeling that it would be inappropriate to question their physicians.
The IMSS urologists felt they were forced to provide a lesser standard of
care at the hospital than they could in their private practices, but they
also reported that "we do the best we can" under difficult institutional
circumstances.

Over the course of my fieldwork, I learned that these circumstances
also presented barriers to the discussion of sexual issues. Patients often

said that they lacked the necessary *confianza* (trust) with their doctors to broach this sensitive topic. Brief appointments that put the focus on life-threatening illnesses and discouraged conversation served as structural disincentives for the treatment of sexual function issues in the IMSS hospital. An IMSS family medicine doctor, who I interviewed when he himself was a urology patient, told me that he was very concerned with providing sexual health care. He routinely raised sexual health issues with his private-practice patients and said that he used to do so in the IMSS hospital. However, he told me that in recent years, as the IMSS doctors have had to see more and more patients each shift, he simply did not have the time to broach the subject. This time pressure made it highly unusual for a general practitioner to ask a man about his sexual function. Because a referral from this kind of doctor was necessary for a patient to see an IMSS specialist such as a urologist, this meant that men were not usually sent to specialists specifically for sexual health concerns. Thus, the urology patients were generally seen for prostate cancer or enlargement or urinary tract diseases, which might cause erectile difficulty, not for ED itself.

Study Methods

Knowing that I wanted to interview men experiencing erectile function changes and aware of the fact that patients were often unwilling to discuss sexual issues with them, the urologists tended to ask any man they suspected might have experienced erectile difficulty if he wanted to participate in a study on sexuality. To my initial surprise, most did. Patients who had undergone long waits for short visits said they appreciated the chance to talk in more depth about their problems and concerns. After a few minutes of conversation, the participants often said that they felt they could trust me, broaching topics that they sometimes said they were too "ashamed" to tell the doctor.

In total, I interviewed 254 male patients, 48 along with wives or other family members who had accompanied them to their appointments. The study participants ranged in age from their late teens to their mid-nineties, although most were in their fifties and sixties. Over 60 percent had come to the urology department because of prostate problems, which usually caused difficulty in urination and pain. About 30 percent of the patients had other chronic illnesses in addition to their urologic complaints, most commonly type 2 diabetes and heart disease. Almost

70 percent of the men I interviewed reported some decrease in their erectile function, although only 28 participants had ever sought medical treatment for this change.

When the patients agreed to speak with me, the urologists led them through the door to "my office" in the break room, and we sat together at the small table. I explained that I was an anthropologist who was interested in learning about the ways people's lives changed as they experienced health problems and related changes in their sexual function.[3] I presented the informed consent letter, stressing that their identities would be kept confidential and alerting them that I would take written notes as we spoke and audio record our interview with their permission. (I subsequently transcribed and translated all of the written notes and the recordings myself.) Although a few of the potential participants declined to participate at this point, mostly related to stated time constraints, the overwhelming majority agreed to participate. The interview lengths varied widely, depending on each participant's desire to talk. Many said that talking about their feelings and fears was a new experience, and they often seemed content but emotionally exhausted after their interviews. The participants often told me that they appreciated the chance to discuss troubling issues; they often made comments like, "this was like therapy" or "it was good to unburden myself."

It became clear to me that my position as a white, American woman helped to establish the *confianza* that the participants said enabled them to tell me things they could not share with their doctors or friends. Despite the stereotype that men, particularly macho Mexicans, will not divulge this information to women, many female researchers have successfully interviewed men about their experiences of sexual dysfunction (Inhorn 2004; Potts et al. 2004; Tiefer 1994) and have interviewed Mexican men about their sexual experiences (Amuchástegui and Aggleton 2007; González-López 2005; Hirsch 2003). Because I am a woman, the participants noted that they did not feel that they had to compete with me to seem manly; along these lines, one told me that he felt more comfortable with female doctors because you can talk to them "like a mother." Being American was also crucial, in that stereotypes about *gringas'*

3   The term *anthropologist* is far better known in Mexico than in the United States because of a long history of publicly funded and widely discussed studies of indigenous cultures and pre-Colombian civilizations and the presence of a well-known anthropology museum in Mexico City.

comfort with sexuality made the participants feel—and state—that they could discuss sex without shocking or offending me.

Speaking American-accented and occasionally grammatically incorrect Spanish also turned out to be helpful in creating *confianza*. I generally introduced myself by saying that I was from the United States and asking potential participants to excuse my language mistakes. This statement shifted the usual balance of power between a hospital professional and a patient. By asking the participants to excuse my language errors, I cast myself as a learner and the participants as people with something to teach. Finally, my clear interest in their life stories was a key reason that patients said they felt comfortable participating in my study. Many of the men who complained that the IMSS hospital was impersonal said that they appreciated my concern.

The structure of the interviews seemed to contribute to the commonly voiced belief of the participants that they were being heard and respected. To gather data on the ways men incorporated medical and sexual experiences into their presentations of themselves as men, I let participants' stories and interests guide the interviews, enabling them to raise the issues they saw as most important. Most of the men's comfort in doing so likely related to my use of established best practices for discussing sexuality, including initially establishing rapport and confidentiality with low-stakes conversation, avoiding assumptions, and using specifics to enhance recall of past behavior (Carrier 1999; Herdt and Lindenbaum 1992; Weinhardt et al. 1998). In addition, I was careful to ask concrete questions, for example, asking men to describe their definitions of a good or a bad husband or father rather than asking about their ideals of masculinity. I also strove to avoid heteronormative language whenever possible, for example, asking about partners rather than wives. However, although the participants spoke freely about affairs, the use of prostitutes, and even committing violence, none mentioned sexual activity with another man. Because other ethnographic studies in Mexico have shown that self-identified straight men may engage in covert same-sex sexuality (Carrier 1995; Lumsden 1991; Prieur 1998), this may have been an area of life that the participants felt they could not discuss with me. Therefore, this book focuses on the female-oriented aspects of avowedly heterosexual men's sexual and romantic lives, a parameter appropriate to its aim of revealing how men construct and present masculinities.

Along these lines, this research method generated a particular kind of data: men's narratives of their behavior and feelings regarding sex, health, and relationships and a view of how they incorporated these narratives into their enactions of masculinity in the interview context. The interviews, like conversations more generally, are intersubjective encounters in which the participants together craft a particular picture of the world and construct context-specific selves (Ochs and Capps 1996). As such, these interviews created a new discursive space for the participants, in which their experiences regarding decreasing sexual function and its consequences for their lives as men became speakable. In this space, they reported reflecting on their lives very differently than they did in conversation with friends, family members, and doctors. My aim in this book is to shed light on the ways that the study participants constructed fluid and context-specific ways of being men in response to decreased erectile function and related experiences, including our interview interactions. Interview data are ideal for this purpose, illuminating on-the-spot construction of a particular form of masculinity suited to a new context. Men's characterizations of themselves as men to an anthropologist in a clinical setting shed light on the ways in which they connect different life experiences into context-appropriate and coherent masculine selfhoods. Rather than seeking to provide a journalistic account of men's sexual, medical, and social activity outside the clinic, this book analyzes participants' interview-based constructions of selfhood to understand how they might link different elements of their lives together into situationally appropriate ways of being men.

Both this aim and the research methods used differ from the traditional ethnographic focus on participant observation, in which a researcher follows the participants throughout their daily lives to understand their social worlds and daily practices through first-hand observation. I performed ten months of observation in the IMSS urology department, observing its daily workings and patient consultations to understand how this context would shape patients' health-care choices, responses to erectile difficulty, and participation in clinic-based interviews. Yet for both theoretical and practical reasons, I chose to center my analysis on interview data, rather than observational data gleaned from following the study participants throughout their daily lives.

Most significantly, developing daily life social relationships with the participants would likely render them unwilling to discuss sexuality because they reported feeling able to do so specifically because we were interacting in a socially circumscribed, medical context. Although observing the lives of the study participants would have shed light on their ways of being men in different settings, it would also have made me a part of their social worlds. Such familiarity would likely have made the men far less forthcoming, possibly leading them to invoke the "sexual silence" used to gloss potentially embarrassing or compromising sexual practices and making asking about their sexual function and practices socially inappropriate.

Practically speaking, participant observation was also not feasible for researching the experiences and the effects of changing sexual function in a large group of men. Although anthropologists have done participant-observation of sex in small and sexually oriented settings such as bath-houses (Bolton 1996), this method was not appropriate for studying sexual practices in the present, mostly married, study population. In addition, daily-life observations would have been distasteful or socially harmful to most of the study participants. Many of the participants made it clear to me that they wanted to maintain a strict separation between their inter-view experiences and their daily lives. Of the hundreds of men I inter-viewed, only two spontaneously invited me to socialize; these men were also outliers in that they were among the small group I interviewed along with their wives, and, unlike most of the participants, reported happy and faithful marriages. It was far more common for the participants to preface revelations with comments such as: "Well, you'll never meet my wife, so I can tell you . . ." Indeed, one man who was friendly and eager to talk about intimate issues, including his infidelity, in our interview looked pointedly at the ground when, later that day, I crossed paths with him and his wife at the food carts outside the hospital.

Despite the unwillingness of many of the participants to share the sexual information that they told me with their wives, I was able to sup-plement the individual interviews with observations of the relational construction of context-specific masculinities in interviews I performed with couples. These interviews provided a venue for observing the ways that the couples jointly made sense of decreasing erectile function. The participants devised this interview format themselves. To maintain con-fidentiality, I never suggested joint interviews. Yet most of the approxi-mately 20 percent of the participants whose wives accompanied them to their medical appointments asked if they could be interviewed together because both had been involved in the medical and sexual experiences that would be discussed. Although the topics they discussed and the ways of being men they presented in these interviews surely varied from what they would have said if we were alone, men's conversations with spouses about how to understand and label bodily and social changes provided important insight into couples' intersubjective constructions of masculinity.

Finally, although this book focuses on IMSS interview data contextualized by observing practices in the urology department, I also draw from supplementary methods. To better understand the sale and the use of ED treatments in Mexico, as well as other forms of health care that the study participants were receiving, I interviewed IMSS and private physicians, pharmacy workers, and ED drug sales representatives. These interviews provided key background data and, like the IMSS patient interviews, also created arenas in which I could observe the interviewees' construction and presentation of specific versions of their selves—in these cases, their professional identities. Whenever possible, I supplemented these interview data with observations, for example, by observing private medical consultations and following an ED drug representative on her rounds. I also drew context from my consumption and review of media during my research period, which focused on topics related to ED, sexual health, and debates about changing gender roles and *machismo*.

Study Ethics

Although most of the patients were happy to participate in the study, differences in understandings of research ethics and confidentiality between the United States and Mexico posed a hurdle. The American idea that doctor-patient interactions are private and secret did not apply in the IMSS hospital. Consultations were somewhat public because family members often accompanied patients into their examinations, and staff, from doctors to janitors, frequently walked through rooms where appointments were in progress. In contrast to the focus in the United States on individual freedom, both the structure and the practice of Mexican law focus on relationships (Adler Lomnitz and Salazar 2002). In this context, legal protections surrounding research in medical settings focus more on preventing coercion and abuse than on keeping information secret. This created difficulty for me as an American researcher as I tried to meet the conflicting ethical standards of my home university and the Mexican field site. Although the American ethics boards that oversee research demand that no one know of an individual's participation in a study, the Mexican ethics boards require that two witnesses sign any informed consent document, to affirm that participation did not occur under duress. I dealt with this problem by asking medical professionals, who already had access to patients' records, to serve as witnesses. Similar to other anthropologists working in urban Mexican hospitals, I found that the participants were unconcerned about confidentiality within the hospital, viewing my questions as a sign of polite interest (Finkler 1991). Most said they felt comfortable talking after receiving assurance that their stories would not "get out," identifiably, to their social circles.

I faced another ethical quandary when some of the urologists, pressed for time in appointments but wanting to offer men help with sexual problems, began to use me as a sort of sexual health counselor. I could often overhear conversations in the consulting rooms from my "office," and I became concerned when the doctors would respond to patients' occasional questions about sexuality by saying, "Go see *la doctora*; she's studying sexuality and health." Despite my repeated requests that the urologists not imply that I was a medical doctor, this situation continued. I explained to the patients that I was *not* a physician but an anthropologist studying the social aspects of erectile function change and related illnesses. Eventually, frustrated that the patients frequently left their medical appointments with unanswered medical questions, or without feeling able to broach sexual health topics, I decided to provide basic answers in these areas when the participants asked me for them. Although at the start of my research I would have seen such interventions as unethical because only physicians and nurses are officially qualified to give biomedical advice, I eventually came to believe that furthering my research by listening to participants' stories but denying them the help they asked for was actually the unethical position.

So when the participants asked me for sexual or medical advice, I first reiterated that I was an anthropologist, not a medical doctor. I said that I had been trained to study culture, so I could offer only an anthropological perspective and give them the medical information that I had learned in the course of my research. When I answered men's questions, I was careful to explain where I had gotten the biomedical facts that I relayed and highlight how my anthropological training shaped my comments. For example, in response to occasional questions about whether men would be able to "have sex again" after a prostate operation, I explained that I had learned from medical articles that the nerves needed to cause erection might be severed during this procedure, but from an anthropological point of view, this would prevent sex only if one thought of sex exclusively in terms of penetration. I always told patients that they should also ask their doctors. When more complex or serious issues arose, I asked the nurse to talk with the participant to provide the needed medical answers. In this way, I negotiated the awkward position of being cast as the sexual health *doctora* by well-meaning but rushed urologists.

Theorizing Changing Masculinities

In this book, I draw on ideas from the anthropology of gender, medicine, and aging, as well as the field of science and technology studies (STS), to make sense of the different ways that men came to act like men as they experienced erectile function change. These fields are rooted in the insight that bodies, behaviors, and selves are culturally contingent. From this perspective, things that may seem natural, such as sexuality, gender, expected life courses, and notions of health, appear so as the consequence of social activity (cf. Bledsoe 2002; Kirkland and Metzl 2010; Rubin 1975) and occur at the confluence of biology and society (cf. Fausto-Sterling 2005). I also build on a new direction within masculinity studies. Although work in this field has long sought to document the constructedness of—and the hierarchical relationships among—various forms of masculinities, it has sometimes had the undesired effect of casting masculinities as static types (Connell and Messerschmidt 2005; Demetriou 2001). In response, recent scholarship in this field calls for attention to emergence, change, and processuality in masculinities (cf. Inhorn 2012; Padilla 2011).

Researchers have developed various models for understanding the mutual constitution of material and social phenomena, aiming to document the real-world consequences that specific physical attributes, contexts, and structures can have on each other without reductively foregrounding or naturalizing one of these realms of experience (McKinnon and Silverman 2005). For example, medical anthropologists have called for attention to the co-construction of individual experiences on three levels: embodiment, social interactions, and political systems (Scheper-Hughes and Lock 1987). STS research, aimed at revealing the sociality of science, offers more spatially oriented approaches for tracking the ways that interactions among multiple actors across social sites produce facts, technologies, and even new kinds of embodiment and selfhood (Berg and Mol 1998; Clarke 2005; Latour 1987). Some scholars taking this approach have moved beyond arguing that bodies and diseases are not natural to asserting that they are also not singular, set things. They argue that the differences in the way something, such as an infertility patient's body, is treated and defined across varying contexts such as medical offices, work, or home, reveal that what seem to be singular entities are actually multiple ones, "choreographed" into functionally cohesive units (Thompson 2007).

Composite Masculinities

My approach for understanding changing masculinities builds on Annemarie Mol's work in this vein, specifically her argument that diseases can be considered "composite objects." By observing the diagnosis and the treatment of atherosclerosis (arterial hardening) across different hospital departments, Mol argues that this condition is multifarious: a set of entities constituted differently by different practices yet called by "the same name" (2002, 47). She demonstrates that different things that "are" atherosclerosis are often mutually exclusive in practice. For example, the diagnosis of atherosclerosis from pain during walking requires patients to use intact legs, whereas the pathology lab detection of the condition based on thickened vein walls requires the inspection of an amputated limb. Mol then tracks the social practices that make these different instantiations of atherosclerosis "hang together" into a coherent and seemingly singular disease (2002, 55). These "practices of coordination" could involve linking up compatible instantiations, such as different tests supporting the same diagnosis, or reconciling conflicting ones, such as keeping disjunctive lab results spatially separate, ignoring some, or assigning them different levels of determinative power (2002, 55). By demonstrating such practices, Mol asserts that understanding medical entities as "composite objects" highlights their context-dependence and multiplicity and the social practices through which they are woven into singular wholes (2002, 54).

I argue that applying Mol's notion of compositeness to gender and understanding men's ways of being men as "composite masculinities" makes it possible to understand how individuals construct and revise their gendered selfhood across time and context. I define composite masculinities as contingent and fluid constellations of elements that men weave together into masculine selfhoods. These elements are drawn from the entire gamut of men's life worlds: their ideas and emotions, experiences, embodiment, relationships, and context. Although someone can thus incorporate a wide range of elements into his way of being a man, various constraints limit the construction of composite masculinities in practice. For example, only certain ways of being a man make sense in a given cultural context. Similarly, the elements available to a particular man are limited by his social and structural circumstances. For example, only a man who has a sexual partner and can afford ED treatment can use it to continue having penetrative sex despite decreased erectile function. In this book, I use the composite perspective to investigate how men incorporate their changing bodies and social experiences into masculinities that make sense in the context of local ideas about gender, Mexicanness, health, and modernity. By focusing on men's experiences of changing sexual function, I aim to reveal how things change when a key signifier of manliness in Mexico—frequent sexual penetration—is no longer available as an element of men's composite masculinities.

This composite perspective makes it possible to map and analyze the ways that men link specific acts, experiences, and forms of embodiment into situation-specific ways of being men. As a tool for identifying the elements a man incorporates into a current enactment of manliness, this approach also helps to resolve long-standing analytical confusion about what masculinities actually are. Matthew Gutmann has documented that scholars conceptualize masculinity in different and conflicting ways, for example, as anything men do or anything women don't do. He intervenes, as mentioned earlier, by incorporating intentionality into his definition, understanding masculinity as what men do "to be men" (1997, 386). This definition has been widely used and offers a good way to identify masculinities in the moment. However, because men must be different kinds of men in varying situations and life phases, it is crucial to not only understand what individual masculinities are at a given time but also why and how they change.

The composite masculinities approach offers a practical framework for tracing such change. Thinking of gendered selves as composites stresses that people continuously create multifaceted selves by linking together different practices, emotions, and experiences through practice, as they live out individual takes on culturally intelligible ways of being men or women. This approach also highlights the ways that individual gendered selves are shaped by context, which limits both the kinds of selves people see as ideal and the potential elements that are available for inclusion in someone's composite self. By identifying the changing sets of elements that form a man's masculinity at certain moments, the practices through which he binds them together, and his reasons for doing so, it is possible to understand not only what masculinities are but also how and why they change over time.

This perspective is also useful for understanding the specific practices through which men enact these changes. Building on Mol's notion that practices of coordination generate objects' seeming singularity, it is possible to identify different ways that men coordinate experiences, actions, physical states, and emotions into composite masculinities. Anthropologists have identified three basic and often interrelated ways that people construct and present selves: through narrative, embodiment, and interpersonal interaction (cf. Jackson 1998; Ochs and Capps 1996; van Wolputte 2004). By analyzing the narrative accounts and experiences of the study participants and my observation of their interactions with myself, their partners, and their physicians, I aim to identify the elements that IMSS patients were likely to incorporate into their composite masculinities when faced with aging, illness, and decreased erectile function and discern the practices of coordination through which they incorporated these elements into particular ways of being men.

The composite approach also helps to account for the reality that, although people usually experience selfhood as singular, someone's ways of being a man can differ so much over time and place that they might seem irreconcilable. Men who perform masculinity in the morning by playing tenderly with their children might enact it in the evening by visiting a brothel with friends. They might also act in ways that differ from their stated goals as men, for example, both critiquing *machismo* and being unfaithful to their wives. Anthropological studies of selfhood have noted that people perform specific acts to create an "illusion of wholeness" among widely varying ways of "being" themselves (Ewing 1990, 251). Understanding gendered selfhood as a composite makes it possible to trace how people maintain this feeling of continuity in the face of lived disjunction, by adding or removing elements of their composite masculinities to be appropriate kinds of men in ever-changing contexts.

Finally, identifying change over time in composite masculinities sheds light on the reasons why this change becomes necessary. Mol argues that when different enactments of a disease are not in conflict, it seems straightforwardly natural and singular. However, when problems arise— for example, when tests measuring a seemingly cohesive disease in different ways show discrepant results—doctors must work to reconcile these different elements. Similarly, when a man's way of being a man is going well, his practices and understanding of masculinity may seem to be straightforward and natural expressions of an essential selfhood. Yet when changing bodies or circumstances make performing a prior style of masculinity difficult, men must work to reconcile their new circumstances with their overarching ideas about manhood.

Extending the composite perspective to other elements of men's lives, including those that form or constrain their composite masculinities, can shed light on the co-construction of masculinities and other elements of men's worlds. Thus, in addition to focusing on gendered selfhood, in this book I also apply the composite approach to men's illness experiences and understandings of health. I use an understanding of chronic disease as composite to trace the ways that bodily changes, social problems, and structural constraints come together into what doctors subsequently define as instances of diabetes or heart disease. This perspective also sheds light on the relationship of decreased erectile function to chronic illness and its structural and emotional consequences and causes. Thus, although many valid analytics exist for understanding gender, selves, and relationships between sociality and materiality, the composite approach is useful because it can track their changing relationships. By revealing how people construct gendered selves from particular elements of their lived experience, this approach enables an analysis of the mutual co-construction of gender and other parts of life.

Johnny's Composite Masculinity

As an extreme example of the loss of the ability to sexually penetrate, Johnny's experience of penile amputation is useful for tracing change in his composite masculinity. He lost a body part—and the social practices it enabled—that had been key to his prior way of being a man. Because having a penis is a basic sign of manhood, a penectomy might be thought to decrease one's manhood; a urologist explaining the procedure told me that after a penectomy, patients urinated, "sitting down . . . like a woman." Accordingly, Johnny feared that losing his penis would threaten his manliness in a way that amputation of less symbolic body parts would not. He said, "Many people lose an arm, a leg, an eye. They keep on being men. But I, thanks to God, I have my arms, legs, but the manly excitement has ended." As someone whose way of being a man centered on penetrative sex, Johnny feared that losing his penis meant losing his manhood.

It was clear to both Johnny and his wife Mayra that his way of being a man would have to change after his operation because he could no longer enact manliness through penetrative sex. Yet Johnny and Mayra had very different ideas about what kind of a man he should become. Through heated arguments that I witnessed over several days in his recovery room, they struggled to define how Johnny would act out masculinity after his penectomy. Shifting among arguing, complaining about one another to me or the nurses within his or her earshot, and simply soliloquizing, Johnny and Mayra used a range of narrative and interactional practices to try to link particular elements of his past, prospects, body, and behavior together into a new composite masculinity.

Mayra, a short, stocky woman with close-cropped gray hair, presented a narrative of Johnny's prior way of being a man as failed. She cast him as a poor provider, describing the economic and physical hardships she had suffered during their marriage. She recounted, down to the smell and feel of a stillbirth, her experiences of bearing twelve children in a doctorless small town, whereas her husband "enjoyed himself," squandering his income on other women in the United States. Often fanning herself with a prayer card, Mayra explained that Johnny needed to become more religious and more responsible. She described the penectomy as Johnny's comeuppance for his irresponsible sexual past and as a chance for him to become a better man now that he was back in Mexico and unable to cheat. While seeking to alter Johnny's masculinity, Mayra asserted her own composite femininity, which foregrounded piety, responsibility, and the suffering often associated with "good" womanhood in Roman Catholic contexts (Melhuus and Stolen 1996). She tended to his health while telling me that he did not deserve such care, leading Johnny to ask, "If I'm so horrible, why are you here caring for me?" She shot him a withering look, explaining, "Because I've suffered a lot." Mayra's mixture of physical caregiving and narrative critique seemed unconsciously strategic, reinforcing their couplehood through the embodied practice of care but putting her in control of their story.

Johnny also used verbal and nonverbal practices, including ignoring or talking over Mayra and yelling back, to assert his head-of-household status despite his physical incapacitation. Although Mayra wanted Johnny to change, he seemed to want to be as similar as possible to the kind of man he was before the operation. Before his penectomy, he despaired about his ability to accomplish this. He told me that he had "loved" his life of work and related sexual success in the United States and feared that it was gone forever. Since falling ill and returning to Mexico, he said, "In my life here, my mind is absent . . . After being a real gentleman (*caballero*)—parties, girls—now I'm missing the most important part of my body." He feared that losing his penis meant losing the trappings of the manliness that it had both literally and symbolically enabled—and thus the erasure of his very self. Yet after the surgery that he had once hoped would kill him, Johnny sought to create a similar kind of composite masculinity despite his amputation by incorporating reminiscence of past sexual successes rather than current sexual practices and focusing on the abilities to work, earn, and travel that had been key to his prior masculinity.

Johnny used the narrative practice of reminiscence to assert his success as a ladies' man in his recovery room. Often shouting over his wife's protestations, he continually repeated his "*gringuitas*, blondes, brunettes" refrain to me. Mayra countered this by foregrounding the limitations posed by his altered body. Seeking to sever the connection between his past and present ways of being a man, she responded to his narratives of sexual conquests with derisive laughter, once pointing to the thick pressure bandage encasing his groin and saying "all that is over." Johnny ignored her, frequently explaining his work and travel plans as a way to highlight these aspects of his intended way of being a man. Ignoring both his wife's and the nurses' protestations that he would not be healthy enough to work, he spoke happily and excitedly about his planned return to the United States and his high-status employment there.

Johnny and Mayra also argued about how to incorporate the amputation of gendered body parts into composite selves. Mayra admonished Johnny for being depressed before his surgery, saying that when she recently had a breast removed as a result of cancer, she had put her faith in God and did not complain. Johnny argued that his penile amputation was an experience similar to a woman losing her uterus and becoming unable to fulfill her social role of bearing children. He said, "It's like when they remove a young woman's womb, they get depressed." She flatly disagreed, saying that he didn't know what women felt and that people who left it to God would feel better. Their different interpretations of these socially symbolic amputations became the centerpieces of their respective arguments about the definition of good masculinity or femininity. For Johnny, the loss of reproductive organs posed a barrier to the sexual practices that he felt constituted his normative gender role as well as the social relationships based on that role. Mayra believed that such amputations were primarily a test of religious faith, foregrounding piety and forbearance in her vision of morally sound enactment of gender roles.

Through such interactions, Johnny reconciled his altered body with his ideals of masculinity. By focusing on work and memories rather than ongoing experiences of penetrative sex, Johnny revised the set of practices through which he could enact manliness. This was not a wholesale shift from one static type of masculinity to another; it was a change in the composite of acts, emotions, and ideas that together formed his way of being a man. Johnny's switch of sexual memories for sexual practices as a key aspect of his composite masculinity illustrates how men might respond to new experiences and constraints by revising the set of aspects that together make up their masculine selves. His memories of past sexual successes took the place of future conquests, linking his selves before and after the penectomy in a way that felt coherent. Furthermore, Johnny's fantasies of future work migration connected past manly work success to an imagined future masculinity, in a seemingly coherent manliness now unlinked from the physical presence of his penis. Thus, although having a penis and penetrative sex seemed crucial to Johnny's manhood before his penectomy, he was able to replace these with the memories of past sexual successes and a focus on work after his operation, revising the set of attributes that he believed made him a man to accommodate his new body. By deciding to conceal his penectomy from his friends, he also took steps to exclude that bodily change from the composite masculinity he would present to his peers.

It is important to note that the composite masculinity Johnny composed in the recovery room was linked to that particular context. After being released from the hospital, Johnny would have to face the fact that his poor health would likely make him unable to work or travel. His plans to lie about his operation and conceal the penile amputation from his friends may also have proved challenging in practice. Johnny's construction of an immediately postoperative composite masculinity thus reflects the changes he was forced to make when a key element of his prior masculinity was literally removed, along with the further changes that his upcoming circumstances would require. Johnny's response to his penectomy was unique, based on his take on cultural ideas about manliness, sex, and work, as well as his own personal experience. However, it exemplifies the process by which men revise the set of elements that make them particular kinds of men, in response to the ever-changing constraints and possibilities posed by their bodies and circumstances.

Overview of the Book

The rest of this book explores the ways that individuals facing similar, though usually less physically extreme, changes attempted to link elements of changing bodies and social worlds into context-appropriate ways of being men. This book focuses on the elements that the study participants most frequently sought to incorporate into new versions of their composite masculinities when faced with aging, illness, and decreased erectile function, along with the aspects of their lives they felt most aided or constrained their attempts to do so. These included ideas about *machismo* and the meanings of being Mexican, about modernity and the need for gender roles to change, locally prevalent ideas of what constitutes a respectable manly life course, and beliefs about health and healing. Thus, although all the study participants' life experiences were unique, here I seek to identify the common patterns, ideas, and practices from which the men drew in response to aging, illness, and sexual function change.

The first two chapters focus on cultural notions about gender and aging, examining study participants' ideas and experiences of the ways that masculinities change over the life course. Chapter 1 presents study participants' understandings of good and bad masculinities, and discusses the ways that these are shaped by what they believe to be their racial and cultural natures as Mexicans. It focuses on the life course narratives adapted by many of the study participants who defined themselves as "older," in which they interpret bodily aging and illness as a prompt to give up youthful forms of manliness and mature into "ex-*machistas.*" Chapter 2 analyzes the ways that men's relationships, primarily with women but also with family members, support groups, and doctors, helped them to make this change.

The subsequent chapters address the different ways that the participants incorporated erectile difficulty and related medical treatments into their composite masculinities. Chapter 3 describes the chronic illness epidemic sweeping Mexico and shows how it engenders erectile difficulty. It argues that, like masculinities, chronic illnesses can be fruitfully understood as composite objects. Chapter 4 shows that, in a structural context that deterred medicalization of erectile difficulty, most of the study participants developed multifaceted understandings of this bodily change that led them to reject and even fear medical ED treatment. Chapter 5 tells the stories of the few study participants who did seek ED treatment, using the composite perspective to show how they understood this as a response to a composite problem of masculinity, rather than a straightforward cure for a purely medical pathology. Finally, the concluding chapter discusses differences and changes among people's responses to decreased erectile function, investigates the relationship between change on individual and societal levels, and highlights the usefulness of the composite approach for understanding these differences and the practice of self-making more broadly.

Chapter One

MEXICANNESS, *MACHISMO*, AND MATURITY IN COMPOSITE MASCULINITIES

Mexican Men Critique "the Mexican Man"

When we discussed sex, marriage, and family, the study participants often made sweeping and surprisingly negative generalizations about Mexican men. Despite the fact that they themselves were members of this group, they would tell me that *Mexicanos* were womanizers, drunks, cheaters, liars, machos, and criminals. Men who strove to live lives they identified as good were often especially vehement in their criticism. One example is Gerardo, a sixty-seven-year-old retired high school teacher who I interviewed with his wife following a prostate checkup. They invited me to lunch at their home, where I was struck by the couple's affectionate closeness as they cooked with their daughter. The family joked together, showed me their vacation photos, and even dressed me up in traditional clothing from their native state of Oaxaca. As Gerardo drove me home that night, we talked about Mexican history—the subject he had taught. When I asked what he found most interesting about the topic, Gerardo replied: "You know, Mexico wasn't colonized like the United States but conquered. Spain opened jails and sent thieves, criminals over. All men, so they took advantage of the indigenous women. That's why *Mexicanos* are lazy, criminals, thieves, marijuana smokers—because our culture isn't clean. It's mixed." Taken aback by Gerardo's damning analysis of his peers, I asked if this could really be true because he himself was a Mexican man and loving husband and father. Looking at me as if I were a disappointing student, he said, "Of course!"

Gerardo's certainty that his countrymen were doomed to enact negative forms of masculinity exemplifies the study participants' views on the abstract Mexican man. Although vocally proud of their heritage, the

participants often believed that it predisposed men to a host of bad behaviors. Whatever their own actions, they generally cast good ways of
being men as learned but described bad aspects of masculinity as essential to Mexican biology or society. The participants almost universally
incorporated the themes of *machismo* or *Mexicanidad* (Mexicanness)
into the composite masculinities they constructed in the interview setting. Many seemed to think that providing me with basic knowledge
about the Mexican man was crucial for my ability to understand their
experiences. In response to my questions about their own lives, the men
often adopted the detached tone of a documentary voice-over and described the behaviors intrinsic to *el Mexicano* in the abstract.

This chapter investigates the ways in which the participants incorporated individual takes on the cultural trope of the abstract Mexican man
into their own composite masculinities. Some directly incorporated this
idea or the closely related concept of *machismo* into their narrative presentations of self, explaining that they did things *because* they were Mexican men. Others used the macho or *Mexicano* as a point of comparison,
incorporating differences from often-naturalized male behaviors into
their composite masculinities. Many did both, for example, when older
men attributed their youthful behavior to their nature as Mexicans but
said that they had changed as they aged.

Although the participants regarded the nature of *el Mexicano* variously as scientific fact, learned behavior, or a stigmatizing stereotype, the
notion was so culturally pervasive that most related it in some way into
their own ways of being men. They often described common assumptions about the *Mexicano* as facilitators of or constraints on their own
constructions of masculinity. Some felt free to perform behaviors that
fulfilled the contested but pervasive cultural expectation that men were
innately macho. Others found that these expectations limited their socially acceptable options for appropriate male behavior. By analyzing
the common ways that men linked understandings of the nature of Mexican manhood into their composite masculinities in our interviews,
along with focusing on how they defined particular traits as good, bad, or
age related, this chapter reveals how the participants incorporated cultural ideas about the nature of masculinity into their ways of being
men over time.

Participants' Ideas of Good Manly Traits

To understand how the study participants defined good masculinities, I often asked them how one should be and what one should do to be a good father and husband.[1] Their answers usually related to the theme of responsibility. The most common forms of responsibility mentioned were working, maintaining the health needed to work, and caring for one's wife and family. Together, their descriptions of good ways of being men reveal a set of manly practices seen as socially positive in Mexican culture. In our interviews, the individual participants frequently asserted particular ways of being men by shifting from describing good men in the abstract to describing their own variations on these positive behaviors. Which of the culturally common aspects of good manliness they sought to live out depended on their specific ideas about what kind of men they wanted to be and were shaped by their social and structural contexts. In a study population of men who were mostly working class but of different ages, generational differences in their understandings of good masculinity contributed to the clearest differences in their definitions of the practices that made a man "responsible."

The participants almost universally described hard work as a key element of good masculinity in the abstract and sought to incorporate it as an element of their own composite masculinities. Work was so essential to being a man for meeting local norms of masculinity that it was the only good trait that the participants ever described as essentially Mexican. For instance, a fifty-three-year-old carpenter said, "We *Mexicanos*, we like to work." Because hard work was seen as so quintessentially manly, men like Johnny who had become unable to continue prior ways of being men often used work to demonstrate their continued manliness. For instance, after explaining that his age and health problems forced him to partially retire from his job, a sixty-nine-year-old construction worker asserted that he continued working without pay for the sheer joy of it: "Work is beautiful; I feel happy working. I do small jobs in the house: painting or gardening."

In addition to demonstrating good manliness, work also enabled men to take on the role of head of household and provider, identities commonly

---

1 Focusing on these practices made sense because most of the study participants had been married and had children, and they described their relationships with wives and families as central to their life stories and senses of self. Even the very few never-married and childless men in the study talked about "men" in the abstract as having wives and children.

linked with manliness in Mexican discourse about gender. A twenty-eight-year-old graduate student said he had been taught that the man provides "fiscal solvency. Earning the money gives you a type of power. You can help your partner more." Inability to work or earn enough money thus became a barrier to enacting good masculinity. For example, a seventy-five-year-old who had retired from a low-paying factory job felt that he had failed as a father—despite trying his best to provide financially and emotionally—because "I earn little, and it's important to provide the comfort of money."

Although the participants described working hard as the cornerstone of being a good man, they defined work differently and saw different types of work as appropriate or possible at various life phases. Most notably, generational differences were apparent in their ideas about whether housework counted as an activity that would demonstrate good masculinity. The younger participants, who had come of age amid cultural calls for increased gender equity, usually said that "helping" with housework was an important part of a man's work. Although most preserved separate gender roles by casting domestic labor as a woman's primary and a man's secondary duty, many said that a failure to perform this responsibility would make one less of a man. For example, a twenty-year-old medical student said failing to help with housework revealed a "lack of masculinity." He said that although Mexico used to have a "macho tradition, I don't say that it has to be that way. The woman fortunately has the same rights as the man; she can work. Both should work to reach their goals together."

Conversely, men raised at a time when the domestic sphere was more strictly feminized often cast housework as a practice that would threaten masculinity. They instead defined work as paid employment outside the home and appropriate domestic labor as overseeing the use of one's income in ways that modeled proper family roles. A fifty-one-year-old university librarian described the role of housework in good masculinity in this way: "One must dole out money in the home, food, clothing, shelter. Secondly, one must be thinking of the family, give them education, recreation, religious training . . . Here in Mexico, it's seen as bad if a man does the housework; they call him whipped. So, one doesn't participate much in sharing housework."

However, men who voiced this notion often also incorporated changing with the times into their composite masculinities, both stating more stereotypically traditional opinions about men's work and calling for them to modernize. After he spoke, the librarian quoted previously thought for a moment and added that because women were now working outside the home, "men are going to have to change their attitude." Men also sometimes shifted their definitions of work to include domestic labor when they became unable to work outside the home. Participants who were similar to the retiree quoted previously included domestic physical labor in the set of acts they did to be men—as a demonstration of their continued will to work after aging out of paid employment. Thus participants of all ages shared the notion of work as a key practice of manly responsibility but revealed generational and situational differences in their definitions of that work.

The participants also saw maintaining the physical strength needed to work as a key element of responsible masculinity. Many of those who worked long hours at physically taxing jobs for low wages felt the duty to push their bodies to the limit to earn money but also to accept blame for their resulting physical deterioration. They also believed that they had failed as men when leisure practices caused bodily damage that might hamper their responsible performance or work and familial duties. For example, a fifty-seven-year-old delivery truck driver said that he felt guilty about a motorcycle accident that damaged his testicles, because even though he did not cause the accident, riding the motorcycle showed a "lack of precaution." He said that if the accident had ended his sexual function or ability to work, he would have felt terrible "because indirectly, I was guilty. I provoked the accident. A good man is responsible, above all else because I have a child." This participant's shift from an abstract definition of a good man to his own case demonstrates the narrative practices through which men incorporated responsibility into the composite masculinities that they presented within the interview setting.

Even more than caring for their bodies, the participants identified caring for one's family as a key element of good manliness. This included working to meet financial obligations, maintaining the bodily ability to do so, and inculcating proper values in one's children. Older men tended to add that being a good example for young people was a key element of good masculinity. A seventy-eight-year-old participant stated, "I feel obligated to be an example for younger people." Many older men described their realizations that this was an important manly duty as part of the shifts from bad to good men that they described in their interviews, which will be discussed later in this chapter. Finally, almost all of the participants said that caring for one's wife and treating her well was key to being a good man. However, participants who enacted different kinds of composite masculinities had varying notions about what this good treatment entailed.

Younger men who had been raised in a society that idealized companionate marriage often characterized emotionally supporting and maintaining open communication with one's wife as central to "treating her well." Many younger men, and the small minority of older men who had been faithful to their wives, also understood sexual fidelity to be an important aspect of caring for one's wife, in terms of both her emotions and her health. The delivery truck driver explained, "Being faithful is part of being responsible, since there are sicknesses, like AIDS."

Most of the older men had very different ideas of what caring for one's wife entailed. They saw treating one's wife well as caring for her in the same general ways that one should care for one's children: providing financially and meeting her social and emotional needs when possible. The older men often understood cordial—though not necessarily emotionally intimate—marital relations to be part of treating one's wife well. In a typical definition of good treatment, a sixty-six-year-old retired driver said, "Don't yell at her, don't hit her, get along well."

Unlike the mostly younger men who incorporated companionate relationships into their composite masculinities, these men saw continued provision for one's wife and family as the key sign of respect and placed little importance on fidelity. A sixty-eight-year-old security guard said, "The most important part of being a good husband isn't to be faithful but to care for the family. I'd never abandon my wife. You have to stick it out for the kids, or it looks bad." Some of these men defined fidelity in emotional, not physical, terms. A sixty-four-year-old retired mechanic, who told me about several extramarital dalliances and also reported caring deeply for his wife, said, "Being faithful is more than anything giving affection to the wife. Infidelity is more of a release." For him, faithfulness meant providing the required resources and care, whereas sex with others was a somewhat unrelated physical act.

Others said that extramarital sex was key to maintaining their ability to care for their wives. The older participants frequently said they had not married for love or had ceased to love their wives and stayed in their marriage "out of responsibility." They often reported that infidelity enabled them to let off sexual steam and made them able to stay in marriages that did not provide sexual or romantic excitement. Thus most of the older participants believed that extramarital sex, if done discreetly, did not represent a lack of respect for one's wife. In fact, because they saw infidelity as a natural act for men, many believed that taking care to keep one's inevitable liaisons out of the public eye was actually a way of caring for one's spouse. For instance, a sixty-five-year-old retired power company worker described going to great lengths to conceal his infidelity, reporting that, "She didn't find out; I had respect."

Such men's methods of concealing infidelity or calming angry wives served as additional ways of demonstrating both innate Mexican sexuality and responsibility. Although many of the men said that they had been taught by their fathers and friends to deny everything if accused of infidelity, they also believed that it was responsible to accept the blame for their actions if they were incontrovertibly caught. A forty-eight-year-old mechanic told me that his wife was angry when she discovered that he was cheating but accepted it after he apologized because he met his husbandly duty of providing for her to the extent that she did not have to work. He explained, "She was always a housewife. I never abandoned her . . . it [infidelity] was a mistake I made." However, although he saw assuming blame for his actions as part of his responsibility and a way to maintain cordial marital relations, he told me that he did not actually feel guilty because "we Mexican men are like that."

The Concepts of Mexicanidad and Machismo

When the study participants talked about good ways of being men, they focused on specific practices that were intended to responsibly support one's family. However, when they discussed being a man in general or talked about bad forms of manliness, they usually spoke of traits that they believed to be deeply rooted in their Mexican bodies and culture. They frequently described tensions between desired practices of responsibility and a *Mexicano* essence that entailed uncontrollable sexual desire and emotional closure. They often characterized this essence as both an innate physical aspect of *Mexicanidad* and a cultural inheritance from which it was difficult to escape.

This idea of an innate Mexican masculinity derives from the cultural notion that Mexican bodies and selves are biologically unique. In the 1920s, as postrevolutionary Mexico sought to define its national identity, public intellectuals promoted José Vasconcelos' idea that the racial mixing of Spanish and Indian ancestry would result in a "cosmic race," ideally suited to participation in modern statehood (Vasconcelos 1997). The notion that the Mexican population has mixed into a unique and special race, often simply called *la raza*, has shaped many aspects of Mexican culture over the past century. "Race" in this conception is broadly defined, indexing shared community and national identity rather than simply reproductive heritage or shared genetics. The notion that Mexican society constitutes a homogeneous, mestizo *raza* has been used to various political ends over the past century, ranging from calls for rights for impoverished members of *la raza* to violent attacks on Mexican nationals excluded from this community, such as Chinese immigrants (Sato 2006). The discourse of *la raza* has influenced debates about and government interventions into both masculinity and health, for example, in health and hygiene programs aimed at encouraging parents to engage in hygienic and modern motherhood and fatherhood practices that would advance the nation, itself figured as a large family (Bliss 1999; Stern 2003). That the idea of Mexican racial uniqueness still shapes health provision is evident in the name of the IMSS flagship hospital: *Centro Medico Nacional la Raza*.

The notion of *machismo* depends on such beliefs about the racial and cultural uniqueness of the Mexican population. The term *macho*, which literally simply means "male," was first used to describe a specific form of masculinity in discussions in the 1930s of rural men's perceived inability to deal with urbanization (Parédes 1967). Octavio Paz's influential 1950s elaboration on this idea into the notion that Mexican men are constitutionally sexually aggressive, dominant, and emotionally closed attributes these characteristics to the same act that founded *la raza*: the conquistadors' coercive reproduction with indigenous women. Paz cast these relationships as a sort of original sin, creating a historical shame that doomed their male offspring to seek self-validation by reproducing their Spanish forefathers' gendered violence and dominance (Paz [1961] 1985).

Paz's arguments were not grounded in social scientific research; they represented his literary interpretation of his own society. Others, such as feminist scholars who challenge this narrative of women's historical subordination, have interpreted the cultural consequences of conquest quite differently (Romero and Nolacea Harris 2005). Thus anthropologists argue that *machismo* is not a naturally occurring or physically innate Mexican trait; it is a construct that has been made real as people believe in and perform it. For example, Matthew Gutmann argues that *machismo* was "partially declared into being" by people's acceptance and subsequent enactment of Paz's ideas (1996, 240). Social scientists have long sought to refute the stereotype that Mexican men are machos, arguing that real men's lives involve complicated relationships with, not simple reproductions of, this discourse (cf. Baca Zinn 1982; García and de Oliveira 2004; Ramirez 2009).

Yet as Gerardo's use of the conquest to explain Mexican manhood shows, Paz's description of *machismo* has become a central way that many people throughout Mexican society understand the nature of the *Mexicano*. Even men like Gerardo who decry bad masculinity and seek to act differently often naturalize *machismo*. For example, Mexican activists seeking to reform men that they see as behaving badly often assert that they have a natural, macho essence that must be combated through deliberate resocialization (Brandes 2003; Garda 2001). The participants frequently incorporated the discourse of *machismo* into their composite masculinities, variously positioning themselves as subject to, or as working against, this form of manhood. They often understood *machismo* as the traditional form of Mexican manliness, which fit badly with modernizing and increasingly egalitarian gender roles but which was nevertheless deeply rooted in Mexican men's biologies and culture.

Mexicanidad and Machismo in Men's Composite Masculinities

The participants drew from the pervasive ideas of *Mexicanidad* and *machismo* in ways that differed based on the kinds of men they wanted to be and the ways that they had felt constrained by these ideas about masculinity. They described *machismo* and its component behaviors in different terms, as biologically innate versus culturally learned, depending on the ways they linked these traits into their constructions of masculinity in our interviews and in their daily lives. This section discusses the ways that men characterized and related to the nature of the abstract Mexican man.

"NATURAL" MEXICAN MANLINESS

Many of the participants incorporated understandings of *machismo* or Mexicanness as natural into their ways of being men. They explained actions such as infidelity by describing them as intrinsic to their Mexican constitutions. A sixty-two-year-old retired glass installer simply said, "The man is not faithful." Similarly, a fifty-six-year-old veterinarian explained, "Here in Mexico, it's something normal. They say the Mexican is passionate. They say the man is polygamous by nature." Many of the participants attributed this nature to a hot (*caliente*) constitution (a health belief that will be discussed further in chapter 3) that led men to desire great amounts of sex, carousing, and hard labor. In a typical statement, a retired state worker told me, "The Mexican is very hot."[2] A fifty-four-year-old retired trucker said, "For me, the sexual appetite has been a daily part of what the Mexican is."

The notion that Mexican men are naturally highly sexual shaped many study participants' expectations about how they should behave. For instance, a sixty-five-year-old retired mechanic was concerned that he had been providing less sex than usual to his wife, despite the fact that she never requested it. He explained, "She isn't demanding, but I know I have to comply. We here in Mexico, it's our reason; our way of thinking." He believed that he was obliged to have a certain amount of sex with his wife not because it would fulfill her stated desires but because it was his natural obligation as a Mexican man. Accordingly, some men who experienced lessening desire viewed disinterest in sex as a bodily abnormality. A forty-year-old construction worker told me that he had lost his "desire," but that he wanted it back: "I want to return to having that because it's normal, the normal life of the man. I think I'm sick; I have a problem. I'm not living normally."

Thus men who believed that "Mexican manhood" had a natural essence nevertheless sometimes found it oppressive or hard to achieve. They often experienced difficulty enacting this essential masculinity as a social failing and felt that the things they could do to be men were limited by their natures. Men commonly voiced this sentiment, by telling me that they enjoyed our interviews because they had no other opportunities to talk about sexuality and emotions. The eighty-year-old participant who asserted that "one as a man is always unfaithful" discussed his fear that his wife would think that he no longer loved her because he could no longer attain an erection and they had not recently had penetrative sex. Compared with many men who reported infidelity, he did not feel that his extramarital affairs had affected his marriage in any way; he described a great love for his wife, whom he called his "destiny," and said they had been happy together since the moment they met. However, he could not bring himself to discuss his sexual problems with her. He explained this by falling back on the nature of the *Mexicano*, saying, "Sometimes one is so hermetically sealed. I don't know why I don't talk to her."

---

2 "Hot" in this and similar quotations should be read as having a double meaning: constitutionally hot in the humoral sense discussed in chapter 3 and also "horny."

He also believed that this inexplicable but inevitable emotional closure prevented him from asking the doctor for ED treatment. A sixty-six-year-old retired driver explained this common idea about Mexican men's emotional closure succinctly by saying, "I prefer to keep my feelings to myself; that's how we Mexican men are."

RESISTING ESSENTIAL MANLINESS

Despite the social harm that many of the men experienced and caused as a consequence of ostensibly natural Mexican masculinity, many of the participants viewed these tendencies as inescapable. For instance, a fifty-nine-year-old retiree laughed and said, "That's how we Mexicans are; a race that—for women, it's something special with women. We want many women, though we don't care for the kids." Similarly, when I asked a thirty-year-old government office worker if he planned to be faithful to his wife, he responded, "Lamentably, the Mexican doesn't have this characteristic. Women yes. But we're very—not machos but—very *conquistador*." When I asked if men were inherently like this or if they were taught to be so—he joked that they were unfaithful, "Recreationally!" However, thinking further, he described variation among men and its possible sources by saying, "Not all are like that. Also, their parents play a role; if the father is a *machista*, with lots of women, the kids pay attention."

In his response, this participant first justified infidelity as a natural Mexican trait. Yet when I pressed him to explain this assumption about natural Mexicanness by clarifying whether it was biologically innate or socially taught, his joking response revealed that he simply saw infidelity as something that men enjoy, which must be natural by virtue of its frequency and social acceptability. Thinking further, he decided that because not all men are unfaithful, it must be a socially transmitted characteristic. The development of this answer demonstrates that although the participants frequently used their understandings of the nature of Mexican men to make sense of their own actions, these understandings were often flexible, situational, or nebulously defined. However, the apparent flexibility of some men's narratives made their beliefs about innate Mexican masculinity no less real; many men experienced these ideas about the Mexican male nature as binding and prescriptive.

Some of the participants who saw Mexican male sexual voracity as a natural bodily characteristic nevertheless believed that men could—and sometimes should—overcome it through mental toughness. Foregrounding responsible masculinity in our interview, a sixty-one-year-old construction worker said that he had to learn to "control my mind" to limit his sexual activity and promote healing after his prostate and kidney surgeries. He said, "You know how Mexican men are—very hot. They want more, more, more. I had to set limits." Others tried to evade what they saw as their naturally macho impulses, for example, avoiding situations that they feared would unleash their inherent *machismo*. A sixty-three-year-old office worker said that he would not discuss sexual problems with his wife because he wanted to avoid the explosive hot-temperedness to which he was naturally prone but sought to repress. He explained, "It's not the case of the macho Mexican. My wife is close with me, but I'm afraid to discuss this . . . we prefer not to talk, so that we don't yell."

Other participants reported lifelong struggles against macho bodily impulses and upbringings, apparently incorporating both responsible rejection of *machismo* and the social dominance offered by traditional masculinity into their composite masculinities in different contexts. Osvaldo, a sixty-four-year-old retired mechanic, said that he has long fought against reenacting the *machismo* modeled by his father, which he fears has nevertheless been transmitted to his son. Osvaldo told me that although he was unfaithful to his wife, he tried not to philander in a sexist way, explaining that "it's *machista* to grab the woman, and that's it. I tried to satisfy them." Explaining why he was not a macho, he said that he had always tried to be different from his father, a professional soldier who eventually abandoned his family. He said, "My father is one of those [a macho]; he beat my mother. I only slapped my wife, maybe two times, with an open hand. My father used to put my mother over his knees and spank her with a belt!" Osvaldo saw rejection of *machismo* not as a wholesale rejection of violence or infidelity but a deliberate tempering of these inherent traits. He said that as a young boy, watching his father, "I thought, I'll be different, but I won't let my wife take advantage of me either."

Thus Osvaldo explicitly sought to retain a certain level of male privilege but rejected the extreme levels of violence and autocratic familial rule that he associated with *machismo*. Unfortunately, he reported that only one of his sons had followed this model, whereas the other treated his wife badly. He said, "The oldest hits his wife; I don't like it, but I don't interfere. It makes me angry; I tell him not to hit her. Don't you think that she feels it? She's not an object!" Trying to explain this son's behavior, he said that despite his attempts to raise him differently, either individual temperament or biologically based *machismo* had won out. He reasoned, "Everyone does his own thing. Or, he has my father's genes." Osvaldo's analysis of his son's behavior demonstrates how men's understandings of *machismo* as biological or social influenced the ways they assessed one's personal responsibility for macho acts.

MACHISMO AS A LEARNED TRAIT

Some of the participants revealed that they saw *machismo* as a performance—one that was necessary for maintaining social status. Such statements enabled them to assert good masculinities, aligned with the cultural discourse valorizing modernization, in our interviews, while also acting in acceptably manly ways with peers. A sixty-five-year-old mechanic who was ashamed about his decreasing erectile function said that he felt he had to act macho to be accepted by his friends, even though he experienced this practice as isolating. He said, "Mentally, one has to force himself. It shames you. They might say—his hand fell [making an effeminate, slack hand gesture]—that you're homosexual." His fear of seeming homosexual, which for him entailed a lack of manliness, meant that he could not discuss his sexual difficulties with friends because he felt that he had to keep up a macho front: "It's shameful for you, as a man. As we say in Mexico, we're macho. When we men get together we're all really macho, but it's not really that way. We have secrets."

Other participants espoused views of *machismo* as a learned trait in order to define their own styles of masculinity against it. They often characterized *machismo* as a bad reputation, a wrongheaded idea, or a deliberate performance rather than a biological imperative. Hugo, a fifty-year-old truck driver whose story will be told later in this chapter, said, "*Machismo* is a reputation, but it isn't true; we're different. It's bad; others have a bad impression of us." A fifty-eight-year-old driver defined *machismo* as the attitude that "the woman needs to be behind," offering the critique that "the wife isn't a thing. She's a person. She's a comrade." He saw *machismo* as an outgrowth of corrupt Mexican politics, which he said left common people behind in an oppressive relationship that mirrored macho marital arrangements. This participant saw distancing himself from *machismo* as a way of repudiating bad politicians' analogous ways of treating the less powerful. Other men sought to demonstrate more modern masculinities by incorporating the origin story of *machismo* into their critiques. A twenty-four-year-old gym teacher said, "A lot of *machismo* exists. They're afraid that if they let their guard down, they'll become whipped [*mandilón*]. That's the closed psychology of the macho man, from pre-Hispanic times." For many men, critiquing *machismo* was a way of defining their own masculinity and linking together various aspects of life, such as self-consciously modern views about gender and politics, into a coherent manly selfhood.

Similarly, some of the participants made rejection of *machismo* a key element of their composite masculinities to assert good manliness after undesired life changes made aspects of their prior practices of being men impossible. Rene, a fifty-two-year-old who had recently been laid off from his job as a television executive, asserted a liberal masculinity as a way to assert his upper class and highly educated status despite his job loss and decreased ability to provide financially for his family. Rene told me, "I'm not a macho," explaining that he had been raised to see women as equals by his non-Mexican father. He said, "My father was a very liberal person. He had freedom of thought." In contrast, Rene said that, "In Mexico, because of tradition, both the man and the woman have a *machista* upbringing, although it has lessened with time." He asserted that *machismo* persists "where there's a lack of education" and used this distinction between educated, progressive masculinity and lower class *machismo* to distinguish himself from the people with whom he interacted after his job loss. Rene was trying to make money by making and selling lamps, and he often traveled to an impoverished indigenous town to buy pottery for this purpose. He said that there, he saw sisters being forced to wash their brothers' clothes and women working hard while men spent the day drinking. By critiquing this "sexist upbringing," Rene both made a political statement about gender and linked his style of masculinity to an elite class status that had been threatened by his unemployment.

ALFONSO: "SLAVERY" TO ONE'S MEXICAN CHARACTER

Alfonso's story illustrates the conflicting and sometimes oppressive ways that men incorporated understandings of the nature of Mexican men into their own composite masculinities. A fifty-nine-year-old carpenter, Alfonso was stooped and wrinkled and looked far older than his age. We met when he came to the IMSS hospital for a checkup following his prostate operation, and I found him eager to talk. He spoke quickly, appearing to repeat ideas and arguments that he had thought through time and again, as he told me about the nature of Mexican men in a way that both excused his admittedly bad behaviors and revealed that he felt trapped into acting out these socially damaging forms of Mexicanness.

Alfonso frequently used the language of slavery to show how he felt bound to particular ways of being. He told me, "I was a slave of work, also of drink." Repeating that he was a "slave of work," he related this bondage to the positive aspects of what he understood to be natural Mexican masculinity. He said that he worked so that "my wife lacks for nothing" and to provide education for their two daughters, who still live with them and now have successful careers. Despite this evidence of his responsible fathering, he commented that he was happy that these daughters had remained single, saying, "They prefer to be single; it's better so they don't marry drunks, liars, like we Mexican men are." When I asked if he himself was like that, he said he was and that "I want to change, but I can't."

He reported feeling trapped in a vicious cycle of needing to work and needing to drink to be able to work. He said he started drinking at 11 a.m. each day, which enabled him to perform his duties in the carpentry shop by preventing his hands from shaking and giving him the will to continue. He told me that drinking helped him not to think, which meant that it helped him to continue his never-ending work. He reported feeling both trapped by this cycle and glad that his work—and thus his ability to provide for his family—could continue. He said, "Now I'm old, but I know how to work. When I work, I know how to do it well. I don't have agility, but the boss knows that I do good work."

Alfonso saw no way out of this "slavery" to work and drink. He believed his drinking and working were interconnected, and were inescapable aspects of his Mexican nature. He said, "Sometimes I want to change my character, but no." He explained that his perceived inability to change caused arguments with his wife that he described as both the fault of his Mexican nature and his spouse: "We, as Mexican men, are jerks. I tell my wife, I want to change. She needs to help; she shouldn't give me money to drink!" He reported that his wife frequently asked him to stop drinking, saying, "Yourself, Alfonso, you have the solution." However, again casting his undesired behavior as an innate personality trait, he said that he would retort, "You knew when you married me that I drink a lot!"

Alfonso believed that his drinking was also caused by the stifling of another physical drive innate to his Mexican male body: his need for sex. Although he said he had frequent sex with his wife and other women early in his marriage, he told me that he began to feel guilty over his infidelities when his wife's health deteriorated, leading him to renounce extramarital sex twenty years ago. He came to this decision when his wife gave birth to their last child; she had septic shock and needed blood transfusions to survive. He provided his own blood and thanked God for her survival, vowing, "I won't go roaming the streets now." However, as a result of his wife's fragile health and resulting disinterest in sex, this vow of fidelity became a de facto vow of celibacy, and Alfonso counted drinking as the only "vice" that remained available to him. He said that he drank not only to get though his workday but also because "I don't have a woman's tenderness."

For Alfonso, drinking and working were both biological and social imperatives. They were elements of a character that he felt he could not escape, particularly because his physical need for sex went unfulfilled. Alfonso's obvious pain, and the contrast between his love for his family and constant fighting with his wife, showed how his stated beliefs about the nature of Mexican men both justified his problematic behaviors and entrapped him into repeating them. Alfonso included current fidelity, guilt over poor treatment of his family, debilitating hard work, and innate desires for drink and sex in a manly selfhood that doomed him to unending sadness. By including the beliefs that he was innately subject to bad desires and that a good man should soberly and responsibly provide in the set of attributes that made up his way of being a man, Alfonso experienced a powerfully raced and gendered unhappiness.

Aging into Mature Masculinities

Although Alfonso felt trapped by the manly traits that he assumed to be natural, many of the participants who understood macho traits to be at least partly biological believed that they might change along with bodily aging. They often described natural macho desires being at odds with the responsible masculinity they valued. A sixty-seven-year-old retiree differentiated between *machismo* and true, or positive, manliness, saying that in Mexico, "We're very manly; we confuse the term *man* with the term macho." I asked him to define these terms, and he said, "Macho: I am, can, do, everything. You as a woman must be restricted. 'Man' for me implies responsibility in all senses: family, wife, children, and with myself." He defined himself as a man, not a macho, but also said that he had been more macho as a youth, when biological urges would bring out macho traits. Offering an example, he said that when he was younger, "I saw a pretty prostitute, with a really nice body. In such cases, the macho comes out of us [*el macho nos sale*]. So I slept with her." Thus he defined his masculinity against *machismo* as an older man but said that macho actions were key parts of his manly self in his youth. This shift makes sense in terms of his understanding of *machismo* as an innate essence, brought out by the application of particular stimuli to a young and vigorous body. Based on such beliefs, the participants frequently characterized bodily aging as a reprieve from macho impulses.

The majority of the older participants included this narrative of changing manhood over time in the composite masculinities they presented in our interviews. Most of them saw the social changes required by bodily aging as enabling a shift to what I will call "mature" masculinity: a set of physical and social practices locally recognized as a good way to be an older man.

Many of the participants said that their youthful bodies once led them into practices such as frequent sex, carousing, and obsession with work, which hampered their ability to be responsible husbands and fathers. Although having once established their masculinity in these ways remained key to their understandings of themselves as men, most of the older participants also saw tempering these activities later in life as equally important to respectable masculinity. They stated that as their bodies aged, urges to carouse and be unfaithful naturally lessened as their sexual potency and physical strength decreased. Although many reported initial unhappiness with these changes, most of them said they came to appreciate them as facilitators of new, age-appropriate practices.

The participants frequently described older age as a time when emotional relationships with romantic partners and family members should come to the fore, as sexual desires and the physically taxing manly acts prompted by youthful bodies faded into the background. Although in Mexican culture women have traditionally been understood to be of "the home" and men of "the street," the sort of mature masculinity that the study participants saw as appropriate for older men entailed a reconfiguring of men's relationships to the domestic sphere (see also Varley and Blasco 2000). Older men reported renouncing more outward-directed self-making practices, such as extramarital sex, partying, and even work migration, and defining their masculine selves more through home-based emotional practices, such as domestic labor and increasingly tender relationships with wives, children, and grandchildren. Thus mature composite masculinities prominently included affective relationships with family members and particular domestic activities.

It is important to note that the categories of mature or older are social, not biological or numeric, classifications. Although in this chapter I have previously used the terms *older* and *younger* to describe generational differences roughly related to numeric age, men's self-classifications discussed in this section relate much more strongly to where individuals saw themselves on their anticipated life paths. Their feelings of being younger or older were shaped by their lived experiences of age, which were powerfully influenced by their bodily health and their progression through expected life milestones, such as marriage and the birth of children and grandchildren. Although many of the study participants shared the understanding that Mexican men would mature over time, when they thought this shift to be personally appropriate varied widely. Some men began to consciously act more mature after getting married in their twenties, whereas others did not do so until having a health scare in their eighties.

MATURE MASCULINITIES

These new practices included evolving relationships with wives and families and new forms of self-care, work, and leisure that reflected the new limitations posed by men's aging bodies. The participants often described their youthful urges for sex and fun as taking them away from their families and thus cast the calming of these embodied urges as a chance to settle into domestic life. A sixty-seven-year-old bakery owner voiced the commonly held notion that cessation of or a decrease in penetrative sex would pave the way for a new, more companionate and affective relationship with one's wife, stating that marital sexuality "is like a plant that dries up over time; the strength [*fuerza*] diminishes. When you get old, you're more tired; spending time together is more important—spending time together happily."

A twenty-nine-year-old prison administrator reported that "as a youth, you're thinking about the future. Now I'm mature. The youthful desires had their time; now one has to adapt to continue onward." As part of this adaptation, he made particular lifestyle changes, including working less and giving up drinking and smoking. He saw these changes as "necessary for my health and my family." In general, the participants saw the cessation of previously enjoyed physical practices, such as sex, drinking, smoking, and even overwork—which they sometimes called "vices"—not as sad consequences of aging but as proactive steps to be taken to mature responsibly.

The participants frequently saw acting appropriately as an older man as a point of masculine pride. In response to my question about whether he continued to have sex, a sixty-eight-year-old barber laughed and told me, "Here in Mexico, we have a saying: 'After old age, chickenpox' [*Despues de vejez, viruelas*]. It means that some things become silly when one is older." Many of the participants felt that desires that were appropriate to young men became inappropriate as they matured and made both new age-appropriate practices and their willingness to age gracefully key elements of their composite masculinities. A seventy-five-year-old retired factory worker said, "Erectile dysfunction isn't important. When I was young, it would have been but not now." Similarly, a sixty-four-year-old retired university staff member remarked, "Now I don't have sex. I don't have the desire; I don't feel that. I don't even try. It gets erased. I don't feel bad—sometimes when I was young, yes, if you couldn't get it, you felt bad but not now. A youth looks for it, but not anymore."

Although the participants believed that giving up vices was a key component of maturation, they generally did not feel remorse for or shame about youthful transgressions. Rather, they saw a youth spent drinking, womanizing, and carousing—as long as it was coupled with responsibility for one's family and a strong work ethic—as age-appropriate behavior that subsequently enabled a shift to mature masculinity. A seventy-seven-year-old retired gardener stated: "As a youth, I was very into women. Time puts everything in order. When there are children, you have to think differently, dedicate yourself to the family. I don't feel bad; I feel normal and content. I was a bad husband in the question of being unfaithful, but I never left my family, she [my wife] was very sickly, but I never left them."

In fact, many of the men told me that the fact that they had enjoyed so much sex, with so many partners, in their youth enabled them to feel satisfied with their experiences and move happily on to a mature masculinity focused elsewhere. A sixty-four-year-old retired mechanic stated that "my sex life now doesn't exist, doesn't exist. But I'm satisfied from my youth. I don't miss it. Thank God, I had a lot of fun before I got married!" After learning from the doctor that a prostate operation would likely end his erectile function, a sixty-eight-year-old retired power company worker reported that he could accept this prognosis because "I'm satisfied; I passed my best years. I'm happy. We've enjoyed ourselves." He went on to say that the cessation of erectile function would mark a shift in his relationship with his wife, and he would strive to support and appreciate her more fully. He stated, "Now, I will completely dedicate myself to her. Recognize that she has done everything for me; whatever I did, she has always been with me. She cares for me, and I care for her too, and we have to get along well."

As this participant's increasingly affective focus on his wife shows, many of the men believed that waning ability to have penetrative sex created room for the further development of emotional relationships with wives, which may have been restricted by aspects of youthful masculinity, such as infidelity, overwork, or overindulgence in alcohol. This emotional attention to one's wife and family, often linked to a shift from a focus on work outside the home to domestic labor, such as home maintenance and caring for grandchildren, was common enough that one participant called it "the Mexican classic" [*el clasico de México*]. A fifty-six-year-old predicted that after his retirement from the public health service, "I will dedicate myself to my wife, the house, gardening, caring for the grandchildren—the Mexican classic." The participants frequently described this change of focus as a "second stage" or "other level" of marriage and life. This second stage was often characterized by a nonsexual love—for wives and other family members—that men experienced as more profound than the sexually mediated emotions they had previously felt for women. A ninety-year-old retired bodyguard, reporting that he had not had sex with his wife for six years, said that, "Life, love, compassion all grow. With time, they are deeper."

The triggers for men to begin enacting mature masculinities tended to be socially significant familial or biological events that they felt required them to be new sorts of men. In addition to a decline in sexual function, these events included the birth of children or grandchildren and the onset of illness. Some of the men also began to incorporate narratives of mature masculinity at life points commonly seen as transitional, such as marriage or retirement. For example, men who had made frequent extramarital sex a key facet of their masculine selfhood often began to focus more on emotional relationships with their wives as they became less able to have frequent penetrative sex. A fifty-five-year-old retired laundry worker told me, "I was a womanizer." When I asked, "Are you still?" he replied, "The truth is, now I don't have the same capacity. I'm fifty-five, I know what I am. I don't want problems with my wife. Like I deserve respect from her, she deserves it from me as well."

Decreasing erectile function was a key bodily change that prompted many participants to make this shift to an older style of masculinity and foreground domestic relationships and activities in their composite masculinities. In general, the IMSS urology patients tended to understand decreasing erectile capacity as a consequence of aging. An eighty-one-year-old retired factory worker, who came to the IMSS hospital for a prostate checkup but also reported changes in sexual function, joked to me that the prostate tests would reveal "what happened to my youth." This equation of the capacity for frequent sexual penetration with youth was common. Most of the study participants reported that their erectile function had to some degree diminished over time, and they accepted this change as natural. Their most common response to questions about sexual function was "it's not like before." Instead of a lament over lost youth or virility, this was generally a matter-of-fact statement that men's bodies, desires, and social lives were not the same as when they were younger. A fifty-five-year-old delivery truck driver reported that he now experienced erections only infrequently, but this was a normal consequence of age and hard work: "My work is a little rough, heavy; I carry a lot, so I feel a little tiredness. Now, I can't have as much sex as before. This is normal. Now it's not the same: when I was young, more potency. Now with my age, not anymore." This understanding of diminishing erectile function as a part of natural aging led most of the participants to accept it as a prompt to reconfigure their composite masculinities, excluding practices that required a youthful body and incorporating new ones.

The participants who shared the general narrative of a shift from youthful to mature masculinity also identified structural constraints as catalysts for this shift. These men often saw decreasing sex or sexual function as consequences of economic change. A seventy-one-year-old cell phone salesman said that with increasing age, it became harder to get work, and his income diminished. This lack of solvency left him without the money needed to wine and dine women for extramarital affairs. He told me that because his wife lacked interest in sex, he used to seek it from others, but "now, not anymore, because there isn't money. It doesn't stretch to cover everything." Although his adoption of fidelity had fiscal rather than moral causes, it shifted the composite picture of his masculinity into one where responsible self-care became crucially definitive of manly selfhood, and frequent penetrative sex no longer was. When I asked if he would start to see other women again if he had more money, he said no because the risk of disease was too great: "With so many things [sexually transmitted diseases], you have to be careful."

Different events prompted other men's shifts toward fidelity. For a sixty-four-year-old retired utility company worker, retirement from formal employment led to physical and emotional proximity to his wife that caused him to be faithful. He said that "before, I worked. I had to travel, one or two months away from home . . . As a youth, it's impossible to resist, like the governor of New York![3] When you're young, away from your family for two months, you sin [laughs]. Now, retired, I work two blocks from my house; I'm closer to my wife."

The onset of chronic illness also encouraged men to mature. A fifty-four-year-old street vendor reported that diabetes made him unable to achieve erections and thus caused him to end his infidelities. When I asked if he would continue to be faithful to his wife if his erectile function returned, he said, "Infidelity comes when one is younger. Now with the illness, I'm totally skinny. I see myself in the mirror, and I scare myself! No woman would be interested." When I asked if that meant that just young people are unfaithful, he responded, "People my age too, but not if they're sick. Then it's not right to go looking."

In addition to frequently identifying illness and its consequences as an impetus to act out new forms of masculinity, many of the men believed that their youthful ways of being men had actually caused the illnesses that later led them to change. For example, a seventy-two-year-old retired bodyguard said that he had changed drastically as a result of a series of heart attacks. He explained, "Before, I was a real womanizer. I always liked the ladies." He recounted that for thirty years, he lived a "violent life," a "fast life" characterized by work-related violence, drinking, and sleeping with as many women as possible. After his heart attacks, which he says were caused by the stress and fast pace of his life, he said he made a "180-degree turn to a tranquil life." Today, he said, "I dedicate myself to the home, working in the garden, caring for my birds. I still think about women, but now I just look." The participants also identified fears of contracting a sexually transmitted infection, which they often asserted were increasing in frequency, as influencing their changes to fidelity.

---

3 New York governor Eliot Spitzer had recently been the focus of a prostitution scandal that was widely publicized in the Mexican media. Sex scandals involving American politicians frequently become popular cultural references in Mexico. For instance, when I taught in a Mexico City middle school during the 1998 Bill Clinton and Monica Lewinsky scandal, students would often taunt each other on the playground by calling each other "Clinton" or "Monica."

Hugo's story exemplifies this Mexican classic shift from an urge-controlled youth to a more circumspect older age. He characterized his life as a learning process, culminating in a change of focus from more primal acts and emotions to thoughtful interaction with loved ones. Hugo said that because he and his wife married young—he was sixteen, she fifteen—"we didn't have much experience," so they made youthful errors. As a long-distance truck driver, he traveled constantly, which encouraged him to stray sexually in what he now considers errors of judgment, saying, "I've made mistakes, been outside the married couple. It's because I'm a truck driver: strange beds, strange women, strange places—one suffers a lot." Hugo characterized these infidelities and the time spent away from his family as "suffering" in hindsight because with the help of his wife, he later decided that a good life would involve a closer focus on his family. He described himself and his wife early on in their marriage as childlike and "inexpert"; he would cheat, and they would fight, "even reaching blows." Now, he said, they don't fight in this way because they don't want to jeopardize their valued relationship. Looking back, he said, "I did think of leaving her, to be with someone else. Thank God I didn't! She put up with me. Thanks to her we're together . . . Now it's not like before, inexpert, and we continue growing, trying to understand each other better. That continues." He recalled an epiphanic moment, when he was driving drunk and thought, "My god, what am I doing? My children are still growing!" He said that he took stock of his life, stopped drinking and smoking, and switched to a local truck route that would enable him to come home every night and "make more of the family."

Although Hugo characterized past acts as "mistakes," like most of the participants who espoused a narrative of maturation he saw that past as a necessary precondition for his current self. Thus both his memories of this past and his current difference from it are key elements of his current composite masculinity. He said, "Now, the past is the past; now is now. I'm different." In the present, tender and communicative relations with his wife enable him to act out a mature masculinity and link new aspects of his life, such as changing sexual function, into that masculinity. He said that his wife's support was key for his previous change: "Alone, one can't change. We have to walk together, have communication, support each other."

When I interviewed Hugo, he had just been told that he needed to have an operation on his enlarged prostate, which might decrease or even end his ability to have erections. He said that he would deal with this change as he dealt with others, by talking with his wife with whom "there is communication; there is trust." Hugo said that he was unbothered by the prospect of decreased erectile function, especially because he believed that his prostate trouble was likely caused by too much sexual contact with other women earlier in his life. He planned to have the surgery and then to focus his remaining sexual capacity on a tender sex life that would satisfy his wife's needs. He said, "The most important thing is to have sexual contact with her. Not punish her. Do my part . . . I understand my wife as a woman." However, Hugo did not think that he would be interested in using medical ED treatment to accomplish this sexual contact. He likened ED drugs to the stimulants that other truck drivers take to stay alert, but which he rejected as physically dangerous, saying, "My work is hard, long hours, and many take drugs to get through it. Not me. If I did, now I'd be like a grandfather! I don't force my body to continue. So, I feel very healthy."

Common Patterns of Change

Hugo's story is one man's version of the life course change from *machismo* toward maturity that many of the participants made a key element of their composite masculinities. Although many of them shared this general idea that aging men should act out manhood in ways appropriate to their changing bodies and social worlds, they lived out very different versions of this trajectory based on their unique life and bodily experiences. Similarly, although many of the men used the language of "before" and "after" to discuss changes from youthful to mature masculinities, they did not experience a binary shift from one static form of masculinity to another. Instead, as changing life circumstances warranted, they added new and removed old practices of masculinity from the set of acts that together comprised their ways of being men. As part of this process, they often drew new comparisons between their former and present selves, adding narratives about the way they had changed over time into their composite masculinities. They lived out versions of this life course change in many different ways, based on their individual experiences, desires, and abilities. Thus the shift from youthful to mature masculinity is not a clean break or a singular event; it is a practice of revising one's way of being a man, in light of cultural norms for respectable male aging, in the context of a changing body and social setting.

Similar to men's incrementally shifting masculinities, their sexual function also tended to change in flexible rather than binary ways. Very few of the men completely lost their ability to attain erections all at once. It was more common for erectile frequency and rigidity to decrease over time and in relationship to specific illness events or social problems. Rather than simply removing the practice and embodied experiences of sex from their composite masculinities, many of the participants gradually replaced youthful forms of frequent, unemotional penetrative sex with sexual practices more centered on emotional connection with their wives or abstinence. In short, the narrative of appropriate masculine life course change did not determine men's actions but provided them with ways of linking acts and attitudes appropriate to their lives into ever-evolving composite masculinities they saw as suitable to their current life phases.

These shifts were powerfully mediated by the study participants' common belief that their Mexicanness entailed innate *machismo*. Many of the men saw their own ways of being men as compromises between good practices and socially destructive embodied urges. They believed that bodily changes that made it easier to resist—or impossible to perform—macho sexual and social relationships would help them to be older men in socially appropriate ways. Thus, although even faithful, responsible, and hardworking participants often believed that Mexican men were inherently macho, most of them saw older age as a time of positive change. The participants also linked particular ways of being men to change over time in the context of cultural narratives of Mexican progress. Just as many believed themselves to have mastered their negative biological urges over time, they cautioned that subsequent generations of men would have to behave differently as their nation moved toward modernity and more egalitarian gender roles. In their own ways of being men and their ideas about their countrymen, the participants saw Mexican men as diverse and ever changing—capable of good and bad—but also physically tethered to a nature hungry for sex and excess.

Chapter Two

SEX, RELATIONSHIPS, AND MASCULINITIES

Sex and Relationships

The understandings of essential Mexican manhood discussed in chapter 1 frame sex as a self-centered act, driven by and demonstrating one's manly nature. Indeed, stereotypes of masculinity around the world often cast men as sexual automatons who seek outlets on which to perform, not partners with whom to engage (Gutmann 2009). Just as most of the study participants characterized the abstract Mexican man as macho, they described Mexican men's sexuality as self-centered and instrumental. In a typical comment, a store clerk described his friends' sex lives as follows: "Yeah, they think about the partner but because of *machismo*, they think more about elevating their ego." Yet despite such characterizations, none of the study participants provided such reductive descriptions of their own sex lives. Instead, they enacted complex social relationships within and regarding their sexual encounters, which meant much more for their ways of being men than simply demonstrating an ability to penetrate. As the participants described them, even quick extramarital encounters with prostitutes were multifaceted relationships through which they acted out many specific forms of masculinity: being a provider of money and physical pleasure, feeling desirable, and engaging in physical acts that made one feel like a man.

The participants reported that changes in their social relationships occasioned changes in their sex lives and vice versa. For example, they frequently recounted how they and their wives had different kinds of sex over time, seeming to have incorporated different practices into varying composite masculinities. A sixty-one-year-old construction worker adopted the narrative of maturation to define an initially troubling decrease in sexual function as socially beneficial. He said that when his erections lessened eight years ago, "I thought, I'll be useless; my wife will cheat on me. But now, I've changed. I don't want to wander the streets; I'm dedicated to the home." He said this shift caused a "beautiful change" in his marital sex life, in which they have sex on the less frequent schedule that his wife desires, and she "sets the conditions." He reported that sex had become pleasurable for both of them; it was no longer an obligation for her, now that he was rid of the "sick mind" that led him to desire it excessively. Men's experiences of the links between changing relationships and sexual practices varied, as did their desired and enacted composite masculinities. Some of the study participants included sex and its surrounding social relationships in their composite masculinities as proof of their virility and attractiveness, whereas others made more "modern" and partner-centered understandings of sex central to their masculinities. All of the men described even brief or paid-for sex as occurring within relationships, which they incorporated into particular ways of being men.

Overall, the study participants' descriptions of their sex lives show that sex is a key practice through which men coordinate particular aspects of their lives—including embodied forms of masculinity, financial interactions, and emotional engagements—into specific composite masculinities. The form those masculinities take is also structured by a range of relationships, with people as well as with their own understandings of others and cultural ideals. This chapter examines the ways that various relationships structure sex and the ways that men link these into changing composite masculinities. It focuses on men's self-making practices through their enacted and imagined relationships with those people and groups that they discussed most in our interviews: extramarital partners, wives, religious and self-help organizations, and doctors. By analyzing both participants' narratives and my observations of their interactions with their wives and doctors, I trace the narrative and interactional practices of coordination through which men linked sex and its structuring relationships into their composite masculinities.

Composite Masculinities and Extramarital Sex

As discussed in chapter 1, the study participants often understood youthful infidelity as an act spurred by one's physical nature as a man or a *Mexicano*. However, their descriptions of extramarital sex revealed that these acts—and the relationships in which they occurred—contributed to their composite masculinities in multiple ways. The participants almost never described their motivation for having extramarital sex as the simple pursuit of physical pleasure. In addition to fulfillment of physical desire, they frequently described acting as a provider—of pleasure, resources, or emotional support—as an important aspect of extramarital sex, showing that it made them feel like men in ways that went beyond the social significance of sexual penetration.

Even those participants who saw penetrative sex as central to their virility understood female sexual satisfaction as a key marker of their successful masculinity. A forty-eight-year-old widowed taxi driver, who had a girlfriend and two "little friends" on the side, reported, "I have little erection; my manly virility is decreasing. It depresses me sometimes not to be able to satisfy the woman." Similarly, a twenty-five-year-old department store clerk who said he was experiencing premature ejaculation told me, "I want to satisfy my partner, so I don't feel bad. If I'm satisfied and my partner isn't, there's no balance." Indeed, the participants sometimes boasted about providing sexual pleasure to women whom they paid for sex and described even overtly financially mediated sex in romantically relational terms—as "beautiful" acts.

In addition to providing pleasure, many of the participants understood themselves as successful providers by financially assisting the women they slept with. For example, a seventy-one-year-old businessman told me that he was beginning to use a penile vacuum pump to try to attain erections, but he did not feel embarrassed about doing so with a thirty-year-old female "friend" who understands his problems. His comfort with expressing sexual vulnerability in this relationship seemed to stem from the fact that although he was unable to achieve reliable erections, he provided regular financial support of about $45 USD a week in exchange for his friend's time. He told me that he disliked prostitutes— "women of the street" (*mujeres de la calle*)—but looked fondly on "little neighbors" (*vecinitas*) or "little friends" (*amiguitas*). He understood the latter as "decent" single mothers in need of financial assistance, who were happy to have sex with him not out of moral failing but "for the help that I offer."

Men frequently characterized money or goods that they exchanged for extramarital sex as charitable contributions, referring to the cash exchanged as "gifts." Although some men visited prostitutes, most preferred to sleep with and financially "help" women who they did not see as sex workers. These women were usually single mothers, who men defined as deserving and "good" women who had fallen on hard times. The participants seemed to define partners as prostitutes based not on whether money changed hands but whether their interactions felt significantly mediated by financial exchange rather than social ties of friendship or trust. Sexual relationships that involved fiscal exchange, which men understood to incorporate fond feelings, provided the study participants with both physical pleasure and the feeling that they were behaving responsibly as successful providers. This common sexual dynamic was likely an economic survival strategy for many single women in Cuernavaca, where one person's full-time wages were often not enough to provide for a family, and unmarried women outnumbered single men (INEGI 2009). Thus, in addition to being an activity through which people act out specific ways of being men or women, infidelity was also a key part of the economic fabric of many people's lives.

Penetrating women in a way that cast one as generous and responsible, as well as virile was important to the way that many of the participants embodied manliness through sex. Furthermore, those participants who subscribed to more recent cultural valorization of companionate relationships reported that they found extramarital affairs to be emotionally gratifying spaces that let them be the kinds of men they could not be in their marriages. For instance, a fifty-one-year-old told me that he began an affair following a frightening surgery to remove a clot in his femoral artery. He said he felt "traumatized" after the experience and was unable to discuss these feelings with his wife. So he started seeing another woman, who helped him to think of things besides his health scare, listened to his fears, and thus "removed the anxiety."

Just as the relationships in which men have sex shape their emotional lives, these relationships also influence their physical bodies. Some of the participants reported that they could achieve erections when thinking about or interacting with younger women but not with their wives. They often hypothesized that these other women were more "exciting," which made it easier to attain an erection. Their desire to sleep with younger women sometimes stemmed from physical attraction, or the desire to incorporate the ability to attract younger women into a sexually vigorous composite masculinity. However, these extramarital liaisons also frequently contained emotional content that counteracted the negative emotions associated with troubled marriages, which could hamper erectile function during marital sex.

For example, a sixty-year-old office worker who came to the IMSS hospital for ED treatment reported the following: "I see a girl in the street. She's pretty; yeah I feel really attracted—I feel my penis growing. I think that maybe my wife doesn't attract me. She's not caring. She's from the country; she learned to be that way [emotionally distant] because she saw her father do it. I told her we're both at fault because you don't get close to me. She didn't say much. She said, 'For me, there's no problem, I'll wait for you.' But I'm afraid as more time passes, she won't wait."

The lack of emotional engagement that this participant felt from his wife, as well as his fear that a lack of sex would lead her to stray, created strong, negative emotions that made it physically difficult for him to attain an erection with her. In cases where partner-specific erectile difficulty was an embodied response to emotionally painful interactions, the men often used their ability to achieve erections with extramarital partners to feel like men. Linking what they saw as successful interactions with these other women into their composite masculinities mitigated their perceived manly failures to maintain happy marital relationships.

This situation was so common that the urologists understood trouble with or a lack of interest in one's wife as a key cause of erectile difficulty. One of the doctors told me that 80 percent of the ED he saw was psychological. Mostly, he said, monotony or boredom with one's wife made it impossible for a man to achieve erections with her, although he could achieve erections with other women. This opinion sometimes influenced doctors' recommendations for ED treatment.

A fifty-eight-year-old retiree who experienced erectile difficulty following prostate surgery told me that a private physician had told him the following: "You know what? Find a seventeen, eighteen-year-old chick; you'll see that you get cured." Aside from its ethical questionability, such advice sometimes had negative outcomes for the patients. One ED treatment seeker told me that a doctor had recommended that a friend with a similar problem see a prostitute, but "he didn't choose well, and she was cruel. She told him that he was wasting her time." Although the medical advice to seek a young, hot chick or an understanding prostitute may seem inappropriate, it fits into an understanding of erectile difficulty as a problem that was as much social as it was biological: the embodiment of negative emotions linked to troubled interpersonal relationships. (This perspective will be discussed in later chapters.) Overall, the advice to seek a more exciting or understanding partner was actually advice to incorporate socially successful interpersonal sexual relationships into one's composite masculinity, thus to remediate the emotional damage done by martial unhappiness and its physical consequence of erectile difficulty.

Thus sexual relationships that may seem on the surface to only be about physical pleasure also constitute relational contexts in which men can engage in practices that form a desired composite masculinity. Extramarital encounters not only enable some men to live out essential Mexican manhood but also provide a forum for enacting other ways of being men, such as providing or sharing emotions, which may be unavailable in their marriages or other life settings. In our interviews, the participants frequently incorporated aspects of their extramarital relationships into their presentations of themselves as men.

PEPE: "YOUTHFUL" AND FULFILLING AFFAIRS

Pepe's story shows how a man can incorporate a range of sexual interactions with women—and the different ways they enable him to act like a man—into his composite masculinity. A sixty-eight-year-old barber, his baldness and hollow cheeks gave him a skeletal appearance that belied his gregarious personality and self-styling as a ladies' man. In fact, Pepe was the only study participant who attempted to start a sexual relationship with me (which I politely declined). Pepe suffered from health problems that had reduced his erectile function, including urethral narrowing caused by complications from prostate surgery over a decade ago. He came to the hospital to undergo urethral dilations, but nevertheless had frequent urges to urinate and was sometimes incontinent, which made him feel "very bad, depressed." Although these urination problems had changed his lifestyle to some extent—for instance, he drank as little as possible so that he could work without constant bathroom breaks—he was more concerned with the sexual side effects. He said that since his prostate operation, "I noted that my capacity lessened . . . My potency lessened." He was one of the few study participants who used ED drugs; he took Viagra to accomplish extramarital sex that enabled him to "feel young" despite his ill health and advancing age.

Pepe reported feeling great affection for his wife. When I asked if he was married, he said, "Yes—fortunately" and told me that they had been together for forty-three years and were nearing their golden anniversary. He stressed his closeness with his large family of children and grandchildren and proudly described the open conversations he and his wife, who was a housewife, had about work, religion, and current events. In general, he said, "We get along well," and their cordial relationship, as well as the way he cared for her diabetes-related health problems, seemed to be key practices that made him feel as if he were a responsible husband. However, he said that he and his wife had sex only "sporadically because it doesn't appeal to her." He believed that this was natural because of her illness and age. At sixty-one, he thought she had reached an age where many women lose interest in sex. However, her embodiment of older age through decreased sexual desire was out of synch with Pepe's desire to appear young and vigorous, partly by having frequent sex. "I'm active," he explained.

Thus Pepe maintained sexual relationships with other women to incorporate a youthful type of sexuality into his way of being a man. He did not see this as a betrayal of his wife, but as a simple consequence of her lack of sexual interest. Because his wife did not want sex, he explained, "You have to find a little friend out of necessity." Pepe was aware that many men his age had abandoned this "necessity," and he eventually expected to make a lifestyle shift similar to those discussed in chapter 1. He said, "The moment must arrive when with age, my capacity will lessen. I will dedicate myself to my wife and to my family." However, Pepe currently sought to maintain a youthful and vigorous composite masculinity by foregrounding the firm erections facilitated by Viagra—and the sex with younger women that they made possible—and backgrounding his aging and ill health.

The character of his relationships with his "little friends" was also a crucial aspect of his current composite masculinity. Asserting his marital responsibility, he said he did not want to catch sexually transmitted infections (STIs), so he avoided prostitutes, who he defined as "public women."[1] Instead, he met weekly with working women who did not demand but nevertheless appreciated "little presents, some little help." He said that he preferred to go out with pretty, young, single mothers, whom he knew were needy and whom he could help. He said, "I give but voluntarily—a help. I help her; she helps me with my problem . . . It's beautiful." Thus, although having extramarital sex was an important component of Pepe's way of being a man, locating that sex within relationships that enabled him to take on the role of charitable provider was equally impor-

---

1 Although most of the participants knew that condoms could protect against STIs, many—especially numerically older men—declined to use them or did so only sporadically. Instead, many reported using the strategy of sleeping with women who were not sex workers and who appeared healthy and "respectable" to avoid STIs.

tant. By entering into these relationships of mutual assistance, the single mothers who dated Pepe enabled him to act out a caring and responsible manliness. The relative youth and beauty of these "little friends" were also crucial for Pepe's embodied practice of male sexuality because he told me that sex with younger women was more "exciting" than with his wife and thus made it easier for him to achieve erections.

Furthermore, Pepe evaluated his success with women on not only the quantity but also the quality of their sexual interactions. It was important to him to sexually satisfy his partners, and he incorporated Viagra use into his embodiment of being a skilled lover. He said that sex with Viagra "is different; my partner is more satisfied." After bragging about an instance in which he gave six orgasms to a woman, he told me that pleasing his partner was important because "that way the experience is more complete, mutual." By understanding Viagra as a sexual enhancement tool rather than a medication for an aging and ill body, Pepe foregrounded his status as a skilled and considerate lover in his composite masculinity and backgrounded the fact that he now needed drugs to attain reliable erections.

Although Pepe saw himself as a considerate man and believed that his infidelities did not make him a bad husband, he also thought that the distress his dalliances caused his wife was responsible for her diabetes. His wife said that seeing him on the street with another woman caused an episode of strong negative emotion that incited her illness. Although Pepe told me that he did not feel guilty for this because he was sleeping with the other woman as a result of his wife rejecting him sexually, he believed her claim regarding diabetes causation. (The common belief that negative emotions cause illness will be discussed in chapter 3.) So because he felt that "I don't want to be the cause that worsens her diabetes," he was very careful to conceal his affairs. He feared that if his wife caught him again, she could get sicker or even die, so he often traveled an hour away by bus to meet women in distant motels. He framed this as a responsible practice that made him a good husband. Despite the inconvenience of going to such lengths to maintain secrecy, and the physical danger he believed his activities posed to his wife, he planned to continue in this way because "you have to keep moving forward." Overall, Pepe's ability to live out a composite masculinity that involved showing responsible financial, emotional, and physical consideration for women, as well as a youthful and vigorous sexuality, entailed both medical intervention and a range of different sex practices and relationships with his wife and his "little friends."

Women's Stated and Imagined Needs

Just as Pepe saw his wife as uninterested in sex but his "little friends" as highly sexual, the participants often held contradictory views of women's sexual needs and desires. On the one hand, they frequently reported that their wives' interest in sex seemed to have declined with age, and often voiced the opinion that women were "naturally" less sexual than men. For instance, many of the participants believed that women's sexual desire lessened greatly with menopause. An eighty-year-old librarian explained, "For men, sexuality doesn't stop; but for women it does, with menopause." On the other hand, many of these same participants nevertheless said that they felt obligated to offer penetrative sex to their aged wives. Considering sex to be a resource that they were obligated to provide, just like money and shelter, many of the men who experienced erectile difficulty feared that their wives would seek sex outside their marriages. Often blaming their nature as emotionally closed Mexicans, the study participants frequently worried that their wives were made unhappy by decreasing sexual frequency but were often too embarrassed to ask their spouses directly whether this lack of sex upset them.

A sixty-five-year-old retired mechanic explained that his wife "isn't demanding, but I know that I have to comply. She never tells me this, but I know I have to comply. We here in Mexico, it's our reason, our way of thinking." The participants commonly read sexual demands into their wives' silences, despite any indication from their wives that they desired sex. Furthermore, these men were haunted by the specter of their wives' infidelity, fearing that if they could not provide the sex that their roles as husbands demanded, their partners would cheat or "put the horns on" them (*ponerse los cuernos*). A fifty-four-year-old salesman told me, "My wife is forty-nine; I think she's still at a good age for having relations. If I can't satisfy her needs, will she put the horns on me?" Jokes about women putting the horns on men are common in Mexican popular culture, especially in television comedies. Such jokes reflect understandings of female infidelity as a gender role reversal that fundamentally unmans the cuckolded partner. Thus, while husbands' infidelities may be cast as a marital problem, wives' infidelities, especially for men subscribing to more traditional gender roles, may pose a threat to one's masculinity.

Often basing their fears on their own behavior, men who used their wives' lack of interest in sex as a justification for their infidelities frequently voiced the fear that their wives would do the same. For example, a seventy-one-year-old salesman said that because his wife did not want to have sex, "one has to look somewhere else. She [my wife] got mad. But I think that she knew it was her own fault." However, both my conversations with women and women's interactions with doctors revealed that husbands' expectations that their wives require penetrative sex were often incorrect. It seems that just as the male study participants held contrasting views about women's sexual natures, these views also contrasted with their wives' stated sexual desires. I heard many examples of this disjunction from Dr. Peralta (a pseudonym), a family-practice physician who lives and works in a poor municipality on the outskirts of Cuernavaca. A warm and gracious woman in her late fifties, Dr. Peralta had lifelong relationships with most of her patients, who reported feeling closeness with and trust for her that was markedly different from the quick, often awkward, encounters I witnessed at the IMSS hospital. Dr. Peralta's patients are demographically similar to those at the IMSS hospital, but they are far more likely to raise sexual health questions. Dr. Peralta believed this was because of the trust they felt, as well as her frank openness about sexual matters (partly learned from her sister, the local Cialis representative).

Dr. Peralta identified a disconnection between what men think their wives want and what those wives actually desire. She said that many times she had older couples sitting in her office, with the men requesting an ED drug and their wives leaning out of their husbands' lines of sight to shake their heads "no." These women often told her privately that they simply did not want to have sex, or they feared that if Dr. Peralta prescribed their husbands the drug, they would use it with other women. Similarly, in my IMSS interviews with couples, the women frequently contradicted their husbands' assumptions that diminishing sex was problematic. Contrary to their husbands' fears, wives of aging or ill men overwhelmingly described decreasing erectile capacity as a "natural" and "normal" occurrence. For instance, when a sixty-eight-year-old laborer told me that his wife "does not like" his decreased ability to have penetrative sex, she corrected him, saying that after he became ill, "it wasn't the same, but it's not serious; it happens with age and health problems." Similarly, a sixty-four-year-old retired mechanic said that he had planned to go to the doctor for ED medicine, but when his wife found out, she stopped him, saying, "No, better [to let things progress] naturally." She explained that she was not eager for her husband to regain full sexual capacity because "I've always had less desire."

Thus the minority of men who eventually revealed their fears of female infidelity to their wives generally received reassurance that a lack of penetrative sex was not a problem. When I interviewed him with his wife, a sixty-year-old farm administrator experiencing erectile difficulty said that his inability to sexually penetrate caused him emotional pain and made him fear that she would cheat. He said, "Imagine living with my wife, without living those beautiful moments . . . and leaving her with needs; I imagined what might happen." However, when he finally voiced his fear to his wife, she told him to try to be happy and not to worry because "my time [for sex] is over." As a fifty-five-year-old housewife, she said that she had lost interest in sex because of aging and health issues: "With age, menopause, they're difficult changes for the woman." She said that she had to reassure him again and again that "there's no problem; I don't have much desire. I'm not going to look elsewhere."

Similarly, a thirty-six-year-old office worker was so concerned about having erectile difficulty at a young age that he assumed his wife would leave him, and he actually told her to do so. He said, "Here in Mexican culture, you say 'man who doesn't function, woman that looks elsewhere' or vice versa. I told her [my wife], 'I'm not going to be well; go with who you want, be free.' She said 'no, cure yourself. We're going to the urologist.' I told her it was expensive; she said it didn't matter."

Even in cases when wives of men experiencing sexual difficulty did want to continue having sex, they usually hoped to work together to seek medical treatment rather than abandon the marriage. Thus men's fears that their wives would be unfaithful or rejecting in the face of erectile difficulty caused them great pain but were rarely borne out in practice.

Perhaps counterintuitively, men's fears that their wives might be unfaithful often coexisted with the strongly held belief that they had always been faithful. Although most of the male study participants sought sex outside their marriages, almost all reported that their wives had not. They generally said that despite the fact that they had concealed their own infidelities, their wives would be incapable of doing the same. For example, a forty-six-year-old optometrist who successfully concealed a long and emotionally tumultuous affair from his wife said that he knew she had been faithful: "I'd know if she was doing something because I know her so well." Exemplifying their contradictory understandings of female sexuality, the male participants frequently voiced both terror that their wives might cheat and utter confidence that they had not yet done so. Thus both lived and imagined aspects of relationships with their wives were available for inclusion in men's composite masculinities.

However, men's fears regarding failure to satisfy their wives were occasionally founded. In some cases, their wives expressed frustration with their changing marital sex lives. This was not usually the case when the marital relationships were good. Instead, the wives most frequently expressed unhappiness with their sex lives in situations where emotional problems in the marriage seemed to be a key cause of their husbands' erectile difficulties. For example, a fifty-six-year-old said that when he got an erection, "it only lasts a short time [and] then goes down." He was seeking medical treatment because this erectile difficulty upset his spouse. He said, "It doesn't satisfy my wife, so it's a problem."

However, he also believed that this erection problem was rooted in the growing emotional distance between the couple. He said they had been married for thirty-four years, and "little by little she has rejected me. I feel that this isn't normal. At times I feel that a relationship should be of two, but sometimes my wife doesn't pay attention to me. She's a little cold." He reported that sometimes when he wanted to have sex, she cruelly said, "No because you can't do it." His response was not to attempt to discuss his feelings with her but to seek medical treatment that would help him attain more lasting erections and "satisfy my wife." In cases such as this, the wives seemed to react negatively not to the simple lack of erection but to sexual difficulties symptomatic of a more broadly troubled relationship. Similar to individual enactments of gender, relationships can be understood as composites in which different elements together shape the whole. Sexual difficulty can be one of a set of mutually reinforcing troubles that add up to an unhappy marriage.

Revising Masculinities with Wives' Help

Although some of the men's notions that wives required sex contributed to their initially negative reactions to decreasing erectile function, conversations with their spouses were crucial to most men's subsequent acceptance of this change as a physical prompt to live out the mature masculinity discussed in chapter 1. For some couples, discussions of their changing bodies led to new styles of marital communication. A sixty-three-year-old retired mechanic said that after an accident he suffered at age fifty-five that marked "the end of my youth," he "totally lost the sexual appetite." His wife asked him why they were no longer having sex, and this occasioned a new openness in their marriage. He said that before, many things went unsaid between them, including the open secret of his infidelities. Frank discussions about the sexual consequences of his accident led to their relationship becoming "more open." In this case, the cessation of penetrative sex led to a different sort of relationship between husband and wife, and the ability to successfully communicate with his spouse became a key element of his composite masculinity.

The study participants also revised other aspects of their composite masculinities in cooperation with their wives. Some of the couples worked together to make lifestyle changes they believed would help them become better partners and parents. For example, a twenty-nine-year-old prison administrator, whose two-liter-a-day soda habit had inflamed his kidneys to the point that he urinated blood, said that his wife was helping him to become more health conscious. He said that they had a good relationship and that "we talk all the time . . . it's like when we were dating." She was currently pregnant with their second child, and he had come to see learning about a healthy diet from her as a way to dedicate himself to their family. He said that in this regard, "She's raising me up."

In many other cases, the wives decided that they were tired of "suffering through" (*aguantando*) bad marriages and made changes or presented ultimatums that required their husbands to alter their behaviors. For instance, I interviewed an eighty-year-old housewife and an eighty-eight-year-old retired office worker who had separated, following her decision to leave her husband after decades of acrimony. Although they did not plan to divorce, and she still cooked for him and accompanied him to his medical appointments, they lived in separate condominiums in the same complex. Her move out of their shared condo was financed by their children, who she said told her that she had already "put up with too much" from their domineering father. She said that during their marriage, "he was neurotic, [and] I was intolerant; but when he worked, he wasn't home much. But when he retired, man, I became a slave! We didn't live together well." For her, the final straw was his refusal to let her engage in her hobby of making and selling artisanal molded gelatins. Although she continues to carry out certain wifely duties related to subsistence and health care that she considers to be her obligation, her decision to separate and move out was a concrete way of altering her husband's controlling behavior. Both her move and his grudging acceptance of it reconfigured their relationship, forcibly removing certain dominant practices from his composite masculinity.

In other cases, husbands and wives attempted to change the nature of their relationships through communication and shared lifestyle changes. As with the previous example, wives sometimes reported coming to feel that they had "put up" with enough. They said that their history of fulfilling their marital duties and overlooking certain types of mistreatment, most often emotional distance and infidelity, entitled them to demand changes as they entered later life. In keeping with the narrative of life course change discussed earlier, both husbands and wives that I interviewed frequently felt that a wife's reward for suffering through her husband's youthful roguishness should be a change in his behavior later on. The wives often reported urging their husbands to make changes that both agreed were appropriate to a more mature masculinity. Such prompts frequently took the form of wives' statements that the couple had moved to "another phase" or a "second plane" of life and marriage, with different attendant norms and standards of behavior. Negotiating with their wives over the kinds of behavior and forms of emotional interaction appropriate to this new life phase was a common practice through which men revised their ways of being men.

Some of the men made these changes after their wives threatened to leave. For instance, a fifty-four-year-old exterminator estimated that he had slept with thirty different women during his marriage, saying he did so because he liked sex and believed that men naturally seek variety. However, his wife threatened to divorce him after she discovered that he had fathered two children with another woman. To convince her to stay, he reported, "I had to make a radical change and dedicate myself only to her." He became faithful and said that he now pays a lot of attention to his wife. He told me that he was happy with this change: "I like it because now I'm older . . . I love her a lot. I will live all my life with her." Similarly, a forty-eight-year-old mechanic told me that he was forced to change his sexual practices after his wife discovered that he had a secret second family.[2] Although his wife did not try to divorce him—he surmised that she stayed because he fulfilled his manly duty of caring for the family so that she did not have to work outside the home—she demanded that he end his other relationship. He saw this as an appropriate change to make "at

2 Although Matthew Gutmann reported finding no evidence of second families, or the "casa chica" phenomenon, in his 1996 study of masculinity in Mexico City, I found this arrangement to be fairly common among the study participants who held jobs such as bus or truck driving that entailed frequent travel along a fixed route and paid well enough to support two households.

my age" because as a grandfather he wanted to model mature masculinity. He remembered thinking, "Now grandchildren are coming, I must be an example." He reported that since he became faithful to his wife, their sex life had improved, and "there is more tenderness" between them. He stated, "I am happy in the house" because "now I'm focusing on the home, the grandchildren. I don't want to complicate things with problems from the street." In general, men who reformulated their ways of being husbands in response to their wives' demands did so after they came to see their spouses' desires as a timely prompt that helped them to act out a masculinity more appropriate to their increasing age.

An interview with a couple in their sixties revealed the active role that a wife might play in helping her husband to construct an age-appropriate composite masculinity based on changes in his body, work, and marriage. When I asked if they had experienced any changes related to his prostate disease, physical or otherwise, she smiled happily and replied, "Now we're old! Like all married couples, it's another era; it's another way of seeing each other. If there isn't sexuality, there's love . . . We always go around together, even to the market. Before, he worked; he didn't have time." Her husband interrupted to assert, "I *do* keep working." She countered, "No, now he's retired. It's another phase that's very beautiful that we've reached together." Her husband groused, "Even though there's no sex." After she discussed the benefits of retirement for their relationship, and he described his lack of erection, she closed the topic with the statement that "now we have no interest in that." She laughed, and he quietly sighed.

This exchange shows how each spouse has crafted a particular narrative of the age-related changes in their lives, sexual practices, and marital relationship. The husband characterized himself as a worker, despite his formal retirement from paid employment, and appeared to some degree to miss the sex that he had been able to perform. His wife had a very different understanding of her husband's life change, casting his aging as enabling a shift from focusing on work to enjoying marital and familial togetherness. She seemed to be working to convince her husband to share her belief that this stage was "beautiful" precisely because it meant that their lives had changed in ways that precluded sex. In contrast to most men's descriptions of being content with the cessation of their sexual function, which I heard after they had time to adjust to this change, this conversation illustrates the ways that couples struggle to redefine their relationships, and their ways of being men and women, when they first encounter bodily and social changes. The following case study shows in greater depth how one couple deliberately sought to change together.

ADÁN AND LETY: REWORKING MARITAL MASCULINITY

Strains of the idea that mature masculinity requires a deeper commitment to family are apparent in the changes that Adán and Lety made to their relationship to enhance their physical health and mitigate Adán's erectile difficulty. I interviewed fifty-four-year-old businessman's assistant Adán and fifty-two-year-old IMSS clerical employee Lety when they came in together for his prostate checkup. They sought medical advice about how to make lifestyle changes that would promote prostate health and improve sexual function as they rebuilt their marriage following Adán's infidelity. They seemed eager to be interviewed, but their answers were often brief, following awkward periods of silence in which they appeared to ponder how to express their feelings. Sitting next to each other but not touching, they seemed determined to openly communicate but were unused to doing so. Both wore shiny, new wedding rings.

They told me that they had been married for thirty-two years and had three adult children. They both said that the cause of Adán's erectile difficulty was likely a combination of aging, his prostate illness, and stress. They believed that this stress was related to not only work but also emotional difficulties they had encountered in their marriage. They had come to believe that open communication, although difficult, would aid both their emotional relationship and their sexual interactions. Adán said it was hard to discuss these things, "but lately we've tried to be more sincere—to have more trust." Lety added, "I believe that we're breaking barriers to communicate more openly, with more trust. In fact, it was hard for a few months, but finally we've been working together to resolve it. For example, now we go together to the doctor."

Lety and Adán revealed that these attempts to communicate and trust each other were a conscious decision they made to reverse the emotional distance that she believed had led to his infidelity. She said, "A little while ago, we decided to face things together. I worked two jobs, traveled a lot; he did too. There was distance." She left one of her jobs to make more time for their relationship, and he said that this enabled them to face his medical difficulties together: "We keep moving ahead, facing problems of age." After this comment, Lety gently corrected him, seeking to put on the record that the problems they faced were related not only to health or work but also his behavior. She told me, "We had a very serious problem.

Serious, serious. A problem of infidelity [she points subtly at Adán]. It was a very serious emotional problem that caused lots of argument—a problem much worse than the jobs." Although Lety cast Adán's infidelity as the cause of their problems, her use of the pronoun *we* highlighted the couple's decision to work together to heal the emotional rift that his behavior caused.

Although many of the wives, particularly older ones, I spoke with expected their husbands to cheat and defined this as "natural" behavior, others held companionate ideals of marriage and believed that both partners should receive emotional and sexual fulfillment within their relationships. Lety saw marriage in this way and thus understood Adán's infidelity as a betrayal that required an emotional solution. When I asked why they did not separate, she told me that they had instead decided to change their behavior and enact a new kind of relationship, which seemed to be the best option for her given her place in life and society. She said, "What happened is that—at our ages, I'm the one who would be alone. So we tried to rescue something valuable. We went to a course at the church. Actually, we just got married in the church a week ago. [Showing her ring] We're trying to live differently, live better, be together." Adán added that they had been married civilly but never in the church, and this church wedding was a meaningful beginning to this new phase of their lives.[3] For him, it represented "a more organized life, being together."

Together, they strove to enact this new relational style in their social and sexual lives. They developed a new group of friends: other couples who were "living well" and with whom they could socialize as a group. They also reported that, although they first focused on the "emotional and spiritual aspects" of their marriage, the positive prostate lab results they received today had encouraged them to, as she said, "renew our intimate life." They hoped that the vitamins prescribed by the urologist, in the context of Lety's new, less hectic schedule and their shared commitment to emotional openness, would help Adán achieve erections and enable them to enjoy a mutually satisfying sex life.

3 In Mexico, civil and religious marriages occur separately, and couples may marry either civilly or religiously or both. Each type of marriage confers different benefits: religious marriages make a union real to the church, whereas civil marriages confer government recognition, benefits, and legal privileges.

Converting Masculinities with Group Support

Although most of the participants described or demonstrated the ways that negotiations with their wives shaped their changing sexuality and masculinity, many also incorporated relationships with peer groups into such changes. Religious and support groups were important to many of the participants, and using group support to move away from macho behavior was a key element of the composite masculinities that many of the men presented in our interviews. Conversion from Roman Catholicism to Protestantism is a growing trend in Mexico and Latin America more broadly (Dow 2005; Steigenga and Cleary 2007); even for nonconverts, the history of the region's conquest has made the trope of conversion a culturally salient way of understanding personal change over time (Brusco 1993). Conversion to Protestantism in particular has been a key recent way through which men self-consciously reform their masculine selves (Brandes 2003). For some of the study participants, increasing religiosity was the catalyst for a shift to mature masculinity. For example, a fifty-nine-year-old retired salesman stated that he was not faithful to his wife when he was young but had become so because "you have to be immersed in the Bible, in the church. As a youth, you don't read the Bible; you try drugs. I gave up smoking; I don't drink as much. Now, I enjoy my children, contact with them. I can talk with my kids about everything."

Some of the study participants also used religious conversion to make sense of illnesses that radically changed their bodies and relationships. For example, retired fifty-two-year-old bus driver Dionísio and thirty-seven-year-old housewife Adelina combined conversion to Protestantism with the understanding that their relationship had moved into a "second plane" to cope with Dionísio's terminal cancer. When I interviewed the couple, Dionísio was weak and thin; his clothing was far too large after a recent drop in weight. His skin was greenish, and his facial expressions revealed that he felt constant pain, but he fought to keep this pain from dampening his determinedly cheerful attitude. Adelina, a pretty, buxom and vivacious woman, touched him constantly as they talked, looking at him with an expression of pure love. They told me that they had met sixteen years ago, when he was a bus driver and she was a bus stewardess. Despite the fact that he was married and older than her, they felt destined to be together. He left his wife and three children, and they moved in together and had a daughter. Both said that they had been very happy.

However, eighteen months before our interview, Dionísio developed renal cancer. Despite the removal of one of his kidneys, the cancer had spread and metastasized throughout his body. The doctors were working to control his pain but had told him that his cancer would be fatal. To deal with this prognosis, he and Adelina underwent a religious conversion and became born-again Christians. Dionísio said, "We met God, and now we don't fear anything. Jesus Christ is going to save us." Adelina added that their religion provided both spiritual and social support: "It was tragic when he was diagnosed, not knowing what would happen. But the congregation helps us in all aspects—as a family, as a couple. We learned to see things differently."

Their shared religious conversion has been a key way that they dealt with Dionísio's impending death and the changes that his illness has caused in their life together. For example, Adelina said that sex used to be an important part of their relationship, but after his illness, they entered a new stage where it no longer mattered. She said, "Before, we tried lots of different ways [of having sex], but now it's better not to look for those. You get absorbed in other things." Adelina also no longer cared whether Dionísio performed tasks that were once central to his way of being a man, such as working to provide money. She joked, "Before, it was he works, we spend! Now we're focused on his health." Thus in the face of terminal cancer, Dionísio and Adelina used a religious conversion to garner social support, cope with emotional pain, and rework Dionísio's composite masculinity to foreground tough, Christ-like suffering rather than provision of sex or money.

Other study participants changed their ways of being men by participating in support and self-help programs. These types of programs are immensely popular in Mexico: Alcoholics Anonymous (AA) alone has over 14,000 Mexican groups (Alcoholicos Anónimos 2012). Such groups often employ conversion narratives to characterize participants' change from bad to good behavior, and even groups focused on specific behaviors, such as drinking or violence, often intervene more broadly in the social practices surrounding those behaviors, which they associate with negative forms of masculinity (Amuchástegui 2009; Brandes 2002).

In general, the study participants linked sex, violence, and alcohol in their descriptions of youthful masculinities. These practices seemed mutually enabling because men often attributed sexual or violent acts to the drunken haze that preceded them. Furthermore, drinking, violence, and sex were all acts that asserted a tough manliness and were thus frequently linked together by men performing macho or hypermasculine composite masculinities. As demonstrated by a Pfizer ad campaign encouraging doctors to reassure men that they could safely combine alcohol and Viagra, many of the study participants said that alcohol was an important facilitator for extramarital sex, both in terms of setting the mood and enabling them to overcome their social or emotional reticence. Because ways of being men that incorporate heavy drinking also tend to incorporate frequent sex, it makes sense that men who stop drinking and become religious in deliberate attempts to revise their masculinities frequently change the character of their sexual relations.

For example, a sixty-nine-year-old retired farmer and construction worker used a quasi-religious conversion narrative to describe changes over time in his way of being a man and the role he subsequently played in other men's life changes. He said that as a youth, "I drank and I forgot everything . . . when I drank, it was hell." Then he found AA and began the first chapter in his town. He proudly told me that there were now five groups meeting in his town, and "I feel very happy. We're saving them [the group members]." As for his own life, during his past twenty-nine years as an "alcoholic," he felt that he has achieved "tranquility" with his wife and children by becoming a better father and a more caring and faithful husband.

Some of the men also used AA to become better men in general, rather than focusing specifically on alcoholism. One day, on a long taxi ride, I mentioned to the driver that I was researching the ways men's masculinities change when they experience sexual problems. Excitedly, he told me that he was currently undergoing a "change in masculinity." He said, "I was neurotic, but I didn't know it." He reported that he was always angry, blowing up at people and yelling at his kids, and he sometimes came to blows with his wife. Family members frequently told him to calm down or change, but he did not believe he had a problem. Then a friend asked him to come to an AA meeting. He responded, "Why? I don't drink." His friend said that it could help him change his life in other ways, and the taxi driver told me that he had found this to be true. After joining AA, he decided to "change my life." Pulling over the car, he took a piece of notebook paper from above his windshield visor and showed it to me; it was a list of all the family members he needed to beg forgiveness from, including the way ("beg forgiveness on knees" or "sincerely beg forgiveness") that he should do so. He told me that he now does the Rosary and has not yelled at or hit anyone for three months.

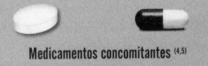

FIGURE 4.
Pfizer ad showing that Viagra and alcohol are "compatible."

He said that this change had greatly improved his family relationships. He chuckled while telling me that his wife and kids at first thought he was crazy, as he begged their forgiveness on his knees, but eventually they saw that he had changed and were now much happier together. Although he used to be unfaithful to his wife, sometimes sleeping with multiple cab passengers a day, he said that since his decision to change, "I have been 100 percent faithful." Both the level of trust between himself and his wife and the quality of their sex life had improved. He remarked that although he was unfaithful, he was careful to do only "routine" sex acts with his wife, for fear that she would wonder where he had learned new moves. Now that she knew he was faithful, he felt that they could be more experimental in the bedroom, and they were both more satisfied. He passed me his phone, showing me a long text message from his wife, in which she told him that she loved him more each day, was so happy that he had changed, and that things were now wonderful. Thus religious and self-help conversions fostered by congregations or support groups sometimes powerfully mediated the ways that men revised their composite masculinities.

Medical Aid for Revising Masculinity

In addition to many men's collaboration with partners and support groups to revise the sets of acts and attitudes that formed their composite masculinities, the study participants often incorporated relationships with medicine and health-care providers into their changing ways of being men. Although most of the older study participants rejected medical ED treatment, some used ED drugs and/or relationships with their doctors to change both embodied and social components of their masculinities. As I will discuss in chapter 5, men who used ED treatments generally saw their erection problems as physical symptoms of a broader social failure to act out the sort of manhood they desired. Thus their relationships with doctors often entailed both pharmaceutical aids for erection and interpersonal forums for working out new ways of being men.

This was especially true in the case of private-practice physicians, who often had more intimate relationships with their patients than the IMSS doctors did. Drug prescriptions for ED formed only a small part of the therapeutic interactions between Dr. Peralta and her patient Ernesto, which also included provision of life advice and suggestions for behavioral change, ranging from new ways to deal with his wife to encouragement for him to have an affair. Fifty-seven-year-old Ernesto worked as a printer of souvenir items, such as T-shirts and mugs, in a working-class town that had been absorbed into Cuernavaca's growing metropolis. He had been a patient of Dr. Peralta for over twenty years, and I interviewed them both alone and together. In both interviews, Ernesto was very talkative, telling me that he felt comfortable with *la doctora* and that she had helped him immensely with his sexual and life difficulties.

Ernesto had work-related physical problems including bad knees, as well as type 2 diabetes. He said that he had been having sexual difficulties, both erectile problems and rapid ejaculation, for about fifteen years. He understood these problems to be partly related to bodily illness and damage, but he also said that he saw them largely as the physical consequences of an emotionally barren marriage. He told me that he and his wife married not for love but because "it seemed like the right thing to do." She wanted to leave her father's house, and he had reached the age of twenty-seven and felt that it was appropriate to marry. He was relatively sexually inexperienced, having been with three women before his marriage, and looked forward to developing a loving and faithful relationship.

Although he had hoped that love would grow between himself and his wife, it did not. He told me that they quickly had children, and his wife paid all her attention to them; he mused that in this way, thirty years somehow passed very quickly. However, increasing conflict between the couple marked these years. He said, "There were always arguments. She doesn't like my way of thinking. I say black; she says white. We like different music, different TV shows. We fought about that, about how to raise the children, etc." These tensions also marked their sexual relationship. Ernesto said, "In marital relations, she doesn't open up; it makes me mad. I was faithful for fifteen years, but when I got close to her with manly needs, she rejected me."

Because of these problems, Ernesto and his wife decided to divorce a year before I spoke with him. He moved in with his mother, but four months later, his wife came to talk to him and convinced him to return to the marriage. He said that they have attempted to become emotionally closer and improve their sex life, stating, "Now, she lets me get closer more. She lets me, but now I don't have erections." Ernesto felt that the emotional damage that had been done was a key factor in his erectile difficulty, for which he sought treatment from his trusted family doctor.

Dr. Peralta told me that she had both prescribed Viagra and engaged in a social intervention with the couple. She spoke, seemingly rather sternly, to Ernesto's wife about the need to be more sexually open. The doctor tried to convince her to engage in sex with her husband even if she did not feel particularly romantic because the lack of affective physical interaction would leave Ernesto feeling used. Dr. Peralta told me the following: "She's very difficult, his wife. And we speak very frankly; I talk to her like an acquaintance, a friend. I'm sometimes defending Ernesto, but I'm also trying to help her. He feels like, I'm just the ATM, but I don't feel desired. It's hurt his self-esteem. He wants to be valued, not just be the provider of money. I tell them [wives] a lot, if you're satisfied with him, he'll work better, earn more money, [and] you'll all be happier."

Although both Ernesto and Dr. Peralta said that his wife made an effort to be more sexually and emotionally open, they believed that the coldness of their previous relations still hindered his physical ability to achieve erections with her. Ernesto said that he got erections in the night, but probably because of fears of rejection and memories of past hurts, "I don't get erections from looking at her." He said, "I couldn't get that out of my mind; you're my wife, but you don't accept me. She's not interested in having sex. She says, 'It's my obligation; I'm married to you.' I hardly have erections. Sometimes I get erections at night: sometimes my wife accepts me, sometimes no, [and] sometimes it just goes away on its own."

Dr. Peralta recommended Viagra and continued medical control of his diabetes to mitigate this problem, but she was also supportive of Ernesto's efforts to find a satisfying romantic relationship outside his marriage. She told me that sex was important for a good life, and a supportive sexual relationship was crucial for sexual function: "The pills don't work if you don't find a response from the woman." Ernesto said that, after the first half of his marriage, in which he tried and failed to develop love with his wife, now, "I'm not faithful because I'm not in love. I've had my little adventures that help me." He told me that fifteen years ago, he found a partner who he was with for eighteen months: "She was very loving. She made me feel like a king. I felt important as a man. But we split because she was separated; she got back together with her husband, and she also became a born-again Christian." Ernesto said that the quality of their sexual relations was very different from what he had encountered previously, in both emotional content and physical pleasure: "The relations were long—three to four hours! Thirty minutes with the others. She was caring, took time, was very artistic, [and] she made me feel good. She was the only woman who ever gave me oral sex."

Thus Ernesto incorporated the emotional content of this relationship into a composite masculinity in which his way of being a man was not limited to being a good husband and a financial provider. He said that he hoped to find another relationship that would make him feel this way: "I'm thinking of looking for another woman to wake me up." He believed that finding a sexually and emotionally open woman, who would not react harshly to his erectile difficulties, might enable him to regain his erectile function. It was also important to Ernesto that this be a woman he met socially, not a prostitute, both to mitigate the risk of disease and because he believed that paying for sex would undo the self-esteem-raising function of being desired and appreciated for himself. He said, "I don't want to go with prostitutes. I had an experience; I got sick with rooster's crest [herpes] and had to go to the gynecologist for treatment. It was before I got married. I'm also not interested in prostitutes because I want to be with someone who wants me for me—not for money—to raise my self-esteem." Supporting his hope of developing a sexual relationship that could incorporate romantic success and noninstrumental appreciation into Ernesto's composite masculinity, Dr. Peralta said, "It's not always that you need to be unfaithful, but that you also only have one life. Do what you have to do."

The Importance of Relationships

The stories told here show that despite the study participants' common belief that the abstract Mexican man simply used sex to prove his manhood, men actually engaged in a range of socially significant kinds of relationships through sexual practice. They included these relationships and sex acts in widely varying composite masculinities. Often, they did so with the help of their sexual partners or professionals, such as doctors, from whom they sought intimate advice. For the many study participants who had multiple partners, sex with different people was not only a way to demonstrate manhood by accomplishing frequent penetrative sex but also an achievement of a set of relationships that provided different elements in their composite masculinities. Although the participants generally believed that sex ideally generated physical pleasure, the men's relationships with multiple partners were not limited to the erotic because the participants also used sexual relationships as forums for enacting various forms of manhood linked to responsibility and the provision of resources.

In addition to relationships with other people, the men also lived out their sex lives in relationship to particular ways of thinking. Their understandings of male and female sexuality in the abstract and in their own lives were key elements of composite masculinities that often changed over time. Some of the participants understood sexuality first primarily through the lens of *machismo* and later through religion. Others applied the quasi-religious logic of conversion found in self-help groups to alter their sexual practices and live out different forms of manhood. Overall, their composite masculinities were powerfully structured by relationships. The interactions that occurred in these relationships, on both the discursive and the physical levels, became key elements of men's ways of being men.

Chapter Three

CHRONIC ILLNESSES AS COMPOSITE PROBLEMS

A Composite Perspective on Chronic Illness

Over the past century, increases in life expectancy and advances in health care have encouraged an "epidemiological transition" in Mexico (Omran 1971). Chronic illness has overtaken infectious disease as the country's most pressing health problem (Frenk et al. 2005). Mexicans born in the 1930s faced widespread communicable disease and malnutrition and died, on average, in their mid-thirties. Today, they can expect to live into their seventies but often contract chronic diseases, such as type 2 diabetes and heart disease (INEGI 2009). Almost one third of the study participants suffered from one or both of these ailments. Such diseases are caused largely by the global spread of unhealthy diets, decreased physical exercise, increased stress, and environmental degradation associated with industrialization (McMurray and Smith 2001). Cancer is another major cause of death in Mexico, which is linked partly to environment and lifestyle; 63 percent of the study participants suffered from prostate cancer or enlargement, often in concert with diabetes or heart disease.

Chronic illness symptoms are thus common among older Mexicans, and the study participants often described the profound effects of these symptoms on their daily lives and senses of self. Most of the study participants had experienced age-related genitourinary problems that were often associated with other chronic diseases. These frequently caused symptoms including weakness, pain, dizziness, shortness of breath, difficulty in urination, and incontinence. In the narratives of change and selfhood that they presented in our interviews, the men frequently highlighted the role that chronic illness had played in their shifts between prior and current ways of being men. The participants reported that feeling ill made it difficult to work and perform physical tasks, which required changes in their daily lives that often made them feel weak, helpless, or ashamed. Chronically ill men had to make frequent visits to their doctors, take medications, and sometimes make broad lifestyle changes. These new practices often compromised elements of their pre-illness composite masculinities, such as autonomy and strength. Furthermore, the illness symptoms sometimes became a source of shame; one study participant borrowed the religious wording often used to describe Jesus Christ's wounds and called his bouts of incontinence "mortifications." The participants often believed that the emotional toll of chronic illness further harmed their health, combining biomedical understandings of health with the local belief that strong negative feelings could physically create pathological "illnesses of emotion" (Rubel, O'Neill, and Collado-Ardón 1985).

Negative emotions and biological pathologies interrelated in different ways for the individual participants. Bodily changes and their social ramifications sometimes caused social suffering, and, conversely, emotional distress often generated or worsened their physical ailments. Medical anthropologists have long sought to understand the lived complexity of illness experiences that occur in both the biological and the social realms, which are shaped by complex contexts (Kleinman 1988; Scheper-Hughes and Lock 1987). Researchers have noted that chronic illnesses, which affect people's lives and bodies over the long term, can cause suffering by disrupting people's expected life paths and plans, and may also be caused by the consequences of such disruptions (Becker 1997; Williams 2000). Overall, people's immersion in changing social and physical contexts over time crucially influences their physical and subjective experience of chronic diseases (Manderson and Smith-Morris 2010).

Similar to gendered selfhood, chronic illness is a composite condition that is lived differently in different social settings. It both shapes and is shaped by individuals' bodies, emotions, social worlds, and structural contexts. In addition to capturing the multifacetedness of chronic illness causation and experience, this composite perspective provides an analytic tool for understanding study participants' heterogeneous understandings of health and sickness. As IMSS patients, all of the study participants saw biomedicine as one valid way to understand at least some forms of bodily distress, which could provide useful ways to treat particular ailments. Yet for most, this medical outlook was only one of a set of ways for understanding health and illness. The participants wove biomedical approaches together with the belief that strong negative emotions caused illness and the humoral notion that health represented a bodily balance of hot and cold (Foster 1994). When faced with bodily changes that they considered to be illness, the participants created composite understandings of illness causation and appropriate treatment, drawing on the aspects of the different understandings of health that seemed most appropriate to their own life situations.

This composite approach to chronic illness is also useful for understanding the gendered consequences of sickness. The participants said that illness made it difficult to perform many of the practices through which they used to act or feel like men. It caused bodily weakness and pain that made working difficult, required men to perform increased (and often feminized) self-care, and frequently hampered erectile function. Because erection occurs when the penis fills with blood, cardiovascular disease and diabetes can damage the vascular system and often make it difficult or impossible to achieve erections (Kubin, Wagner, and Fugl-Meyer 2003). The pharmaceutical treatments for these diseases, as well as the surgical treatments for prostate ailments that can damage genital nerves, have the same effect (Melman and Gingell 1999; Walsh and Donker 2002). In addition, the shame that some of the participants felt over becoming weak, ill, or unable to perform tasks that had been important to their prior ways of being men created emotional distress, which itself is a key cause of erectile difficulty (Rosen 2001).

To show how different aspects of composite chronic illnesses come together to influence men's lives, this chapter will focus on the intersection of three elements that the study participants highlighted in their narratives of sickness and related life changes over time: their most common chronic diseases and symptoms, the emotions that they identified as causes and effects of these illness experiences, and the relationships between these experiences and structural context. It will then discuss the study participants' own understandings of these events and experiences as composite wholes, concluding with examples of the ways men related chronic illness experiences into composite masculinities they often saw as less than ideal.

Biomedical and Experiential Understandings
of Common Diseases

This section briefly overviews type 2 diabetes, cardiovascular disease, and prostate enlargement and cancer from biomedical and epidemiological perspectives and in terms of study participants' experiences of these conditions. Biomedical understandings of disease focus on biological change, whereas epidemiological approaches look at disease prevalence and causation. This information is useful for understanding the changes taking place within the bodies of chronic illness sufferers and how these common diseases affect the Mexican population as a whole. However, although biomedical definitions of disease suggest the kind of bodily symptoms a sickness might cause, the lived experience of illness includes powerful social and emotional components that range beyond the realm of biology. To paint a picture of the study participants' chronic illness burdens, this section also includes multiple perspectives to describe their embodied experiences of chronic disease.

TYPE 2 DIABETES

Type 2 diabetes, in which insulin resistance leads to elevated blood sugar, causes a variety of symptoms, including fatigue, thirst, and increased urination. This disease can lead to blindness, persistent wounds, limb amputation, coma, or death (National Diabetes Information Clearinghouse 2012). Vascular damage caused by diabetes is also a widespread cause of decreased erectile function (National Institute of Diabetes and Digestive and Kidney Diseases 2012). Type 2 diabetes is among the top three causes of death in Mexico and is one of the most common causes of morbidity; it is estimated that almost twelve million Mexicans will suffer from this disease by 2025 (Dirección General de Información y Evaluación del Desempeño 2003; INEGI 2009; King, Aubert, and Herman 1998). Urban men, like the study participants described here, are at particularly high risk for type 2 diabetes, as well as for high rates of complications and extended hospitalizations (Lerman et al. 1998; Phillips and Salmerón 1992). Although sufferers often seem to have genetic predispositions to diabetes, occurrence of the disease is strongly linked to poor diet, a lack of exercise, and obesity (National Diabetes Information Clearinghouse 2012). These conditions encourage the development of metabolic syndrome, a set of risk factors for both type 2 diabetes and cardiovascular disease that is prevalent in the Mexican population (Aguilar-Salinas et al. 2004).

When I asked the study participants to describe their illnesses, they tended not to list the individual symptoms of type 2 diabetes but instead discussed it as an added "burden" that exaggerated the "complications," "problems," and general bodily degradation associated with aging and a hard life. For example, an eighty-one-year-old retired factory worker said, "Diabetes brings a lot of problems. It made me tired, irritable; your whole body falls apart . . . I was a man who had a lot of energy, so it was hard to become sick." The participants stressed that these problems and burdens were not only physical and psychological but also logistical because it was often difficult to make the recommended lifestyle changes or perform interventions such as insulin shots. In many cases, the care necessitated by a participant's or family member's diabetes required radical lifestyle changes. For instance, an eighty-five-year-old retired driver told me that although he was married, "now I don't have a wife." Because his wife's severe diabetes required that she receive multiple daily injections that he was unable to administer, she had lived with their daughter for the past decade. He lived alone, and another daughter brought him daily meals. Thus the participants saw diabetes as one burden among many, although the physical care required by this particular burden could be especially disruptive of their daily lives.

CARDIOVASCULAR DISEASE

Cardiovascular disease, the leading cause of death in Mexico (INEGI 2009), was also prevalent among the study participants and their spouses. In this condition, fatty buildup and plaque narrows arteries, slowing or stopping blood flow to the heart. Similar to type 2 diabetes, heart disease occurrence entails both genetic predisposition and lifestyle factors. The risk factors include diabetes, high blood pressure, high low-density lipoprotein (LDL) or low high-density lipoprotein (HDL) cholesterol, sedentism, obesity, and smoking (Wilson et al. 1998). The symptoms of heart disease range from chest pain, decreased energy, and shortness of breath to heart attacks. Both heart disease and its pharmaceutical treatments can cause erectile difficulties. Drugs for high blood pressure are particularly likely to hamper erectile function (Melman and Gingell 1999). In addition, factors such as obesity and smoking that contribute to heart disease also increase the risk of erectile difficulty (National Institute of Diabetes and Digestive and Kidney Diseases 2012).

Because cardiovascular disease is the leading killer in Mexico, the participants tended to see it as such a common problem that it was to be expected with age. For example, a ninety-year-old retired bodyguard told me, "I've got high blood pressure, but so does everyone else." The participants were frequently on medication for some type of heart disease, and they understood the condition to be a function of poor diet, obesity, and heredity. However, in addition to these epidemiological factors, the participants tended to understand heart disease as most powerfully related to the difficulties of life in economically unequal Mexico. They usually characterized heart disease, especially high blood pressure, as at least partly a function of stress and other life problems that "raise the pressure." For instance, the wife of a sixty-year-old retired window installer said that "when there are problems, worries, the pressure rises," and others reported that a key symptom of high blood pressure is "agitation." Thus most of the participants related this biomedical diagnosis to illnesses of emotion, which will be discussed later in this chapter.

PROSTATE PROBLEMS

Although heart disease and type 2 diabetes are the most common chronic diseases in the general Mexican population, the most prevalent health problems among the study participants in the IMSS urology department were prostate related. Prostate enlargement frequently occurs with aging because this gland, which surrounds the urethra and produces seminal fluid, grows over time. This can create pressure on the urethra that causes difficulty in urination, frequent or painful urination, and incontinence, which can be treated pharmaceutically or surgically (National Library of Medicine 2011). This is an extremely common problem; in the United States, more than half of the men in their sixties and 90 percent of the men in their seventies and eighties have some symptoms of prostate enlargement (National Kidney and Urologic Diseases Information Clearinghouse 2012). Although statistics on the population-wide prevalence of prostate enlargement in Mexico do not exist, a nationwide study of Mexican urology patients found that almost 70 percent showed some degree of this condition (Jaspersen-Gastelum et al. 2008).

Prostate enlargement is not a cause of prostate cancer, although both may cause similar symptoms (National Institutes of Health 2011). However, prostate cancer is a major cause of mortality for Mexican men (INEGI 2009). This form of cancer is generally slow growing but can be fatal, especially if left untreated (Tovar-Guzmán et al. 1999). The causes of prostate cancer are unknown, but risk factors include age and a family history of the disease (National Institutes of Health 2011). Prostate cancer, like type 2 diabetes and heart disease, appears to be a "disease of devel-opment" that occurs most commonly in urban zones marked by environ-mental degradation and largely sedentary populations consuming un-healthy diets (Tovar-Guzmán et al. 1999). Diet seems to play a particular role in prostate cancer occurrence, which has been linked to a high con-sumption of meat and dairy; risk for the disease is decreased by a vitamin-rich diet (Penson and Chan 2009). Both prostate enlargement and cancer and their surgical treatments can hamper erectile function. In particular, prostate surgery can damage or sever the nerves necessary for erection (National Institute of Diabetes and Digestive and Kidney Diseases 2012). Prostate surgery may also cause the physically harmless but potentially psychologically troubling condition of retrograde ejaculation, in which semen is released into the bladder during ejaculation, not out through the urethra (Penson and Chan 2009).

Many men expressed frustration about the bodily changes resulting from prostate problems and their treatments. Although many of the par-ticipants who had undergone prostate surgery remarked that it had re-duced their erectile function, prostate enlargement and cancer sufferers reported greater distress about the resulting frequent urination. Describ-ing this nuisance, a sixty-two-year-old architect said, "You have to think before you go out, about whether there will be bathrooms." A seventy-eight-year-old retired utility company worker, who had undergone a prostate operation one year before our interview, said, "It's like milking a cow! My member is left for dead. It's like a hose. It clogs up; there's no pressure. I have to pinch it to pee—like milking a cow!" Many who were upset by urinary problems were also embarrassed by incontinence. A seventy-five-year-old retired factory worker said he had to make an effort to get all the urine out but often could not, so "I can't even walk or run—little drops come out. I can't move, and no one can touch me." Thus, al-though the participants were frightened by diagnoses of cancer and frus-trated by difficult or frequent urination and, less frequently, decreased sexual function, they generally characterized the shame of incontinence as the most troubling problem related to prostate disease.

Overall, although the study participants were often aware of the bio-medical definitions of their diseases, they usually responded to my re-quests to "describe your sickness (*enfermedad*)" in terms of life experi-ences, not biological changes. They sometimes placed great importance on biomedical diagnoses and prognoses, for instance, when they had been diagnosed with prostate cancer and wondered if it might be fatal.

However, the majority of the men experiencing chronic illnesses that they did not see as immediately life threatening were most concerned about how the symptoms would affect their daily lives. Biomedical diagnoses and the daily experience of illness thus represented particular elements of composite chronic illnesses, which became more or less important for understanding their bodies and lives in different circumstances.

Illnesses of Emotion and Emotional Responses to Illness

Emotion was a key element of the study participants' composite chronic illnesses because they frequently saw negative emotion as both an outcome of sickness, and a cause of disease itself. In Latin America and its diaspora, people often recognize illnesses of emotion as an important kind of sickness. Illnesses of emotion occur when strong negative feelings create physical distress. Throughout Mexico, and among the study participants, many people believe that emotional experiences—such as *susto* (fright), *nervios* (nerves), and *coraje* (rage)—trigger bodily pathologies ranging from trembling and fits to incidences of or increased susceptibility to biomedically recognized sicknesses, such as heart disease and type 2 diabetes (Baer et al. 2003; Finkler 1991; Guarnaccia et al. 1996; Rubel et al. 1985). In this view, psychological and emotional troubles are inseparable from bodily distress because emotional pain is thought to cause organic physical pathology and vice versa (Congress 1992).

These pathogenically negative emotions generally arise from problematic interpersonal relationships or life hardships, and people frequently relate them to gender. Strong negative feelings are often caused by hardships specific to a person's struggle to be the sort of man or woman he or she strives to be or to suffering related to the gendered social lot assigned to them (Finkler 1994; Rebhun 1993). It is in this context that Pepe's wife's claim that her husband's unfaithfulness incited her diabetes (discussed in chapter 2) makes sense because both Pepe and his wife believed that his gendered betrayal caused her powerfully negative and illness-inducing feelings.

Thus the participants often understood negative emotion to cause illness in its own right. When I asked about their sicknesses, they often discussed illnesses of emotion in addition to the biomedical ailments for which they were receiving IMSS treatment. For instance, a forty-five-year-old gardener said that his worrying about the deterioration of his marriage had done bodily damage because these worries made him feel "stress and nerves." He clarified that although these conditions were caused by emotion, "'nerves' is physical." In his case, he said that the symptoms of *nervios* were trembling and a predisposition to high blood pressure. Likewise, a seventy-one-year-old businessman told me that *coraje* had physical symptoms that were similar to the hormonal changes he had experienced after a prostate operation: "I feel a heat; I start to sweat for ten or fifteen minutes."

The participants also frequently said that negative feelings worsened or triggered the onset of chronic diseases for which they subsequently received biomedical treatment. For instance, the wife of a sixty-two-year-old retired salesman reported that he had been healthy until his diabetes was triggered by a "very strong rage over family problems." Similarly, a fifty-seven-year-old furniture deliverer, who characterized himself as "very sentimental," told me that he became deeply depressed after three of his close relatives died. He concealed his sadness from his wife, fearing that it would cause her to worry and "make her sick," possibly worsening her hypertension. He finally became so depressed that he sought the help of an IMSS psychologist, which he said helped considerably. Although his depression had lifted, he said that it had caused lasting physical changes, making him susceptible to various health problems, including prostate enlargement, gastritis, and decreased erectile function. In addition to the damage done by his depression, he believed that these illnesses also lingered because of his diabetes. For this participant, negative feelings and biomedically recognized physical and psychological problems were powerfully interrelated.

Biomedical practitioners also sometimes ascribed physical symptoms to emotions. When I asked one of the urologists about his lingering cough, he explained, "It's psychosomatic, caused by stress and problems" with his wife and their finances. Although this doctor's language was tempered by his medical training, which is evident in his use of the term *psychosomatic* to draw a line between psychological and organic etiologies, his understanding of his illness as rooted in emotion reveals his own enculturation in local ideas of health. Similarly, a fifty-four-year-old IMSS family medicine doctor, who I interviewed when he himself was a urology patient, described the physical consequences of rage thusly: "When one gets angry, the nervous system secretes toxic substances. You get a bitter taste in your mouth [and] your back hurts." Because of this link between anger and ill health, he told his patients to make life changes that would make them happier. He said, "Sometimes they come in sad, depressed, unstable. I tell them that they'll have better health if they make changes in their life, so that they have more energy and strength. God wants people to be happy." He added that, unfortunately, negative emotions were often rooted in difficult life circumstances that were hard to change. IMSS doctors' understandings of emotions and physical symptoms as powerfully interlinked also influenced their treatment recommendations for decreased erectile function, which will be discussed in the next chapters.

Although the participants often spoke of emotion causing biomedical illnesses, they also believed that illnesses of emotion could be consequences of biomedically recognized diseases and their treatments. In these cases, sadness and fear related to illness symptoms or medical encounters were thought to develop into related disorders of emotion. For example, an eighty-one-year-old retired factory worker reported that his wife "has a serious nerves problem" because she "has suffered many [medical] interventions" and now has a constant fear that she will need to undergo more. This fear has concrete physical consequences, such as making her weak. Likewise, a seventy-eight-year-old retired utility worker said that his diabetes made him more susceptible to fright, to the point that he had begun to tremble constantly.

The participants saw high blood pressure as especially connected to disordered emotion because many said that "pressure" in life and in the body were intimately linked. For instance, a sixty-seven-year-old veterinarian said that he and his wife both have hypertension that was "rooted in a scare . . . A tree fell on our house ten or fifteen years ago." He told me that this was one key cause of their high blood pressure, along with age and being overweight. He characterized the scare as the "catalyst" that set off an illness process that came to involve multiple physical and emotional factors. Similarly, a fifty-six-year-old prison worker had been taking high blood pressure medication for ten years. He told me that because the physical aspects of his illness were under control, only emotional changes now caused his fluctuating pressure. He said that his pressure "only rises if I have a rage. Then I feel a headache." This rage-headache correlation shows the extent to which many of the study participants understood emotions to be expressed through bodily sensation and sickness.

Humoral Understandings of the Body

In addition to ideas of biomedical diseases and emotions as sources of ill health, the study participants tended to include humoral notions of health and illness in their composite understandings of bodily function and disease causation. In humoral understandings of the body, food, medicines, and activities are ascribed hot or cold properties, and health is achieved when people take in a balance of hot and cold that results in bodily equilibrium (Foster 1994). In many cultures, people ascribe properties of literal or metaphorical hotness or coldness to substances, illnesses, injuries, acts, remedies, and personality traits (Anderson 1987). Classical Greek medicine was based on this humoral notion, which still influences some Euro-American beliefs about sickness; this humoral legacy is the reason that Americans call common respiratory infections "colds" (Rebhun 1999). In Mexico, humoral notions of bodily function may have been present in the health beliefs of preconquest indigenous societies and were also promoted by colonizing Spaniards (Messner 1987). To varying degrees, many people worldwide believe that excesses or inappropriate mixes of even metaphorical hot or cold can do real physical damage (Manderson 1987).

In both humoral and emotion-based understandings of illness causation, balance—whether it is bodily or emotional—is the defining component of good health. Descriptions of balance and imbalance were thus key elements of many study participants' composite understandings of chronic illness. They saw imbalances in their environments, behaviors, feelings, social relationships, and patterns of consumption as bad for their health. For example, some of the participants believed that extreme hot or cold weather caused bodily harm, such as the fifty-five-year-old gardener who said that more than thirty years of working outside in the early morning chill had made him permanently "cold" and caused urinary problems. He said he saw the doctor because "I wanted something to warm my body." Likewise, a seventy-one-year-old factory worker reported the following: "I worked for a long time in the heat—the lime ovens. That heat caused prostate trouble. About five months ago, I felt really bad when I peed. It burned, and I woke up a few times in the night. When I was working in the strong heat, I drank lots of water but with ice. I didn't feel bad then—I was burning, and it felt refreshing. But that could have done harm."

Accordingly, some of the participants attempted to change their behaviors in ways that would protect them from extreme hot or cold, sometimes on their doctor's recommendation. For instance, a sixty-five-year-old gardener started showering at night rather than in the morning "because the doctor says if I'm going to bathe, then I shouldn't go out; I could catch a cold."

People subscribing to humoral understandings of the body also often believe that one's humoral balance dictates their personality or nature, as in the case of the "hot" Mexican man. Similarly raced and gendered ideas of hot bloodedness are both used within and are stereotypically ascribed to the populations of other postcolonial countries, such as Brazil (Parker 1991). Many of the participants spoke of having hot or cold constitutions that they interpreted as either symptoms or causes of physical changes and social behavior, most frequently when they discussed their interest in sex over time. I interviewed a security guard and a homemaker in their early sixties who had not had sex for over a month as a result of his prostate problems. The wife explained that her cool constitution made her amenable to this change, saying, "I'm content; I'm not affected by the lack of sex. I'm very cold." She also believed that her husband's extreme "hotness," evinced through his desire for frequent sex, was the root cause of his prostate disease. She reasoned that "he's too hot, so this time without sex will improve his health."

The participants frequently combined biomedical, emotional, and humoral illness beliefs into composite understandings of health. For example, people frequently told me that very hot or cold weather exacerbated biomedically defined chronic illnesses such as diabetes, increasing symptoms such as thirst or swelling by subjecting ill bodies to unbalanced environments. A fifty-two-year-old lawyer attributed his hypertension and diabetes to a combination of genetics, emotions, and lifestyle. He characterized himself as "extremely anxious" and said that his stressful work exacerbated his "problem of nerves." Thus he saw his chronic disease as an inheritance worsened by his life situation and fragile emotional state. He said, "I have family with [hypertension] and diabetes. It's hereditary, though of course work helped the hypertension to develop more quickly." This participant also feared that his nervous state would make an upcoming prostate operation more difficult because related emotional and physical problems predisposed him to a negative reaction to anesthesia. He told me, "I'm afraid, primarily because general anesthesia affects me a lot. They have to use different drugs with me. After previous operations, I felt like I was in an abyss, falling fast. If I don't grab the rocks on the sides, I'll die. I get sick from nerves."

Structural Causes of Illness

Along with negative emotion, humoral imbalance, and biological pathology, structural factors also played a key role in chronic illness incidence and in study participants' narrative explanations of their sicknesses. Experiences of life as structurally and emotionally difficult, as well as the commonness of later-life chronic illness among their peers, led many of the study participants to see chronic disease as a somewhat inevitable product of aging in Mexico. This section examines the ways that structural forces influenced men's daily life activities, such as eating and working, in ways that promoted chronic illness.

The participants often believed that their chronic illnesses had been augmented or worsened by poor bodily health linked to economic hardship and its consequences. They frequently described lives marked by illnesses and injuries that were exacerbated by a lack of consistent access to health care. For example, a sixty-five-year-old retiree came to the IMSS hospital to seek treatment because "my sexual acts aren't very good." He surmised that this resulted from a "lack of desire" caused by the chronic pain he experienced as a result of a series of accidents and the lack of good medical treatment in his youth. He said, "Ever since I was a boy, I had many illnesses." His parents were farmers, and they lived in a rural area without access to health care. He suffered an inexplicable paralysis when he was between eight and ten years old; he received no treatment for it but eventually recovered. A few years later, he fell from a tall tree, landing chest first on a stone used to wash laundry. He raised his shirt to show me the resulting indentation in his chest, joking, "It's not that I have a big belly; it's that the top part is pushed in." He has had back pain ever since this accident and believed that this constant pain led to a lack of sexual desire that made it difficult to attain an erection.

Poor diet and the unhealthy consumption of substances such as tobacco were also key causes of diabetes and heart disease. This was especially clear in the case of a sixty-eight-year-old retired office administrator who attributed his four heart attacks largely to pork and secondarily to smoking. He told me that he was "obsessed" with *carnitas* (braised pork chunks); he ate a kilo of them and smoked three packs of cigarettes per day in the year before his first heart attack. After each attack, he halved his pork consumption and cut out one daily pack of cigarettes. He eventually stopped smoking, although he told me that "I can't live without red meat," even though he knew it might cause further heart problems. Many of the participants were unwilling to change their diets because they saw eating what they wanted as a quality of life issue. A jovial seventy-year-old retired bus driver said that he liked soda, so despite his diabetes, "I have a Coke once in a while. We all have to die of something!"

The participants also often revealed that they maintained poor diets after chronic illness diagnoses, linking their eating habits to financial constraints in their descriptions of their chronic illnesses. For example, a sixty-eight year old retiree told me that for his diabetes medications to work, "it's necessary to eat the correct diet, but because of economic concerns, we can't always have special foods in the house." Similarly, an eighty-one-year-old retired factory worker said that he believed his diabetes to be partly hereditary but also caused by being overweight. However, he had never kept to the diet his doctors recommended because "I can't." He said that his family could not afford to provide different food for "the sick one in the house," so he ate a special diet only when he was in the hospital for diabetes-related complications. Although the individual foods that the participants described as healthy, such as produce and nonfried items, were locally affordable, they understood these foods to be special and inaccessible because they differed from the normal diets of most families. The participants rarely saw healthy diets as lifestyle possibilities for their whole families, casting them instead as remedial responses to sickness. This belief made healthy foods seem impossibly expensive because they would be purchased in addition to the family's normal meals.

The participants' work lives also fundamentally influenced their bodily health. Particular career paths require specific daily life routines that often involve sedentary or dangerous activities; stress; and a lack of opportunity for exercise, adequate sleep, or healthy eating. For example, a fifty-nine-year-old truck driver who has had diabetes for eighteen years said that it was caused by the lifestyle he lived as he prepared for his career: "I went for my truck driving license because Mexicans want to earn more, more, more. While I was studying, I didn't take care of myself, so I was struck with diabetes." A twenty-nine-year-old prison administrator, who considered changing his diet after finding blood in his urine, said that he disliked bringing a lunch to work because it had to be inspected by the security guards, which made him feel uncomfortable. So he preferred to buy food inside the prison, even though all the options there were unhealthy.

Many of the study participants' jobs required unhealthy levels of sedentism. This was especially true for older men, whose employment options were very limited. Because it is legal to make hiring decisions based on age in Mexico and most of the job ads call for young applicants, many of the older participants turned to taxi driving after being forced to retire from their previous jobs. Taxi driving is one of the few professions that recruits older men, because their older age is thought to make them more reliable drivers. However, this work entails spending long days seated in a car, which makes it difficult to exercise.

The participants also identified work as a key cause of negative emotions that might contribute to chronic illness. A fifty-three-year-old gardener believed that the mental and physical effects of overwork caused both his diabetes and erectile difficulty. He had been diabetic and had taken insulin for fifteen years. He said that for about a year and a half, his erections "aren't the same." He told me that the diabetes came on because he works too much and being "exhausted and tired doesn't help." He said that if the erectile problems were caused directly by the overwork, he could fix them by simply working less. However, because the problems were also caused by his diabetes, "it's not so easy." Similarly, a fifty-eight-year-old office worker saw his prostate problems as the cause of his erectile difficulty, with stress at work as the cause of this prostate trouble. He said that "work pressures" caused negative emotions that had partly caused his prostate enlargement. Because of both this ongoing stress and the physical damage done by his prostate problem, he believed "my erections aren't that firm." Employment-related stress weighed especially heavily on many of the participants because work was central to most of their composite masculinities. Because many of the men used workplace success to assert successful manliness, subordination or failure at work often caused stress that led to embodied illness. This illness further hampered their work, fueling their emotional distress.

In the workplace, interpersonal relationships often combined with structural constraints to promote behavior that hurt people's health. Although diet and exercise may on the surface seem to be easily changeable personal decisions, individuals' choices about what to eat and even when and how to move around are powerfully shaped by particular constraints. I learned this myself when, after months of breakfasting with the urologists each morning on tacos and cola, I decided to learn from the cautionary tales I was hearing and switch to drinking juice. Mexicans consume more Coca-Cola per capita than people of any other nation (Coca-Cola Company 2008), and my hospital field site was located next to a Coca-Cola factory. The IMSS urologists were no exception to this national love of cola, and they not only noticed but also felt personally offended by my beverage change. They first teased me, but after a few days, they began to warn me that juice in the morning would unsettle my stomach and harm my health. Despite their biomedical knowledge that soda consumption can have negative health consequences, they seemed to understand my switch to juice with breakfast as a personal insult to their own dietary choices. Furthermore, because sharing food is an important way to cement social bonds and express intimacy, I believe they felt that by declining soda, I was rejecting a communal experience (Mintz and Du Bois 2002). Thus the urologists continued to offer me cola each morning, and I resumed drinking it to preserve harmony at the breakfast table. Similar social pressures to share unhealthy foods must have weighed even more heavily on my study participants, who were living their lives in their workplaces, whereas I was just a visitor.

Composite Chronic Illnesses and Treatments

Chronic illness sufferers' multifaceted understandings of disease causes and consequences lend themselves to a composite analysis. The study participants believed that their conditions had a range of interrelated social, emotional, physical, and structural causes and outcomes. For example, many said that diseases such as diabetes were partly hereditary and partly a result of unhealthy lifestyle choices and bodily aging. An eighty-year-old retired factory worker asserted, "My diabetes is an inheritance; my mother and sister had it. But it's also because I'm overweight." Similarly, a fifty-five-year-old grocery deliverer and recovered alcoholic believed that diabetes ran in his family, "but drinking slowed the treatment." Other participants attributed changes that could be understood as chronic disease symptoms, such as erectile difficulty, to familial predispositions to chronic illness. For example, a forty-nine-year-old plumber believed that his trouble achieving an erection was a result of a propensity to diabetes: "My mother died of diabetes. I'm not diabetic, but I have her genes—my mother's blood in me." These men believed that multiple problems and predispositions combined together to generate their illnesses.

This perspective led chronic illness sufferers to attribute their diseases to a range of causes that could not be reduced to discrete component parts. The eighty-one-year-old retired factory worker quoted previously said it was impossible to determine whether his erectile difficulty was caused by "sugar or aging." Along these lines, a sixty-three-year-old retired industrial mechanic said that his erection problems were part of an overall "bad process" in which biological, lifestyle, and social problems had "bonded together." Many of the participants had been diagnosed with multiple chronic diseases, including diabetes, cardiovascular disease, and prostate disease, and they often saw these as parts of a composite illness whole. They often reported not knowing which problem was responsible for which symptom, instead seeing different ills as complexly interconnected.

Just as men saw illness causes as multiple and interrelated, they understood their illnesses to have complex and wide-reaching consequences. They reported embodied consequences of chronic illness that ranged from physically observable symptoms, such as erectile difficulty, to emotional changes. Many of the participants stated that chronic disease made one more susceptible to other illnesses, especially illnesses of emotion. A seventy-eight-year-old retired utility company worker said that his diabetes has made him prone to *susto*, as evinced by his trembling hands. Others, such as a seventy-one-year-old retiree, who called his diabetes "a terrifying type of cancer—it eats you, affecting sight, feet, kidneys," spoke of stress caused by their fears about chronic illness harming their mental and emotional states. The participants also described vicious cycles in which emotional distress caused by chronic disease could exacerbate the illness. The retired mechanic quoted previously said, "Though [my diabetes is] controlled, there are occasions when I get angry; my blood sugar rises."

The participants also reported that the experience of chronic illness could cause negative personality and attitude changes. In some cases, lifestyle changes that were recommended to alleviate illness did social harm or were at least assigned blame for unhappiness related to the effects of chronic illness. For example, an eighty-five-year-old retired factory worker said, "I used to be happy. I drank a lot. But now I can't, and I've got a temper." His daughter, who accompanied him to his doctor's appointment, said that the changes they made to his diet made him tired, and now he's "neurasthenic; everything makes him mad." She said that these changes dated back to the time when diabetes-related headaches forced him to retire from his factory job.

Men's treatment responses to chronic illnesses also reflected their belief in composite etiologies and effects. The study particpants' most common response was to take the chronic disease medications that their doctors prescribed. But because they understood the causes of chronic illnesses as multifactoral, many of them combined pharmaceutical interventions with other treatments, such as holistic or *naturista* (naturopathic) remedies. They told me that these different treatments dealt with specific aspects of their chronic illnesses, such as specific physical or emotional symptoms, which the pharmaceuticals did not. For example, a sixty-eight-year-old retired truck driver reported that he had been diabetic for fourteen years, so he supplemented his medication with "a natural medicine that I take when I don't want to be sleepy. It wakes me up." Some of the participants also took natural medicines designed to alleviate conditions that underlaid their chronic illness, such as strong negative emotions. A fifty-eight-year-old electrician, for example, drank natural teas to supplement his diabetes medication. One tea treated diabetes, and the other calmed "rages."

This use of natural treatments sometimes extended to diet. A seventy-five-year-old retired factory worker took diabetes pills but also ate "vegetables that do me good . . . smoothies made of grapefruit, pineapple, nopal, alfalfa, parsley, or tomato. With that, I lower myself [my blood sugar level]." The participants who were not focused on natural medicine sometimes also changed their diets in the face of heart disease or diabetes, often on the advice of their doctors and loved ones. A fifty-nine-year-old retired driver said that since being diagnosed with diabetes, "I've changed my way of eating. Before, I ate ten to twelve tortillas, now only one or two. Before, soda, all carbohydrates." He joked, "Now, no soda, only beer!" The participants who made such dietary changes often accounted for the composite nature of chronic illness in their reasoning, saying that the trouble of dietary change was worth it to avoid physical deterioration and related life and emotional problems. The retiree who compared diabetes to cancer both took medication and watched his diet. He explained, "You have to eat on a diet because if you don't take care of yourself, you get worse, and the medicines don't work." Similarly, a forty-eight-year-old taxi driver feared that his diabetes would impair his sexual function if left untreated. He said, "If I don't take care of myself, nothing [no erection]. That's why I'm here. You have to watch the diabetes . . . that's why I'm going to change my diet."

Some patients made other healthful lifestyle changes, such as adding exercise to their daily routines. This change was most common among retired men who had the free time to walk or do calisthenics or among the few men who lived close enough to their job sites to begin walking or cycling to work. As with the structural aspects of chronic illness causation, particular work and financial contexts shaped men's ability to perform physical activity that would improve their health. For instance, a forty-two-year-old welder whose diabetes has been controlled with medication and diet for nine years said that he also stopped drinking, which was facilitated by a change in work sites. He reported that giving up beer was easy after returning to Mexico after working in the United States: "While I was working there, I drank six beers a day because I was so hot from the work."

The men who successfully made lifestyle changes after a chronic illness diagnosis usually had social motivations to do so, above and beyond the desire to promote physical health. For instance, a forty-six-year-old utility company worker with a twenty-six-year-old wife began to swim and jog after becoming diabetic. Pointing to his wife and laughing, he said, "At my age, imagine! You have to exercise to be with her!" Other participants considered emotion management and work on interpersonal relationships to be health-promoting lifestyle changes. For example, married retired teachers in their late sixties reported that to control their blood pressure, they tried to "live a tranquil life . . . we try not to have rages or scares." Treatment responses that included physical, social, and emotional components thus reflected participants' understandings of chronic illness as the aggregate outcome of multiple kinds of problems.

Composite Masculinities and Chronic Illnesses

A composite approach also sheds light on the interactions between men's chronic illnesses and composite masculinities. Chronic diseases present gendered challenges, making it difficult for men to work, requiring increased self-care that might be locally viewed as unmanly, and frequently causing erectile difficulty. Because feelings of failure about fulfilling gendered norms can be key causes of illnesses of emotion, physical changes that prevent men from performing practices once central to their composite masculinities can combine with negative feelings about their perceived failures and become self-perpetuating composite problems of both illness and manhood.

The participants frequently blamed themselves for their chronic conditions in specifically gendered ways. Men who saw particular lifestyle choices as key causal elements of their illnesses often blamed themselves for acting badly or irresponsibly. When I asked why he thought he had diabetes, an eighty-five-year-old retired driver replied, "I drank a lot and didn't eat well. I would rather have drunk than eaten. And I got angry a lot. That's why I've fallen apart." Along these lines, the participants sometimes cast the emotional causes of illness as gendered failures, for instance, to irresponsibly fail to control one's innately Mexican "hot temper."

The participants also said that the emotional distress and physical deterioration related to chronic illnesses had consequences for their senses of manly selfhood. They often became upset about physical changes that made them unable to perform actions they saw as key to their ways of being men. This disappointment sometimes related to penetrative sex. Describing his erectile difficulty following a prostate operation, a seventy-two-year-old retired bodyguard said, "The prostate problems disarmed me." Often, this sort of distress related to a man's inability to work. The eighty-one-year-old former factory worker quoted previously said that he was forced to retire from his manufacturing job in 1984 because of complications from his diabetes. He said that the disease "brings many problems; your whole organism falls apart," and his bodily distress was worsened by his sadness about leaving his job. He eventually made past rather than ongoing work success a key element of his composite masculinity, to the point that he always carried his old factory identification card, which he proudly showed me during our interview. He said that despite diabetes-related problems like infections, he strove to remain "active" and became depressed when he was unable to do so. He explained, "I was a man that had a lot of energy. It was hard to become sick."

Similarly, the study participants often feared that their chronic illnesses would hamper their ability to control themselves bodily and mentally, which many saw as a key requirement for successful Mexican masculinity. In one doctor's visit, a fifty-six-year-old heavy machinery operator discovered that he needed prostate surgery and had diabetes. He said that the operation did not worry him too much because "you have to face the problem." However, he said he was more concerned about the diabetes because it was a "permanent sickness" that you could control but not cure. This threatened his ability to continue the emotional practice of self-control that was a key component of his composite masculinity; he noted that both emotionally and physically, "I try to control myself." Although he believed that he would be able to control his diabetes with frequent clinic visits and a change of diet, he was worried that his declining health and the related need to spend time at the IMSS hospital would affect his ability to work. He said, "I have to work to sustain my home. That's the problem . . . Now, nothing will be the same because I have to take more care of myself."

The composite approach is also useful for understanding the role that decreased erectile function plays in the mutual construction of illness experiences and gendered selfhoods. Erectile function change is often implicated as both a cause and an outcome of illness and men's difficulty in performing their desired forms of manhood. Erectile capacity diminishes for a variety of often-interrelated reasons, which are linked to men's physical bodies, life experiences, and social and structural contexts. Because sex is often a key element of their composite masculinities, the sets of factors that shape illness also shape their gendered selfhoods. Although most of the study participants who considered themselves to be older at the onset of chronic illness incorporated erectile function change into composite masculinities foregrounding the maturity discussed in chapter 1, men who saw themselves as too young to have such diseases struggled to reconcile the social and physical consequences of their conditions with their desired ways of being men. Chronic illness experiences became a key aspect of their composite masculinities, as did related fears that their ill bodies prevented them from being ideally or successfully manly. The following case study demonstrates the composite natures of chronic illness and erectile difficulty, including the ways one man related them into ways of being a man that changed according to context.

MANUEL: CROHN'S DISEASE, SHAME, AND BACHELORHOOD

Manuel, a slight fifty-six-year-old who was studying to be a tailor, wore large glasses and walked with a cane. Excitable and very talkative, he kept leaning forward as we spoke to emphasize his points, and having to push his thick bangs out of his face. For most of his life, he had suffered from Crohn's disease, an inflammation of the bowel that causes diarrhea and chronic pain. Because of what he called the "burden" of his disease, the shame he felt about it, and his assumption that no woman would want to saddle herself with an "unwell" man, Manuel said that he decided in his youth that he would never marry. He moved to the United States in 1986, eventually gaining legal residency and working in a Miami clothing factory for twelve years. Despite the fact that he sometimes had girlfriends in Miami, he held to his belief that his illness, which over time necessitated intestinal surgeries and a colostomy, was off-putting to women. He felt sure that no one would want to marry a man "with so many problems." His illness became a key facet of his composite masculinity, significantly constraining his romantic, familial, and sexual possibilities. This situation led Manuel to focus on work rather than romance as a source of manly pride, but he nevertheless reported overall feelings of shame and low self-worth.

The sexual consequences of his illness were a key factor in both this shame and his decision not to marry. He said that he felt embarrassed about his colostomy bag and a chronic bladder infection that made his urine smell and stain. Most of all, he was constantly afraid that his general ill health would make it impossible for him to get an erection. This fear began when, fifteen years earlier, he had failed to achieve an erection with a prostitute. He went to a doctor, who said there was nothing wrong with him. However, he reported being "traumatized" by the incident and kept repeating that he still felt "shame" and was "embarrassed" about it. He recounted the details of the fifteen-year-old encounter vividly, and it was clear that this moment of erectile failure had become a key part of a composite masculinity in which shame related to his illness and fears of sexual inadequacy supported his declaration that it was inappropriate for him to try to marry.

However, having recently returned to Mexico, Manuel told me that he was reevaluating this decision. Now in a social context where everyone he knew was married and had children, he said he had come to feel that he missed out on a key part of life. He told me that he saw his siblings married, with grown children, and wished that he had done the same. In this new context, a composite masculinity centered on avoiding shame by limiting potentially unsuccessful intimate relationships made less sense. Furthermore, although bachelorhood during work migration in the United States did not seem particularly odd, in Mexico the lack of a romantic relationship marked Manuel as different in a very public way. So he found a local girlfriend who was in a similar situation—like him, she had never married or had children—and he told her about his sexual difficulties. They had not yet attempted sex, but he said that she was very supportive and encouraged him to see a urologist for an ED medication. He was prescribed one and told me that if it worked and they could have sex, he planned to marry his girlfriend. Manuel thus decided that if he were able to add one new, valorized way of demonstrating manliness—sexual penetration—into his composite masculinity, he would have the courage to add new, related manly practices such as marriage.

The Utility of the Composite Approach

Manuel's experience shows that both chronic illnesses and particular ways of being men can be fruitfully understood as composite conditions. This perspective helps to reveal that illness experiences and gendered selfhood are mutually constituted and depend on relationships among experiences, emotions, social interactions, and structural limitations. This composite approach generates a multifaceted account of illness occurrences and experiences, which sheds light on the logic of chronically ill individuals' actions, illness beliefs, and self-care choices. It also highlights the ways that people fit composite illness experiences into composite gendered selfhoods. In addition, this analytic makes sense for understanding individual reactions to chronic illness in a cultural context where multifaceted understandings of bodies and health are prevalent, and where people often experience multiple chronic health problems, including illnesses of emotion, not as stand-alone problems but as facets of broader, more holistic experiences of ill health.

This composite approach is also useful for bridging the divide between biomedical and individual understandings of health and the body. Rather than requiring researchers to conform to the linear models of disease causation prevalent in biomedicine, the composite perspective is useful for mapping how different life events combine into and mutually reinforce illness. This approach makes room for both the biomedical understanding of chronic disease as a physical pathology caused by specific lifestyle or organic factors and study participants' understandings of emotional and humoral imbalance as key additional causes of sickness. It also offers a way to understand how these different ways of thinking about health interrelate in individual lives, providing a way to map interactions between multiple chronic illness experiences and explanations.

Finally, this approach sheds light on the specific ways that men incorporate chronic illness experiences into their composite masculinities, and on the concrete consequences that different composite masculinities can have for men's health. Men who incorporate practices such as dietary change into their notions of selfhood after becoming ill have very different social and physical outcomes than those who seek to maintain existing forms of masculinity by refusing to make life- or persona-altering changes, such as eating healthier or exercising. Men's willingness to perform certain health-promoting behaviors is thus linked to the set of practices that form their composite masculinities. In short, although structural constraints related to work, finances, and food availability are key to the incidence of chronic disease, the way that men incorporate these conditions into their senses of themselves as men is equally salient to their health outcomes. Just as men's ways of being men shape their health status, the stories told in this chapter show how men's composite chronic illnesses often come to form key aspects of their composite masculinities.

Chapter Four

REJECTING ERECTILE DYSFUNCTION DRUGS

Rejecting Erectile Dysfunction Drugs

This chapter will explore why, in a country where ED drugs are major sellers and penetrative sex is often described as crucial to Mexican masculinity in the abstract, most of the study participants who experienced decreased erectile function chose not to treat it medically. Although about 70 percent of the study participants reported decreased erectile function, only about 9 percent had ever used a medical ED treatment; in addition, most of those who had tried an ED drug did not continue to use it. Rather than simple disinterest in ED drugs, many of the study participants expressed disdain for or fear of the drugs, to the point that some warned that "Viagra will kill you." Presenting the range of reasons why the study participants usually believed that ED drugs were the wrong treatments for their complex bodies and ills, this chapter demonstrates how the notion of erectile change as a medical pathology might be unappealing to men experiencing erectile difficulty, even if they are receiving biomedical treatment for other urologic ailments in a context rife with ED drug marketing.

I analyze the men's descriptions of their responses to erectile difficulty, along with their comments about the nature and the dangers of ED drugs, to identify the social and structural factors that encouraged most of the study participants to develop negative views of ED treatment. Through such analysis, this chapter shows how their understandings of ED treatment were frequently shaped by the holistic understandings of health and illness described in chapter 3. Composite understandings of health that combined medical, humoral, and emotion-based ideas of illness led many of the participants to view pharmaceuticals as too narrow a treatment for their multifaceted bodily changes.

Many study participants' views regarding the inappropriateness of ED drugs developed in concert with their common assessment of decreasing erectile function as a signal that they should make the shift to an appropriately mature style of masculinity. Thus I argue that most of the study participants also rejected medical intervention because they believed it would threaten, not support, composite masculinities that they had crafted to be mature, respectable, and age appropriate. For most of the study participants, it did not make sense to adopt the notion of decreasing erectile function as a medical pathology because drugs such as Viagra would not help them to be the kinds of respectable older men they strove to be.

Together, these ideas about the social and physical inappropriateness of ED drugs led many of the study participants to believe that these drugs were physically dangerous. Because they saw illness and aging as potential causes of erectile function change, the participants usually did not understand diminished erectile function itself as a chronic illness or a medical concern. Thus they believed that applying strong pharmaceutical treatments to a nonmedical change might cause bodily harm. Overall, many of the participants who self-identified as older saw artificially prolonging youthful sexual embodiment with drug treatment as both silly and physically risky. They frequently described the dangers of ED treatment, for instance, discussing rumors that Viagra use had killed their neighbors and arguing that it would unnaturally "accelerate" one's body. The participants tended to see "fast" living as appropriate for young men and youthful sexuality but dangerous for older, slowing bodies. For these men, the social inappropriateness of ED treatment to mature masculinity translated into clear physical risk because it required pushing one's body to perform acts that were no longer age appropriate.

Understanding men's reactions to erectile difficulty and ED treatment as composite objects, this chapter also examines the role that the structural context of IMSS health care played in their understandings of the appropriate ways to treat and understand decreased erectile function. Based on both interviews with the study participants and a broader survey of the IMSS patient population, I discuss the ways that the IMSS institutional setting shaped men's ideas about whether ED drugs were accessible, affordable, and appropriate. I argue that the IMSS urology patients faced structural disincentives for seeking medical ED treatment that, along with familial encouragement to give up youthful sexuality, made them more inclined to incorporate mature sexuality than medically mediated penetrative sex into their composite masculinities.

Erectile Dysfunction Drug Use in the IMSS Patient Population

This section provides background information on the popularity of ED drug treatment in a broader sample of the IMSS hospital population. At the start of my research, I was surprised by the very low frequency of ED drug use among the IMSS urology patients because drugs such as Viagra were so widely available in Cuernavaca and were reportedly very popular throughout Mexico. To discover whether other IMSS patients shared the study participants' view that ED drug treatment was unnecessary, I worked with local public health researchers and the IMSS hospital's nursing staff to survey 750 male IMSS patients between the ages of 40 and 60—who were not patients in the urology service—about their knowledge and use of a range of ED treatments.[1] We recruited these survey participants from the waiting area of the hospital's family medicine division. Some of these men were seeing their family doctors for their own health problems, whereas others had accompanied family members to appointments. We focused on this group of men because they provided a cross section of all the men using IMSS health care in Cuernavaca.

Survey participants' responses revealed that although virtually all of them had heard of medications for treating ED, this did not translate into high levels of drug usage. Forty-four percent of the survey respondents who experienced erectile difficulty had tried some intervention that they hoped would increase erectile function, but they focused largely on nonpharmaceutical treatments, which most considered "more natural" and "more healthy" than the drug treatments. The most common response to decreased erectile function was lifestyle change: over 65 percent of the men who had sought a nonmedical intervention sought to exercise more

---

1 Details of the study methodology and findings have been published elsewhere (Wentzell and Salmerón 2009a, 2009b). Briefly, we found that 337 of the 750 men surveyed reported decreased erectile function. Of those men, 212 agreed to complete self-administered surveys; research nurses assisted them if they could not read or had poor eyesight. The three-page surveys included eighteen questions and collected four types of information: basic demographic information, information on change over time in the frequency and the quality of sexual relations, the social and emotional effects of these changes, and respondents' use of—and satisfaction with—various ED treatments.

or eat healthier diets. Taking vitamins was also a popular response among men in this group. Almost 57 percent of them did so, believing that vitamins would promote general health and vitality without dangerous side effects. Nonpharmaceutical treatments, such as herbal supplements marketed to stimulate erectile function rather than general bodily health, were perceived as somewhat similar to ED drugs and were far less popular. Less than 17 percent of the men who used nonpharmaceutical treatments took dietary supplements, such as "MForce" or "Himcaps," and about 13 percent took potency-enhancing medicinal herbs.

Pharmaceuticals for ED treatment were the least popular kind of intervention among the men who responded to decreased erectile function with a change in health-care practice. Less than 13 percent of the men who reported decreased erectile function had ever used an ED drug. Furthermore, these men rarely continued using the treatment. Only 10 of the respondents who had tried an ED drug continued taking it after their initial trial. The survey respondents reported abandoning medical ED treatment for four key reasons: the cost was too high, the drug did not work, it was no longer needed, or it had undesirable side effects. Overall, only a small percentage of the IMSS patients experiencing decreased erectile function experimented with pharmaceutical treatment, and very few incorporated ED drugs into their standard health-care practices.

Findings about where the men who tried drug treatment obtained the drugs suggest that the IMSS setting itself may deter men from defining erectile function decrease as a health problem and treating it medically. Most of the men surveyed who had tried an ED drug had it prescribed by a doctor. However, although these survey participants received free health care at the IMSS hospital but had to pay for private-practice consultations, almost all of their medical encounters in which ED drugs were prescribed took place outside the IMSS system. The fact that men were willing to pay to receive private medical ED treatment suggests that they felt unable to ask—or were uncomfortable about asking—for such treatment at their IMSS appointments. This situation also contributed to the survey respondents' common characterization of ED drugs as expensive because despite the ostensible availability of free ED treatment within the IMSS hospital, the vast majority of ED medication users felt the need to seek private medical treatment for this condition, requiring them to purchase the prescribed drugs out of pocket. Overall, these findings show that ED drugs were an unpopular response to decreased erectile function among the IMSS patients, who saw nonpharmaceutical interventions as more appropriate and IMSS ED treatment as inaccessible. These survey responses demonstrate that the Cuernavaca IMSS patients as a group experienced the same structural and social deterrents to ED treatment use that similarly aged study participants encountered in the urology service.

Structural Disincentives for Using Erectile Dysfunction Drugs

In our interviews, the study participants described their medical encounters in ways that made it clear that ED treatment was difficult to access in the IMSS system. The structure of IMSS referrals and consultations generated medical interactions that focused on specific diseases, which left little time or social space for the discussion of other ills. Most of the urology patients were referred to the service for serious conditions, such as prostate enlargement or cancer, which became the main focus of the time-limited doctor-patient interactions. Despite the fact that many of the chronic diseases that the patients suffered could hamper erectile function, the urologists usually did not ask about IMSS patients' sex lives. When observing consultations, I noted that when the urologists did raise such questions, it was usually as the coda to a series of cursory questions following a physical exam: ". . . How are you peeing? . . . And any pain? . . . And your sex life?" It was also likely that the doctors asked this last question more frequently than usual during the times I was in the urology department because they were seeking out patients with sexual function change for me to interview. In the hierarchal culture of the hospital, many of the patients told me that they felt uncomfortable trying to steer their appointments toward any particular issue, especially a sensitive one.

Thus, even when the doctors asked the participants about their sexual function, the rushed and often impersonal feel of the appointments prevented some of the men who did want medical ED treatment from feeling the *confianza* necessary to ask for it. During our interviews after their medical appointments, men who had not been diagnosed with ED sometimes told me that they were having trouble attaining erections and wanted advice. When I asked why they had not told their doctors, the answer was usually "because of shame" (*pena* or *verguenza*). The participants frequently said that a "foundation of trust" was necessary for them to broach sensitive topics with their physicians, but it could not be built in hurried interactions where they were unsure if their doctors cared personally about them. Even men who told me that they desperately wanted medical ED treatment often felt there had been insufficient time to build the rapport with the urologist that would allow them to ask about potentially embarrassing sexual issues. The limited time and personnel resources in the IMSS hospital thus created an atmosphere that was not conducive to treating nonurgent health problems, particularly sexual problems that many of the patients needed to work up courage to discuss.

A lack of financial resources also limited ED drug treatment in the IMSS system. IMSS hospitals are required by federal law to dispense a standard set of pharmaceuticals at no cost to their patients whenever an IMSS physician prescribes such drugs. The ED drug sildenafil is included in this set of cost-free pharmaceuticals (Comisión Interinstitucional del Cuadro Básico de Insumos del Sector Salud 2009). However, the financial constraints that the Cuernavaca IMSS hospital faced meant that this law was simply not followed. According to the urologists, the hospital pharmacy could not afford to stock all the medications that it was required to, so it often failed to offer drugs—such as sildenafil—that were infrequently prescribed or not used to treat life-threatening conditions. Knowing that their patients often faced financial hardships, the urologists said they preferred not to prescribe drugs that the pharmacy would not dispense. In what was likely a self-perpetuating cycle, the urologists tended not to prescribe ED drugs, so the pharmacy tended not to stock them. In cases where the urologists felt that ED drugs were necessary or when patients requested them, the urologists sometimes gave patients free samples of ED drugs that they received from pharmaceutical sales representatives. Otherwise, the patients were forced to buy the pills on their own, and they often told me they found them prohibitively expensive. Although it is unlikely that the drug cost directly deterred urology patients from seeking IMSS ED treatment, because none of the participants mentioned prior knowledge that the legally mandated drugs would not be available, it seems that the doctors' knowledge about drug unavailability combined with the patients' reticence to seek IMSS ED treatment to deter both parties from medicalizing erectile difficulty.

This state of affairs also encouraged the IMSS doctors to maintain holistic understandings of erectile difficulty. Physicians are trained to heal using biomedical understandings of the body; in addition, they may also promote this perspective because of their personal beliefs and the social status often linked to biomedical knowledge and employment. Yet similar to other people, doctors may be exposed to a range of health beliefs and generate their own, context-specific composite understandings of illness etiology. Although the IMSS urologists privileged biomedical explanations for disease, their view of the causes of erectile difficulty was fundamentally holistic, including both emotional and physiological etiologies. They were partly encouraged toward such beliefs by the structure of IMSS appointments because they often lacked the time and the resources to diagnose and treat decreased erectile function as ED. Furthermore, unlike private-practice physicians, the IMSS doctors had no financial incentives to promote medical understandings of erectile difficulty. Especially because most of the patients who experienced it believed it to be a natural part of aging, decreased erectile function was rarely seen as a purely biological phenomenon in the IMSS setting, even in cases where it was treated medically.

The biomedical definition of ED itself can be interpreted to lend support for such holistic understandings of the condition's causation. Rather than seeking to disprove the widespread conventional wisdom that negative emotions can decrease erectile function, biomedical researchers working after the advent of ED drugs have sought to clarify the roles played by different causal factors to distinguish cases in which biomedical remedies might be effective (Melman and Gingell 1999). Such investigations are nevertheless used in pharmaceutical company attempts to define men experiencing psychologically based erectile function change as potential ED drug consumers because these treatments are now being touted as useful even in cases where feelings, not physiology, are presumed to be at fault (Olsson et al. 2000). Although it is inherently medicalizing, the suggestion of using biomedical treatments for psychogenic erectile difficulty nevertheless entails a composite notion of this condition, in which social and physiological events are intimately related. This means that physicians who are facing disincentives to adopt strictly biological understandings of ED etiology may find support for holistic approaches within the medical literature. This interpretation demonstrates that the context in which medical knowledge is used powerfully influences the ways that people interpret it.

Erectile Dysfunction Drugs as Inappropriate and Dangerous

Along these lines, the relative inaccessibility of ED drugs in the IMSS hospital appeared to be a key aspect of the participants' composite beliefs about the nature of erectile difficulty and ED treatment. The fact that medical ED treatments, unlike drugs for other commonly known conditions, were rarely prescribed resonated with the study participants' common belief that pharmaceuticals were not always appropriate responses to bodily change. Furthermore, the study participants commonly told me that they thought carefully about whether specific drugs were necessary for them, describing the interlinked social and physical dangers of pharmaceutical misuse. Most of the study participants rejected ED drugs as radically inappropriate for both their bodies and social situations. In keeping with the common ideas of life course change that cast decreasing sexual function as a key aspect of mature manhood and normal aging bodies, most of the men saw ED drugs and the sex that they would fuel as socially off-key and physiologically abnormal. They also believed that using these treatments would encourage behaviors that they and their wives no longer saw as aspects of appropriate ways of being men or couples. In short, most saw using ED drugs to artificially prolong the sexually active phase of their lives as simply wrongheaded.

Many of the participants saw continued penetrative sex as inappropriate for their life situations. Their belief that maturity was incompatible with frequent sex was often compounded by social situations that encouraged them to call a halt to their sex lives. In cases where men's wives were no longer interested in sex, or where relationships with sexual partners had soured, ED drugs seemed to be an inappropriate choice because men's social situations no longer provided opportunities for sex. For example, a sixty-eight-year-old retired administrator told me that his wife had discovered his infidelity and remained angry with him, even though he was no longer unfaithful because his ability to attain erections had decreased. I asked why he had not tried an ED drug to resume having sex with his wife or other partners. He responded as follows:

> That's the most difficult question that's ever been put to me. Why not? Because I love women . . . Look. Because the only person I could use it with would be my wife; I can't go back to my lover and ask forgiveness. And I'm certain my wife would reject me. She also can't respond physically. There's no lubrication, and the last few times, it hurt her a little—the lack of lubrication. And it was more

like an obligation, physical necessity but not psychological—she's thinking of Tom Selleck! Possibly that's why. At my age, I'd look ridiculous going out with young girls! I don't want to gross anyone out; it hasn't been important to find a cure for this situation [decreasing erectile function].

For this participant, the lack of a willing sexual partner was compounded by the belief that seeking sex at his age would seem silly or repulsive. This perceived social pressure not to seek out "ridiculous" sex provided an incentive for him to understand his decreased erectile function as a normal and socially appropriate bodily change, and it discouraged him from seeking medically mediated erections that he would have no place to use.

Other participants believed ED drugs to be inappropriate because they thought that having sex in times of fragile health or in older age could lead to bodily harm. The participants frequently told me that they believed that their older bodies could no longer withstand youthful levels of sexual activity. This was especially the case for the majority of the participants for whom aging was marked by chronic illness. A sixty-four-year-old retiree said: "I've had prostate cancer for two years, so nothing sexual because I'm taking care of myself . . . I don't know if it's because of the medications or what, but I haven't felt—for example, I don't even have erections. No desire, I'm calm. I feel good. Very calm, and the only thing that worries me is my health." Similarly, a forty-six-year-old Spanish teacher told me that since her boyfriend's prostate troubles began, "we've tried to avoid sex, so we don't have it very much. He doesn't want to hurt himself." She told me that since his health problems had given him *nervios* that impeded his erectile function, avoiding sex at times of health stress was quite easy. Even one of the youngest study participants, a twenty-three-year-old nursing student awaiting the removal of a testicular cyst, reported that he was having less sex before his operation "so as not to do damage." He feared that having too much sex during a time of illness would reduce his future fertility.

Overall, men suffering from urologic ailments often feared that sex might exacerbate their conditions. They generally expected to have to lessen or stop their sex lives at the onset of health problems to preserve their overall bodily health. For example, a seventy-year-old retired government worker who suffered from prostate enlargement told me that he planned to ask the doctor if sex was "prohibited" and, if so, to put himself on a "disciplinary order" to abstain for the foreseeable future. Most of the participants saw abstinence for health as a responsible move that supported, rather than undermined, good masculinity. A sixty-four-year-old small-business owner told me that he was abstaining after prostate surgery and related complications, but this change did not make him feel less manly: "I don't have much sex because of hygiene, for health, because I'm bleeding, etc. That doesn't mean that I'm no longer a man."

Other participants associated sex with the risky lifestyles in which they had indulged as youths; thus they believed that drug-enhanced erectile capacity would lead to dangerous behavior inappropriate for their older selves and bodies. For instance, a sixty-eight-year-old retired truck driver told me that he would not consider using ED drugs "for fear of an [sexually transmitted] illness" because the only sex available to him was with prostitutes. Many others abstained from marital sex out of concern for their wives' fragile health. A seventy-four-year-old retiree, who reported that he had been faithful to his wife for the past twelve years because he was too sick with diabetes to pursue affairs, told me that they were abstaining because of her hypertension and recent stroke. He said, "We don't have sex because my wife is sick. But I'm not going to die. It's not necessary; it's not urgent. In my youth, I enjoyed it enough."

Most commonly, the study participants understood ED drugs to be physically dangerous *because* they were socially inappropriate. Understanding decreasing sexual function to be an appropriate embodiment of respectable older age, they saw pharmaceutical disruption of this decline as causing an "unnatural and thus dangerous embodiment of youthful sexuality. Many expressed fear of the drugs, making comments similar to a sixty-eight-year-old retiree's observation that "Viagra scares me." Men frequently described their bodies and sex lives as "slowing" over time, moving from an "accelerated" state fueled by their "hot" Mexican male natures to a calmer, less sexual state more appropriate to older and weaker bodies. A sixty-year-old farm administrator explained, "I was very accelerated as a youth. But my wife has started menopause; we're calmer. I'm more patient. We have sex once in a while."

Along these lines, the participants often cited age-inappropriate bodily acceleration as the key danger posed by ED drugs. Elaborating on the cause of this fear, a seventy-eight-year-old food vendor stated that ED drugs "accelerate you to your death. Many friends have told me [that] they will accelerate you a lot; then you'll collapse. That stuff will kill you." The participants sometimes worked this idea into perhaps apocryphal stories of ED drugs harming relatives or neighbors. For example, a retired couple in their late seventies told me that they had heard that a neighbor took Viagra, and it caused a terrible health problem. However, they were not sure which neighbor it was or what health problem he endured. Nevertheless, this led them to believe that "Viagra isn't worth it." More bombastically, a plumber in his late fifties reported, "People are dying of Viagra! They get excited [and] have heart attacks. I had an old uncle; he 'got Viagraed.' He stayed there on top, like a sea turtle—with the girl under him! . . . There are lots of rumors about Viagra here in Mexico—lots of fear."

The idea that the possible dangers of ED drug treatment outweighed its benefits was thus rooted in the notion that youthful levels of sex were simply inappropriate to—and perhaps physically harmful during—older age. Some of the participants said that the potential side effects of the ED drugs made taking them not worth the risk. For example, César, a sixty-four-year-old retired utility company worker who had experienced decreasing erectile function following kidney disease, whose story will be told later in this chapter, said that he hadn't tried an ED drug "principally because of my kidney; it could hurt my kidney." The dual perceived risks of ED drug effects and the physical demands of sex outweighed the benefits of physical pleasure for most of the older participants. Relatedly, some believed that ED drugs and the vigorous sex they might enable would do enough damage that they should be used only a few times. A forty-five-year-old bus driver had been prescribed Levitra but had never used it because "It might make your kidneys work more; it's bad to take it a lot. You should use it maybe four, five times in your life."

In general, the participants told me that ED drugs would unnaturally disrupt the bodily functions natural to a particular life stage. A fifty-six-year-old heavy machinery operator stated, "I don't like to use things that aren't normal. I don't like to force my body." In keeping with this view, many of the men who had decided not to seek treatment for diminished erectile function believed that it is "part of the process" and, as an eighty-two year old retired accountant said, "something that I've lived. It's nature; I'm diminishing, and I take that as something normal." A retired electrician in his late sixties joked that his cessation of sex was "part of being retired; I can't work anymore!" Many others saw lessening erectile function in men as akin to menopause in women, which they understood to entail a reduction of sexual desire. Thus the majority of the participants understood diminished erectile function and sexual activity in older age as part of a healthy life cycle. They feared that thwarting these natural changes through medical intervention might cause bodily harm or hasten death.

A minority of the participants rejected ED drugs for reasons other than the belief that they had aged out of now-dangerous youthful sexuality. Some of the men who still considered themselves "young" rejected pharmaceutical assistance for erectile difficulty, even though they still wanted to have sex. They saw the need for ED drugs as incompatible with the manly sexuality that they believed should come naturally from masculine bodies. For example, a fifty-nine-year-old Spanish teacher said, "It's *machista* to think so, but I don't need foreign substances [for sexual function]." Conversely, some of the men felt that because diminished erectile function was associated with older age, using drugs to treat it would mark them as prematurely old and disrupt the normal social path of their life cycles. A forty-seven-year-old pool installer took Viagra once and found it effective but did not use the drug again because "I don't want to feel that I need it. I don't need it, really. I'm older, not elderly. That's not life. I don't want to take it; I don't feel good taking it." He said he had been taking vitamins instead, and he believed that they had helped. Overall, most of the study participants believed that ED drug taking, and the sex it would inspire, would not fit into the sorts of composite masculinities they wanted to construct, and many believed that they would be physically negative additions to their composite illness experiences.

CÉSAR: ABSTAINING FOR HEALTH

César's story demonstrates the common belief that continued sex was simply not worth the physical toll that it—and the drugs needed to achieve it—might take. A sixty-four-year-old retired utility company worker, César said he used to pride himself on his "active" life. "I was the guy who climbed those utility posts," he said, and he told me that his work took him away from home for months at a time, during which he frequently engaged in extramarital affairs. (He was quoted in chapter 1 comparing his sexual temptation to that of former New York governor Eliot Spitzer.) However, since his retirement, he had been both spatially and emotionally closer to his wife, and he told me that they were in a wonderful phase of their relationship characterized by the freedom to "travel, enjoy each other's company, [and] take care of the grandchildren." César had thus wholeheartedly adopted the common local idea of mature masculinity.

So César told me that when he began to suffer from serious kidney stones and had to have one kidney removed, he and his wife decided jointly that they would prioritize his health over their sex life and abstain. His erectile function decreased but did not disappear, and César said he knew from ED drug marketing that this meant that pharmaceutical treatment was an option. However, he told me, "There was no reason to [use ED drugs] . . . At our age, sex isn't so important; it's a false satisfaction . . . Sexual satisfaction is great, but you just can't ask so much of the body; you'll do damage."

César and his wife's rejection of medical ED treatment did not mean that they rejected pharmaceutical intervention or illness-related self-care more broadly. They sought medical treatment for those bodily changes that they believed fell under the purview of biomedicine. In addition to the pharmaceutical treatment he received for his kidney disease, and her surgical treatment for a hernia, they strove to make lifestyle changes that would mitigate César's diabetes. They changed their diets, eating more vegetables and cutting out red meat. César also began to exercise, adding walking, biking, and swimming to his weekly routine. Despite their interest in using medical and lifestyle treatments for other ailments, they both agreed that César's decreased erectile function should be understood as a normal aspect of aging, so trying to treat it to have more sex would be harmful to his health. César said, "We take it as something normal because of age, because of illness. My wife, a very healthy person,[2] understands." For César and his wife, "healthiness" involved treating bodily changes they interpreted as pathological and accepting those that they saw intrinsic to normal aging. Foregrounding responsibility for health in his composite masculinity, César eschewed medical ED treatment and the sex he saw as physically taxing for older bodies.

Erectile Dysfunction Drugs as Oversimplistic Solutions

As demonstrated by César and his wife's decision to categorize only certain bodily changes as medical problems, while rejecting the medicalization of other changes in the name of health, study participants' rejection of ED drugs does not signal disinterest in biomedicine. As IMSS patients, all of the study participants sought biomedical treatment for certain

---

2 The adjective "healthy" (*sano*) as used here refers to both physical and moral or spiritual health.

health problems. Furthermore, most were amenable to particular pharmaceutical treatments, and many took drugs for prostate problems, type 2 diabetes, and heart disease. Their use of biomedical interventions for particular age and illness-related changes—but not for decreased erectile function—made sense in terms of their specific composite understandings of health. Believing that biomedical disease, negative emotions, and humoral imbalance all contributed to illness, the study participants chose interventions that they believed would redress those physical changes they saw as dangerous, while promoting overall bodily balance and emotional well-being.

For example, many of the men saw both erectile difficulty and diabetes as consequences of aging, physical damage, and emotional problems. They believed that although decreased erectile function was a normal consequence of older age that could be socially positive, unbalanced blood sugar was a continuing source of bodily harm. These men said they were happy to take medication to regulate their blood glucose levels and thus achieve more healthy bodily balance, but they rejected ED drugs that they feared might unbalance them. Many of the study participants believed that it was important to consider the effects a drug might have on the entire body before deciding to take it. They frequently stated the maxim that "the body is complicated" (*el organismo es complicado*) and voiced fears that ED drugs were dangerously simplistic treatments for a multifaceted condition. Rather than viewing pharmaceutical treatment as an unconditional good, the participants characterized it as an action that would have positive and negative consequences. They weighed these in their decisions regarding which bodily changes to treat and how to do so.

Likely influenced by the perceived inaccessibility of ED drugs and the social encouragement they received to accept decreased erectile function as natural, most of the study participants told me that the harm of ED drugs outweighed the good. They often characterized the ED drugs as brute-force treatments that could cause damage when applied to one aspect of a complex and person-specific set of interrelated bodily and life changes. The participants often felt that their health problems were highly individual and feared that standard, nonpersonalized treatments would be inappropriate to their bodily needs and thus harmful. Speaking from experience, a fifty-nine-year-old retired businessman who grew breasts after taking a prostate medication explained that "things can affect people differently; not everyone has the same body." Thus the study participants distrusted drugs that were used in the same way for each patient.

For example, a sixty-one-year-old retired electrician rejected ED medicine because it would treat the symptom of erectile function change without revealing or addressing its root cause. He reasoned, "If I don't know how my body functions, it won't accept what I do [for treatment] well."

The notion that bodies are unique and complex led the participants—even those who self-prescribed interventions such as antibiotics and vitamins for bodily ailments that they believed to be straightforward and purely physical—to decry the idea that one could use ED treatments without a prescription. Although nearly all medications, even those that technically require a prescription, are widely available over the counter in Mexico, the participants singled out the availability of ED medications as a dangerous public health problem. They often told me that the complexity of the human body and its sexual function changes demanded careful scrutiny by a doctor who knew his or her patient well—both physically and psychologically. A fifty-two-year-old carpenter who had lost his job when he developed a hernia said that he did not want to use Viagra because "I don't know where my problem comes from . . . I don't want to get medicine from someone who doesn't know me deep down, who doesn't know my system." Similarly, a seventy-four-year-old retired economics professor believed that only specialists should prescribe ED drugs, people "who will get to know me—how I am physically, how I think." Then they could prescribe more appropriate and effective medications. He said that "the human body is very complicated" and taking the wrong drug could do great damage. For this reason, he defined the ED drug ads on television and radio as a public health problem. Some of the participants even felt similarly about the self-prescription of natural or alternative treatments. For example, a forty-nine-year-old plumber stated that choosing one's own treatments could be a waste of money and could hamper one's doctor's efforts to identify the right treatment. He said, "I don't want to self-prescribe, especially with the socioeconomic problems that I have, and if you go to a lot of different doctors, they tell you different things; it's hard to find a solution. It's like cheating on your spouse!"

Despite their stated respect for biomedicine and its practitioners, the study participants often invoked these ideas of bodily complexity to question their doctors' advice. This was especially the case in terms of ED treatment, which many of the men considered to be a risky intervention that required thorough knowledge of a recipient's body and social context. Because their visits with the IMSS urologists were brief, many of the participants did not believe that their doctors knew them well enough to fully understand the interaction between their physical changes, life courses, and social worlds. Thus most of the participants felt free to ignore medical advice that they thought did not fully account for their bodily complexity. For example, a fifty-nine-year-old retired bus driver ignored his doctor's suggestion that he use a vacuum pump to attain erections, explaining, "With my diabetes, it [decreased erectile function] is a consequence of my body—diabetes and hypertension. I'm not a doctor, but I know my body—how I feel. I'm good friends with the doctor, and he suggested that I use the little pump, but I don't think it's a good idea. I'm conscious of the risk." Similarly, although few of the participants were prescribed ED medications, many of those that were declined to fill their prescriptions, viewing the drugs as inappropriate for their state of health. For example, a fifty-nine-year-old truck driver said, "I was prescribed pills, but I haven't used them. As a diabetic, I could have a heart attack."

Thus, although the majority of the participants were taking daily medicines for chronic conditions such as diabetes, heart disease, and prostate enlargement, which they believed encouraged overall bodily balance, they were generally unwilling to add ED drugs to their regimen. Men using other treatments frequently saw ED drugs as potentially dangerous overloads to their system. They believed that the ED drugs had benefits but also caused collateral physical damage, so on the whole it was best to avoid additional medications, particularly ED treatments that would treat only the symptoms of more complex problems.

The participants' situational acceptance and rejection of particular medications related directly to their composite understandings of the causes of illness. Many who experienced erectile function change saw it as predominantly caused by factors such as humoral imbalance that were not susceptible to pharmaceutical intervention. For example, many of the participants who were experiencing erectile difficulty blamed their "hot" Mexican temperaments, fearing that their overactive sex drives may have led them to physically damage their genitalia through overuse. A sixty-eight-year-old retiree told me that "I don't have erection; it leaves after a second," a condition caused by "my hot character—there's no balance."

In keeping with their multifaceted understandings of health, some of the participants also saw erectile function change as having partly behavioral roots. For example, some believed that youthful overuse of their bodies' sexual and energetic resources had created a dangerous bodily imbalance. These men asked me if I thought that frequent sex or masturbation had "unbalanced" their bodies. Along these lines, one participant revealed to me that he had a "very small member," which he viewed as a sign of a naturally limited sexual capacity that he feared he had overextended by having frequent sex in his youth. Similarly, a fifty-three-year-old office worker whose prostate surgery caused retrograde ejaculation, a condition in which semen enters the bladder at orgasm instead of leaving the body, told me that he thought a vasectomy might cure his problem. He believed that a vasectomy would improve his bodily state "because I wouldn't spend the semen. There would be less biological expenditure." Summing up humoral views of bodily balance as health, a sixty-one-year-old retired electrician explained that attempting to have more sex was healthful but only if done in moderation. He said, "I'm not immoral, but I don't have prejudices; sex is something God gave us to use—as long as it's healthy, not homosexual or perverted. And excess is always bad; if you eat too much, you get indigestion. Everything in moderation." As these examples show, the different versions of the commonly held belief that erectile function decrease was a composite problem, involving not only biology but also emotions, acts and social context, often led the participants to reject ED drug treatment as an oversimplistic and thus inappropriate response.

Choosing the Right Treatment for the Right Situation

Although many of the men rejected all forms of ED treatment, some who viewed pharmaceutical interventions as dangerous were willing to consider alternative interventions. A few men who thought that ED drugs would be harmful when they were experiencing general ill health said that they might try the drugs if their health improved. Similar to the survey respondents discussed earlier, some of the urology patients saw non-biomedical interventions as healthier alternatives that might also be more suitable for treating complex ills. Overall, the participants made context-based treatment choices, considering the effects they believed different remedies would have on their bodies in their current states. For example, a fifty-six-year-old garbage truck driver who took blood pressure medications but rejected ED drugs explained that the appropriateness of various remedies was situational and based on both immediate needs and long-term safety concerns. He told me, "Whether you use herbs or medicines depends on the situation. Medicines act faster than herbs, so you'd want them for a strong pain, but in the long run, herbs are better." Understanding their health as a composite object composed of a range of changes, feelings, and interventions, the men evaluated whether a particular intervention was appropriate based on the other elements with which it would interact.

The participants who considered trying to mitigate their erectile function changes sought to select the correct intervention for their current health status and social situations, based on ideas about the relative merits and risks of pharmaceuticals, natural medicines, and nondrug interventions such as lifestyle changes. For example, the wife of a fifty-nine-year-old retired metalworker said that her husband, who had experienced diminished erectile function following a heart attack, had been eating almonds and peanuts to restore his "strong temperament." However, now that his general health had improved, they were thinking of seeking pharmaceutical ED treatment. She said, "When all this started, he was dying of medicines. But now that he's stable, we'd like to try it." Similarly, a participant who had received a free sample pack of Levitra said that he would try the drug as a last resort if vitamins did not help. He explained, "I hope that I function with [the vitamin]. If not, I'll try the Levitra." When I asked why he preferred the vitamin, he replied "because I've always been normal. Also, I'm not the type of guy to be with many women." This man saw ED drug treatment as possibly incorrect for his present situation because it marked a bodily abnormality that he did not wish to claim and because he felt it incorrectly matched his level of libido. Conversely, a few of the participants were planning to start their search for treatment with a pharmaceutical and then try alternative remedies if the drug failed to work.

Frequently, the participants believed that lifestyle changes would be the most appropriate response to erectile function changes that co-occurred with chronic illnesses. They told me that eating more healthily or exercising would do no harm and might improve their overall health and mitigate a range of chronic disease symptoms. Many of the study participants suffered from chronic diseases, such as diabetes and hypertension, which often seemed to have caused the changes they experienced in erectile function. For instance, one participant said that because of his high blood pressure, "My sexuality is very bad. I don't have erections; they leave in a second . . . There's no [bodily] balance." Some of these men used alternative treatments for these co-occurring illnesses, such as eating *nopales* (cactus leaves) or using herbal treatments to control their blood sugar. Others saw lifestyle changes as double-duty treatments for their ED and chronic illnesses. A forty-eight-year-old taxi driver who had resisted changing his diet to mitigate his diabetes because "eating salad gave me headaches" said that he would make those changes now that he had developed erectile difficulty: "If I don't take care of myself, I won't have any [erections]. I hope that won't happen; that's why I'm going to change my diet." A seventy-seven-year-old retiree started to exercise and eat healthily as he began to experience decreased erectile function and other "problems of age," explaining that although he saw these changes as normal, he also hoped to mitigate them. He said, "Your body is like a car; the older it gets, the more problems you've got." He saw these lifestyle changes as akin to car maintenance; routines that might not prevent but could minimize age-related changes.

Overall, many of the study participants saw acceptance tempered with lifestyle change as the most appropriate and safest response to decreased erectile function because they believed this change to be a symptom of multiple lifestyle issues, including social interactions and behavioral factors such as diet. Some of the participants saw lifestyle change as the only safe treatment for decreased erectile function. For example, a sixty-two-year-old retired glass installer reported, "I'm not interested in Viagra because it could damage my body, for example, my kidneys. All medicine is dangerous. For example, I had a spine operation in 2000. My back hurt if I tried to carry things, so it was better to rest than to take medicine."

Similarly, when discussing potential treatment options, a fifty-two-year-old book salesman said, "We'll seek to find out if there's medicine, but I don't like allopathic medicine much. Better to exercise, take vitamins; I take Omega 3. I like to take vitamins, although I read a lot of scientific magazines and they say some allopathic vitamins do damage. Better to eat well." This participant went on to recount a frightening experience involving a combination of allopathic and herbal medicines, which caused him to rethink the advisability of any drug treatment: "I don't like medications—natural ones or not—because they have lots of contraindications, and natural medicines don't have much oversight. I prefer to exercise. My wife had a bad experience with natural medicines. She has an artificial heart valve and takes anticoagulants, and they reacted with a natural cholesterol medicine she was taking. She had hematomas in her leg. So I'm really scared of natural products." Fearing that even seemingly benign interventions could have unintended consequences when introduced into complex bodies, such participants saw lifestyle changes as the only fully safe treatment response. Unfortunately, as discussed in chapter 3, most of the participants also felt that a range of social and structural constraints prevented them from making the healthy lifestyle changes that they considered.

Many of the participants also saw vitamins and herbal treatments as gentle interventions that could promote erectile function as a consequence of improving general health. They saw these treatments as socially appropriate because they would improve bodily function but would not erase the physical changes associated with respectable male aging. For instance, the sixty-one-year-old retired electrician quoted earlier on the benefits of moderation was a firm believer in natural medicine; he asserted that a traditional healer had saved his infant son's life. He reported using a remedy for decreased erectile function that he found in a natural healing magazine. He said that mixing honey and cinnamon in water—"a Mayan recipe"—had brought back his erectile function: "Every night, I wake up with an erection. This recipe helps with many things; cholesterol in your veins hurts your circulation and that hurts your erections, and this recipe helps with that." When I commented that I found it interesting that improving blood flow was the same action that drugs akin to Viagra have, he responded, "Yes, but Viagra causes harm."

The participants who used alternative treatments generally understood them to broadly balance and revitalize their bodies and embodied selves but to be free of the dangerous side effects of pharmaceuticals. The seventy-eight-year-old retiree quoted earlier stated that vitamins could work like but more safely than Viagra by "strengthening the blood" and promoting "a fertile life," similar to the hot, revitalizing vegetable soup he drank at the market. The participants tended to say that vitamins and herbs "wake me up" or "energize me," promoting general health conducive to improved bodily function rather than directly causing specific bodily reactions, such as erections. The sixty-eight-year-old retired truck driver quoted earlier said that although he took allopathic medicines for his diabetes, "I also take a *naturista* medicine, powdered *guere* root, in water when I don't want to be sleepy any more. When I take it, I wake up." Likewise, a sixty-three-year-old retired salesman experienced erectile difficulty following prostate enlargement and said, "I went to the pharmacy, and got vitamins I've taken before, B complex and B2. They revitalize me a little, nothing more."

Some of the participants explicitly used vitamins or herbs to balance bodies that they believed were damaged by the drugs they had to take for other chronic illnesses. A seventy-three-year-old retired farmworker said that his diabetes and heart medications "make me feel a lot of heat, deflated . . . I take vitamins to reanimate myself." Finally, some of the participants believed that vitamin or herbal treatments could also help with the illnesses of emotion that precipitated chronic illness and erectile difficulty. A retired office worker in his late fifties quoted previously is diabetic and takes three "natural teas" in addition to his diabetes medication; two address diabetes symptoms and one treats *corajes*, the rages that are commonly believed to harm one's health.

Based on composite understandings of bodily function that included emotional and humoral with biomedical ideas of disease causation, the study participants drew from multiple healing traditions when deciding which intervention would be most appropriate for a particular bodily change. Different participants claimed different levels of knowledge about and acceptance of these healing systems. As biomedical service users and urban dwellers, the participants generally reported learning about health from school, television shows, and doctor visits and said that they knew more about medical than other forms of healing. Yet they often proudly explained to me that Mexico has its own traditional ways of healing and frequently reported using *naturista* and herbal remedies. Although the majority felt that seeing a doctor was important for deciding which medical treatment to use, they felt comfortable self-prescribing vitamins, herbs, or other natural remedies, such as particular foods, because they believed that these could do little harm. They said that they learned about these treatments through magazines, word of mouth, natural or traditional healers, stores or marketing, and occasionally the Internet. For example, a seventy-seven-year-old retired construction worker was taking medicine to control his high blood pressure but said, "I'm also taking some herb that my son found on the Internet. I'm not sure if it will work—we'll see."

Only a few of the study participants told me that they or someone close to them had systematic knowledge about traditional or natural healing. In these cases, that person had grown up in a rural area underserved by allopathic medicine and was accustomed to relying on shared cultural knowledge of nonbiomedical treatments. For instance, a seventy-five-year-old retired factory worker was eating particular foods to control his blood sugar at his wife's suggestion. He explained, "I didn't know [about these treatments], but my wife is from the country; her relatives used them." In keeping with the cultural pride surrounding traditional healing, a few urban dwellers took classes to become certified in or knowledgeable about such techniques. For example, a seventy-five-year-old retired factory worker's wife was treating his erectile difficulty with herbal poultices, massages, and specific foods that she learned to use when she was trained in traditional medicine techniques to become a local health promoter. It is also probable that some of the participants incorporated nonbiomedical self-care practices into their lives as a matter of course, failing to note them in our interviews because these practices were so habitual. However, in Cuernavaca's urban context, patients' statements that particular treatments were natural and traditional most often appeared to reflect the marketing claims attached to the treatments, not a basis in culturally shared treatment knowledge. Nevertheless, many of the participants prided themselves on their recognition of multiple healing systems and their ability to make appropriate treatment choices from these choices; they did not believe that biomedical treatments were universally applicable or desirable.

GUILLERMO: COMFORT IN SCIENCE BUT
NOT ERECTILE DYSFUNCTION DRUGS

Guillermo's story illustrates how even participants who made knowledge about science and medicine key elements of their composite selves might see medical ED treatment as inappropriate to their individual bodies and needs. Guillermo, a seventy-two-year-old civil engineer, began treatment for bladder cancer with a private-practice doctor a year before our interview. However, after he retired and money became tighter, he sought treatment for a recurrence of this cancer in the IMSS hospital. He told me that he was not frightened about the cancer treatment because of both his stoicism and intellectualism. He kept a tight rein on his emotions, explaining, "It's my personality. I make myself—I don't let myself fall apart, I don't cry. I don't like to suffer or to worry other people. What would I gain by worrying or crying?" Guillermo told me that his interest in science helped him to be strong in the face of cancer, explaining, "I have information. I watch scientific programs; the history of humans, where we came from, where we're going and why. Medical information programs. This helps me keep my feet on the ground." This interest in science provided a bigger picture in which Guillermo could make sense of his illness experience and specific information about his disease and the medical treatments he was receiving.

In addition to his focus on intellectual life, Guillermo also reported a keen interest in sex that had a largely emotional basis. Divorced but currently living with a partner, he said that he periodically slept with other women in search of additional "human contact." He believed that this would not hurt his partner, saying, "If the eyes don't see, the heart doesn't feel." He also felt that the risk of his partner finding out was worth the emotional rewards of infidelity. He told me that he saw other women "only sporadically, but it is an important part of my life. This exchange—I have great affection for them. They're not objects; it's emotional. More emotional, more *human*, than sexual." Thus the reduction in erectile capacity that he had begun to experience after his first cancer treatment greatly concerned him.

Although Guillermo's interest in science, the use of biomedicine, and desire to maintain an active sex life would seem to make him an excellent candidate for ED drugs, he saw ED treatment as inappropriate to his situation. He believed that chemotherapy, together with natural aging, might further inhibit his erectile function. He said, "I'm seventy-two years old. As natural consequences, all my capacities are lessening: sexual, I can't run as fast. And everybody is different, so I don't know what my response to chemo will be." However, he did not believe that ED drugs were the correct type of treatment to help him maintain a sex life focused on emotional connection. When I asked if he might use the drugs, he replied as follows: "I don't know if I would use ED drugs. I might if my sexual response lessens, since they're energizers, or stimulants. But they don't make a permanent change, a cure, since they're stimulants . . . I don't have to use stimulant medications. My conditioning is mental—talking, looking, a drink of whiskey—a disinhibitor. Conversation, sight, tactile, hearing, taste, touch. For me, this is important. I might not use medications because that's nothing more than boom, on to the next thing."

Even as a self-described "open-minded" person with a scientific bent, Guillermo saw ED drugs as an option that he might consider but would likely reject. He did not believe that ED drugs, as "energizers," would facilitate the sort of sex he desired. He thought that ED drugs that reduced sex to a quick "boom" would be antithetical to the sensuous and deeply emotional experience of human connection that he sought in his sex life. So Guillermo linked his sexual function changes to the narrative of mature aging common among the study participants. He said that although he had "recuperated much of my potency" after his first operation, he knew he would never "return to being young," and this knowledge did not bother him. He said that if he completely lost erectile function in the course of his cancer treatment, "I'll do what I always do—look for other forms of satisfaction. Conversation. I like to cook, other activities. If there's no solution, there's no cause to worry about it." In short, rather than wholly accepting all biomedical offerings, Guillermo saw ED drugs as an option for restoring a certain kind of sexual function but not for supporting the sort of sexuality that made sense in his own life.

Assessment of Erectile Difficulty as a Composite Object

The IMSS patients and urologists created composite explanations for individual cases of decreased erectile function, through which they defined this change as either a normal occurrence or a medical pathology. These explanations linked elements of men's physical and life experiences to specific culturally intelligible understandings of health, aging, and male sexuality. The patients crafted these composite understandings in a context that offered ample—and conflicting—medical and other narratives regarding the cause, nature, and consequence of decreased erectile function. The IMSS doctors, influenced by structural constraints, supported such holistic understandings of erectile difficulty. Overall, this chapter has shown that for a range of social and structural reasons, the study participants were predisposed to understand erectile difficulty in nonmedical ways.

The men's descriptions of their experiences of decreased erectile function and their views on ED treatment shed light on why nonbiomedical explanations were so popular among the study participants. In our conversations, they tended to connect their experiences of erectile difficulty to narratives of natural aging, age-appropriate changes in Mexican male sexuality, and the notion that health entailed bodily balance. As discussed in chapter 2, many received encouragement from their partners and families to adopt this view. In addition, the IMSS health-care system posed disincentives for adopting a medical view of decreased erectile function. The brief, impersonal urology appointments—made necessary by overscheduling—deterred men from asking for ED treatment. This lack of trust made the survey respondents feel they might need to seek expensive private health care if they were to receive ED drugs. Although cost did not seem to function as a primary deterrent for patients already receiving urologic care, who did not appear to know, unless they were prescribed the drugs, that the IMSS hospital might not meet its obligation of providing them, the doctors' knowledge of this situation likely influenced their treatment recommendations. The IMSS hospital's failure to meet their legal obligation to provide free ED drugs thus deterred the urologists from prescribing these drugs and presented a cost barrier to patients who wished to use them.

This context influenced their composite explanations of erectile difficulty. Each participant presented a unique narrative for understanding this change, based on his life history and experiences, which fit into the composite masculinity he sought to construct. Although their understandings of erectile difficulty varied, these explanations also shared common elements because they were crafted from a basic set of ways of understanding aging, health, and masculinity that made sense in their cultural contexts. For example, the study participants' frequent rejections of ED treatment often entailed understandings of bodily change and illness causation as multifactoral, involving not only biology but also emotional distress and humoral imbalance. Although very few of the urology patients identified drug cost as a reason for not medicalizing erectile difficulty, it is possible that men who learned that ED drugs might not be freely available feared that a failure to afford treatment would threaten composite masculinities that foregrounded the ability to earn and provide, so they protected these masculinities by avoiding financially compromising attempts to seek treatment. This chapter has shown that, when drawing from shared experiences of IMSS treatment and being aging and ill Mexican men, the participants often developed understandings of decreased erectile function as a natural event.

This phenomenon demonstrates that receiving biomedical treatment and using pharmaceuticals do not necessarily predispose people to identify a given bodily change as a biological pathology. All of the study participants were under medical care, and the majority used pharmaceutical treatments for diseases such as diabetes. Although they saw treatments for some diseases as compatible with their holistic understandings of illness causation and consequence, such a response to erectile function change seemed radically inappropriate to most of the men. This was especially true for participants receiving pharmaceutical treatments for other illnesses, who often thought that both those diseases and their treatment would weaken their bodies. Such men believed that forcing their bodies to perform age-inappropriate sexual behavior would cause physical damage. The participants thus saw their sexual function not as a simple biological process to be medically treated when compromised but as the embodiment of masculinity appropriate to a specific phase of the life course.

Rather than simply ignoring the notion of ED, many of the study participants who assessed their erectile difficulty as natural incorporated critiques of ED treatment into their composite understandings of their sexual health. Drugs akin to Viagra are a major topic of conversation in Mexico, and the study participants frequently told me that they knew that they could use these treatments. Yet although well-publicized medical treatments for a particular bodily change encourage people to relate such options into their composite explanations of their own embodied experiences, it does not necessarily lead to their adoption. In support of their explanations of decreased erectile function as natural, normal, and often socially positive, many of the participants included the rejection of ED drugs into their composite understandings of their health. They cast ED drugs as silly, unnecessary, and physically dangerous. Based on their other beliefs about health and aging, even the minority of men who did want some kind of intervention to increase erectile function generally saw ED medication as the wrong treatment for their situations. They believed these drugs to be a narrowly focused pharmacological attack on a physical symptom, not a treatment for its complexly biosocial causes. Thus those who hoped to enhance erectile function tended to prefer lifestyle changes, vitamins, or herbal/*naturista* treatments to pharmaceuticals. Chapter 5 discusses the experiences of those few study participants who, despite experiencing the same deterrents to understanding erectile difficulty as ED that most of the other men incorporated into nonmedical understandings of this change, sought medical treatment to restore their erectile function.

Chapter Five

MEDICAL ERECTILE DYSFUNCTION
TREATMENT IN CONTEXT

Erectile Dysfunction Treatment among the Study Participants

For the reasons described in chapter 4, only a minority of the study participants—11 percent—had used medical ED treatment, despite the ubiquity of ED drugs in Mexico. Those few who used ED drugs described being aware that other men in their situation might accept decreased erectile function as a natural consequence of aging, often stating that a time would come when they too would be "too old" for sex. However, they did not believe that this time had arrived. For these men, engaging in penetrative sex was an important part of their composite masculinities, and they were unwilling to exchange this element in favor of a focus on more mature activities. These treatment seekers differed from the other participants in that they maintained ideals of manhood that were centered on continued sexual activity, even as they became less physically able to sexually penetrate. Unlike peers who incorporated decreased erectile function into reconfigured composite masculinities, these men strove to change their bodies rather than their ideals for their ways of being men, using ED drugs in the hope of reversing their erectile function decrease.

Medical anthropologists have noted that people may use pharmaceuticals to embody particular kinds of selfhood, and their attempts to do so are shaped by their social and structural contexts (Clarke et al. 2003; Nichter and Vuckovic 1994; Petryna and Kleinman 2006). This chapter discusses the reasons that the participants sought ED treatment, which they usually presented as part of a broader project to become a different and better kind of man. In keeping with their composite understandings of health and despite their use of biomedical ED treatments, these men rarely understood decreasing erectile function as a purely biological issue. Instead, men who were distressed by changing erectile function believed it to be caused by an interrelated set of biological and social problems, which had a similarly wide range of consequences. Most of the participants who sought medical help for decreased erectile function saw it as an element of a failed composite masculinity constrained by life difficulties, structural inequalities, physical illness, and social problems. Rather than understanding medical ED treatment as a straightforward cure for a physical problem, most described it as a way to instigate a physical change that might have a ripple effect on their lives, causing positive emotional and social changes that they could incorporate into a more desirable composite masculinity.

This chapter focuses on the ways these men described their ways of being men as failed and made plans for change by drawing links among the physical, interpersonal, and narrative elements of their composite masculinities. It presents their narratives about the related development of erectile difficulty and less-than-ideal masculinity in which sexual, social, economic, and other life problems added up to undesirable ways of being men. Analyzing their discussions of treatment, I argue that most of these participants hoped that ED drugs would alter their physical function in ways that would generate new kinds of interactions and experiences from which they could craft new composite masculinities. Here, I draw from their descriptions of the causes of their erectile difficulty and their experiences with and hopes for ED treatment to explore how certain men sought to incorporate pharmaceutically enhanced erectile function into new composite masculinities. The chapter begins with a discussion of the reasons why few men attributed their ED to biology alone, instead identifying failed masculinity as a key cause of erectile difficulty. It next describes the reasons why patients and the IMSS urologists were likely to understand erectile difficulty holistically rather than only biomedically. It then describes the various ways that the study participants sought to alter single elements of undesirable composite masculinities using ED treatment, in the hopes of embarking on a broader set of gendered life changes. The narratives presented here reveal the context dependence of both the physical and the social experiences of decreased erectile function, demonstrating how medical perspectives and treatments can become elements of composite treatments and selves.

Biological Understandings of Erectile Dysfunction

Only a few of the study participants who sought ED treatment ascribed their decreased erectile function to only biological causes. These were men who described their lives and relationships as happy, so they did not believe that negative emotions or experiences had influenced their erectile function. In their narratives regarding the cause of their erectile difficulty, they ascribed their physical change to a medical event, most frequently the severing of penile nerves during prostate surgery. Because they reported being unready for a decreased sex life, it made sense to these men to seek pharmaceutical treatment for a change they defined as a medical problem. In keeping with this view, these men regularly took ED drugs, unlike those patients (who are discussed later in this chapter), for whom imagining the positive consequences of ED treatment seemed to be as or more therapeutic than actually using that treatment.

These drug takers described pharmaceuticals akin to Viagra as addressing a biologically based symptom in a way that would enable them to continue their normal bodily and social function. For example, a sixty-three-year-old retired salesman saw ED treatment as a remedy for a change he saw as a symptom of prostate cancer, saying, "I know that [the ED] is a product of the prostate, so it [the ED drug] is one medicine more, to keep me functioning. It will normalize me." He felt that ED drugs would thus help him return to "the normal—return to my own rhythm of relations." People in this situation described ED drugs as a way to maintain positive sexual and social lives. For instance, a couple who had been using Cialis twice a month described their relationship as supportive and characterized by mutual understanding and reported that redressing the husband's physical changes with medicine had allowed them to return to a "normal life." When I asked how they liked the Cialis, the wife reported, "It has been good. [Using it seems] normal—if there is hypertension, diabetes, it's normal that there isn't erection. When you're young, you're healthy; things change. One has to adapt to one's body." By "adapting" their bodies with a pharmaceutical aid, rather than constructing a new normal for sexuality and manliness, these ED drug users were able to continue the practices of masculinity that they found satisfying. Thus they tended to report very positive experiences with drug treatment.

Rather than experiencing erectile difficulty or its treatment as a jarring change, these participants used the ED diagnosis to limit the effects of erectile difficulty to the physical realm, defining their bodily changes as a biological event that need not alter their sexual or social lives. Despite this definition, these men expressed fears that decreased erectile function could cause problems beyond the realm of biology. They understood ED treatment as a physiological intervention that would not only cure a pathological change but also prevent emotional and social distress that might stem from sexual difficulty or deviation from their desired ways of being men. Although they adopted biomedical understandings of erectile difficulty, they saw ED drugs as a social intervention: a maintenance treatment for their normal and successful ways of being men. Despite the fact that many of these men lived on very low incomes or pensions, none described the cost of the drugs as problematic; it likely seemed worthwhile to pay for a functioning cure.

Erectile Difficulty and Failed Masculinity

Conversely, the vast majority of the treatment users and seekers attributed their decreasing erections to both bodily and emotional causes, most significantly what they perceived as a general failure of masculinity. They believed that such failures were caused—and subsequently compounded—by a combination of physical weakness and social strife. They characterized decreased erectile function as a symptom of this broader failure, as well as a key part of the composite problem of their continuing inadequacy as men. Most of the participants described having reliably firm erections as not only a source of physical pleasure but also a way to fulfill certain manly duties. They described having sufficient sex with one's wife—and with other women in the case of men who believed their Mexican natures demanded it—as a manly responsibility. For these men, providing what they imagined to be adequate sex was a key way to demonstrate being a good provider, a hard worker, and a true Mexican man. In our interviews, most ED treatment seekers related their erectile difficulty to the problems they encountered in enacting these practices of masculinity, which they described as key to being a good man in Mexican culture, and to the emotional distress these perceived failures caused.

For example, men seeking ED treatment often attributed their erectile difficulty to a failure to undertake responsible self-care. A thirty-six-year-old office worker worried that his erectile difficulty might be a "failure on my part" because he had not finished the course of antibiotics he was given after the surgical removal of a varicose vein in his scrotum. Even when they could not point to a particular action that had caused their sexual difficulties, many of the participants described feeling generalized guilt linked to their perceived failure to perform the manly trait of responsibility. An eighty-year-old retiree said, "I am guilty" for the infrequent sex with his wife because "it's my deficiency. I don't have the erection I'd like to have." In general, the participants felt that being good men required them to push their bodies, in contexts such as work, in ways that made self-care difficult. However, they also felt the need to take personal blame if this resulted in the inability to physically perform tasks, especially work and sex, which they saw as their duty. For some, using drugs to enhance one's erection became a way to demonstrate manly responsibility, remedying the prior lack of self-care that had contributed to their erectile function change.

Many of the ED treatment seekers understood their erectile difficulties to be caused partly by a failure of confidence within themselves, brought about by problems in areas of life key to successful masculinity and selfhood. A sixty-year-old retired window installer, who believed that hypertension had caused his ED, commented that he could achieve erections when things were good, but "if there are life problems, no." A seventy-one-year-old vendor contrasted his belief that he was naturally sexually attracted to women with emotional problems linked to aging: "Women are like an appetizing fruit. But the mind—the nerves—kill that. As an old man, I'm useless." A fifty-four-year-old office administrator said that he had become blocked by fear, and his treatment entailed changing his attitude: "Emotionally, one thinks, I won't be able to. It blocks you. The pleasure is less. The doctor says that I need to change my attitude; fear is blocking me." A fifty-three-year-old study participant summed up the idea that ED treatment aids confidence and improves one's perception of his masculine selfhood. He was experiencing erectile problems during a separation from his wife, which was caused by her discovery of his infidelity and which he said was "my fault, really, due to lack of care, for everything." He said that from ED treatment he hoped to gain, "more than anything else, confidence. Dysfunction is a problem of the head—of not having confidence."

Many of the men also linked these problems of confidence to problems at work, a key area for the construction of Mexican men's selves. They often identified work problems as the direct causes of ED. A sixty-year-old farmer who had bad harvests two years running said, "Pressured finances contribute to sexual problems." Similarly, the pool installer quoted earlier said that his ED was directly "related to work and cash flow problems." Furthermore, the participants frequently described practical ways in which work problems caused erectile difficulty, identifying stress or nerves as the conduit by which employment and financial problems became embodied as sexual troubles. A fifty-year-old taxi driver, who was prescribed a vitamin following prostate surgery and "a little bit of impotence" reported that the doctor had said that work stress might also be causing his ED. He said, "I'm a taxi driver; there's stress, it's badly paid, money pressures. Lots of pressure. I think that's at the root of this [impotence]. I was ferocious when I had a different job [laughs]!" A thirty-six-year-old union leader said that work and related financial stresses must have caused his ED because his physical health was good: "I have responsibility for many projects and stress. Lots of pressure. It's the fault of stress, work stress, and little time with the family. That is at fault because I don't drink—I hardly drink—I don't smoke; there's nothing else [to cause it]. Economic problems, children in school, paying school fees." Thus the participants seeking ED treatment identified work, financial problems, and difficulty providing their families with necessary resources—including their own time—as sources of stress that inhibited erectile function.

In addition to stress, these participants saw problematic relationships with romantic partners as a key linkage between life problems and their embodiment as ED. For instance, a carpenter forced to close his shop because of a hernia reported shame that his wife, a lifelong housewife, had to take work as a cleaner, and they had to accept financial help from their son. He sought ED treatment to redress his erectile difficulty and to "be useful to my wife" in at least one requisite way because he was unable to work, provide financially, or maintain his health and strength. Other participants saw problems with their partners as potential causes of their sexual difficulties. An office worker told me, "I have erection problems. I've seen two doctors. The problem is . . . an issue that's more than physical; it's moral. I hope this isn't it, but probably my wife doesn't interest me. Or it could be age. I'm sixty. Yes, I've failed my wife five times now. She's young—forty-two." This participant implicated multiple problems as both causes and consequences of ED: emotional problems with his partner, physical aging and its social consequences, the pressure to provide sexually for one's wife (especially because she was younger), and the idea that not providing sex represented a failure of resource provision. Although a few of the study participants, mostly chronologically younger men, explicitly mentioned love or good communication with one's wife as key aspects of good masculinity in the abstract, the ED treatment seekers frequently described failures in these areas as key sources of negative emotion that affected their embodied sexuality.

Based on understandings of health that fused biomedical perspectives with belief in illnesses of emotion, the treatment seekers often saw stress and sadness as the links that transformed social or psychological problems into physical, sexual difficulties. These sexual problems were then understood to start a vicious cycle, in which a generalized loss of confidence sustained both ED and depression that made it difficult for men to salvage their work, financial, and familial lives. Unprompted, many of these men defined their sexual difficulties as failures of manhood, an understanding that made sense given that they often understood ED as being caused by failings in the life areas crucial for good masculinity. For example, an unemployed fifty-two-year-old study participant said that he wanted medical ED treatment so that he could "serve as a man." He told me that in light of the work and life disruptions that had caused his sexual problems, when he was unable to achieve firm erections, he felt small; he demonstrated this by gesturing as if he were cupping something very small and shrinking with his hands. It seemed that this participant's flaccid penis had come to signify his reduced strength in the areas of life he saw as keys for being a good man.

Patients' and Doctors' Composite Beliefs about Erectile Dysfunction Treatment

The study participants' common belief that erectile difficulty was intimately related to broader life problems led most of the ED treatment seekers to view the drugs as a treatment for one physical symptom of a larger problem of masculinity. This perspective made sense in light of the local prevalence of composite understandings of health that incorporated biomedical, humoral, and emotion-based perspectives, as well as the deterrents against adopting medical understandings of erectile difficulty, discussed earlier. Even when diagnosing and treating ED, the IMSS patients and doctors usually took a holistic approach, believing that medical treatment addressed only one aspect of this multifaceted issue. They often saw decreased erectile function as part of a larger whole, not as a discrete illness, ascribing it to a person-specific mix of bodily and social problems and changes. This composite often included physical changes such as chronic illness and aging and negative emotions stemming from these changes, life stresses, bad relationships, and structural hardships.

This perspective shaped ED treatment practices in the IMSS hospital because the urologists also had holistic ideas about the causation of erectile difficulty. Although the urologists told me that organic changes such as diabetes or prostate surgery could hamper erectile function, they also believed that occasional erectile difficulty was "normal because of the stress people have." However, they warned that this emotionally driven erectile difficulty could become a "psychological trauma" and a "vicious cycle" in which men felt they were sexual failures and thus would be unable to attain an erection. Dr. Cárdenas, the jovial urologist who developed the closest relationships with his patients, sometimes gave me therapeutic assignments to undertake during my interviews that illustrated his belief that erectile difficulty was often rooted in life and emotional problems. For example, before one interview he whispered, "This patient does not feel confident in himself; he had problems with his wife, and his self-esteem decreased. He thinks he needs pills, but what he needs is to feel better about himself, so you should talk to him about that."

Although both patients and doctors often drew differently from the array of local understandings of the causes of ill health, their views on the nature of ED were closely aligned. Patients usually described all their health complaints as being mediated by a mix of biological, social, and emotional issues. In contrast, the urologists were led by their medical training—and the social status conferred by being men of science—to describe most diseases as discrete physical pathologies that might be influenced by lifestyle factors but were primarily biological. Yet the urologists were far more likely to identify social and emotional factors as causal of erectile difficulty than of the other bodily ailments they treated. Their exceptionally holistic understandings of ED seemed to relate directly to their own experiences of sex and masculinity. They often told me that as men, they understood how life pressures and problems could make it hard to attain an erection, and they also understood how socially compromising and emotionally painful this difficulty could be. They saw decreased erectile function during men's youths as an embodied problem that could be caused by either physical or emotional difficulties or both. Furthermore, they stressed that although the physical symptoms of ED might respond to medical treatment, this did not imply that the problem was purely physiological in most cases.

Based on their views of erectile difficulty as a condition rooted as much in emotion as in biology, plus being faced with time-constrained consultations and the unavailability of ED drugs in their hospital, the IMSS urologists offered medical ED treatment only if a patient specifically requested it. They described this treatment to me as not only a physiological intervention but also an attempt to intervene—in one of the few ways possible—in a composite illness caused by social and structural factors beyond individual control. For this reason, the doctors often prescribed vitamins, especially multivitamins containing ginseng, rather than ED pharmaceuticals, as a first line treatment for men upset by erectile difficulty.

VITAMINS AS A FIRST-LINE TREATMENT FOR COMPOSITE PROBLEMS

Similar to those participants discussed in chapter 4 who rejected ED treatment but saw vitamins as beneficial, the ED treatment seekers also often preferred to try vitamins before pharmaceuticals. Both the doctors and the patients saw these treatments as interventions that might "revitalize" them in body and spirit. They thought the act of pursuing treatment would provide emotional uplift, whereas the ginseng would physiologically promote erectile function by improving circulation. This more holistic approach meshed with their beliefs that erectile difficulty was a symptom of general malaise and emotional distress that was expressed through but not reducible to a vascular disorder. Although the urologists also usually ordered tests for the ED treatment seekers to determine whether prostate problems were organically contributing to erectile difficulty, they believed that vitamins could do major good by promoting bodily vigor and functioning as a placebo to give men more sexual confidence. The urologists saw the vitamins as a physically beneficial and side effect–free way to provide a psychological boost that could help a patient break the cycle of emotion-based erection problems.

Even patients willing to use ED drugs preferred vitamins to pharmaceuticals, believing the former to be safer. Some of the IMSS patients also believed that ED drugs and vitamins functioned in similar ways, by improving general bodily health. For instance, one patient said, "A buddy says that a vitamin is like Viagra—strengthening the blood for a fertile life!" He illustrated his comment by jokingly posing as a bodybuilder and flexing his biceps. In general, the IMSS doctors prescribed—and patients sought—pharmaceutical treatments only after vitamins failed to restore erectile function. This happened most frequently with men who also suffered from diabetes, high blood pressure, or other chronic illnesses that physiologically impeded erectile function. The practice of beginning treatment with vitamins was also shaped by structural factors because both doctors and patients who learned that ED drugs might not be available at the IMSS hospital saw them as a much more cost-effective treatment than pharmaceuticals.

The Objective of Erectile Dysfunction Treatment

As with vitamins, patients and doctors often considered the ED drugs' psychological impact to be as important as their ability to cause bodily change. Many of the participants, particularly those whose romantic relationships had been disrupted by their sexual difficulties, described the drugs as a treatment for a mental illness. They often characterized ED medications as restoring function that had been "blocked" by social and emotional circumstances. A twenty-one-year-old law student, the youngest ED patient I interviewed, told me that he believed that his three-month period of inability to achieve firm erections stemmed from nerves, and that: "I got blocked; I couldn't do it." Other patients reported experiencing similar blockages caused by feelings of social awkwardness or a lack of tenderness from their female partners. Some of the men identified a placebo effect at work in this process. A sixty-year-old office worker reported that simply being prescribed ED drugs, which he did not purchase because of their cost, was enough to reassure him and thus restore his sexual function for a time. He said, "The pills were to unblock me."

That this participant reported being cured by receiving a prescription—not by actually taking drugs—illustrates how ED treatment seeking often functioned as a remedy in itself. With the exception of those men who saw their ED as a purely biological issue, the treatment seekers were far more likely to discuss using medical treatment than to actually do so. Although cost and fears about drug side effects were likely key deterrents for many of those who sought but did not use the drugs, they rarely discussed these issues. Instead, it appeared that most of the treatment seekers experienced talking about their interrelated health and life problems and imagining how they might change as a therapeutic activity.

Overall, the urologists and most of the ED treatment seekers believed that erectile difficulty was significantly related to emotional turmoil, so the treatment seekers viewed drugs such as Viagra as treatments for a symptom of a broader problem, not a cure for a discrete biological pathology. To understand why these few participants requested medical ED treatment for their complex life problems, it is necessary to investigate how their lives and composite masculinities differed from those of other men who experienced decreased erectile function as natural. Most strikingly, the men I spoke with who wanted ED treatment were overwhelmingly unhappy. Many shared a sense of hopelessness, telling me that they felt unable to alter most of the negative aspects of their lives. With the exception of the very few men who attributed ED to a clear biological cause, the treatment seekers explained their erectile difficulties as generated by a range of manly failings, hardships, and stresses that had caused and perpetuated their failures to be the kinds of men they wanted to be. None believed that ED drugs alone would cure their problems. Instead, they told me that they hoped that making the small and achievable change of taking ED medication—and hopefully being able to have penetrative sex again—would start them off in a better direction. They saw the treatment as an aid for one aspect of a composite problem and hoped that by altering one element of an undesirable composite masculinity, they could begin to have new relationships, experiences, and feelings from which they could build more positive ways of being men.

These participants saw ED treatment as the step they could most feasibly take to begin improving lives troubled in a variety of ways. In our interviews, they described unique composite problems that had hampered their ability to be particular kinds of men. These problems often involved financial hardship, troubled interpersonal relationships, illness, and sadness about failing to live up to a particular standard of masculinity. Some of these men felt powerless to change most aspects of their situations, such as their socioeconomic status, and thus saw erectile difficulty as an easier problem to tackle. Others were unwilling to take the actions necessary for changing the situations that made them unhappy. For example, men guided by beliefs about how Mexican men should naturally act were sometimes loathe to improve their health by making lifestyle changes that they saw as gender inappropriate, such as performing better self-care. The following examples demonstrate how individuals faced with very different composite life problems, composed largely of elements that they felt powerless or unwilling to address, turned to ED treatment in the hopes of creating change.

For Gabriel, erectile difficulty occurred at the intersection of diabetes, financial woes, job stress, and increasing fear that a lack of sex would harm his romantic relationship. A neat and polite forty-seven-year-old gardener, he described himself as quiet by nature and was one of the few study participants who reported being faithful to his wife. He spoke of her with great affection, saying that they came from a small town, had known each other since they were children, and that "we have a special love." They had each only had sex with the other, and although he said his wife had been very supportive and understanding about his erectile difficulty, they missed the closeness of lovemaking. Thus Gabriel came to the doctor "to see if there's a medicine that can help me to have normal erection again or if I have some negative mentality [that is causing erectile difficulty]. The doctor says that I'm demoralized." Gabriel also believed his erection problems were linked to his type 2 diabetes. He had been diabetic for over a decade, but he maintained stable blood sugar levels with the help of medication and reported "no symptoms, besides the erection problem."

Although he classified his erectile difficulty as a diabetes symptom, he also said that his overall good health led him to believe that this particular symptom was more closely related to "mental pressures" surrounding work and finances. He liked his job of over twenty years, acting as the gardener in a condominium complex, but felt continually stressed by his low salary. He said, "The economic aspect is difficult; they pay me very little. I have worries, since sometimes the money isn't enough." On a weekly salary of 1,300 pesos (about $100 USD), Gabriel supported his wife and three daughters, paid the university fees for his eldest two daughters, and helped his parents financially. He told me he wanted to get a second job, but his employers would not let him. So he said he spent a lot of time worrying about money and his family's welfare. In Gabriel's case, diabetes played a role in his erectile difficulty, but poverty, work, and related stresses led more directly to his embodied sexual problems.

Gabriel said that he had only recently begun to experience erectile difficulty with his wife. Because he often awoke with an erection in the morning, his urologist judged this problem to be largely of psychological origin. Dr. Cárdenas told me that he believed that Gabriel's erectile difficulty was caused by a "vicious cycle" of fearing that he would not achieve erections and thus failing to do so. Before our interview, Dr. Cárdenas asked me to talk with him and see if he could express—and begin to work through—these emotional difficulties. Asking about these problems proved easy because Gabriel believed that his erectile problems were rooted in negative emotions. However, he saw no remedy for these feelings because they stemmed from financial and work pressures that had no clear remedy. So, he asked for medication, knowing that taking pills would be much more feasible than reducing life stress or finding better-compensated employment.

RENALDO: PILLS FOR A RANGE OF PROBLEMS

Renaldo's story illustrates how erectile function change can represent one aspect of a broader chronic illness experience encompassing bodily aging, poor nutrition, and sedentary work. Similar to Gabriel, Renaldo's ability to make changes in these arenas was curtailed by structural factors beyond his control. But unlike Gabriel, Renaldo held ideas about sex and the legitimacy of male privilege that also circumscribed his ability to revise his understanding of ideal manliness, although his divergence from this standard caused him pain and powerfully shaped his lived experience of erectile function change.

A talkative forty-nine-year-old truck driver, Renaldo was very vocal about his multiple chronic diseases and the ways he believed they had affected his life. He was overweight and suffered from diabetes, prostate enlargement, and kidney disease. These diseases caused a range of symptoms, including difficulty in urination, testicular and abdominal pain, nausea, a buildup of pressure in his eyes that threatened his vision, and erectile difficulty. Although Renaldo found some of these symptoms more bothersome than others, he was particularly upset about his changing erectile function, which he said "now isn't the same—it's little" and made him "feel very bad." He was unsure whether to attribute this problem to his prostate enlargement, diabetes, or aging, but he said that he had hoped to receive medical treatment for it at the IMSS hospital. He was frustrated when the doctor said that his chronic illnesses were causing the problem, did not offer him pharmaceutical treatment, and sent him to me to discuss his problem. He joked pointedly, "Are there treatments—other than shooting yourself?" and mimed firing a gun at his head. Unhappy with his doctor's visit, he told me that he believed poor health care and lack of appropriate treatment was to blame for his erectile problems, because his diabetic friends living in the United States had received better care.

Although Renaldo saw his decreased erectile function as the consequence of many factors, including a health-demoting lifestyle, he had sought drug treatment because he felt unable to make lifestyle changes. He believed that his diet was partly responsible for his ill health, telling me that his diabetes was "from my belly! Because of Coke and tacos." Although he had reduced his Coca-Cola intake from eight to four bottles a day, he believed that he could only make healthful lifestyle changes to the extent that his job allowed. He said, "Yes, I'd like to eat well—I know how to eat well. But as a driver, I eat and I stay seated. I get home, I eat, [and] I sleep. I need to leave this job." Unfortunately, changing jobs was not a realistic option for Renaldo because he was approaching the retirement age and would be unlikely to find other work.

Renaldo's desire to take medication rather than make lifestyle changes was reflected more broadly in his approach to his sexual problems. He said that he desired not only an ED drug but also a medicine that would make his wife more sexually receptive. He asked me if ED drugs could also work for women, saying, "My wife is older, and she's frigid. She said, 'get me something.'" He explained that his wife had always lacked sexual desire and had been considering using a medication to increase her sex drive. When I asked why she wanted to increase her desire, he said, "Because I tell her to comply!" Renaldo said that when they first married, over twenty years ago, they had sex daily, and she seemed to enjoy it. He hypothesized that "maybe it's because I'm fat; now I don't stimulate her." He thought his erectile difficulties might also exacerbate her lack of desire.

Thus Renaldo attributed multiple physical and emotional causes to the problems of desire and sexual function that he and his wife experienced. However, he felt that circumstances beyond his control foreclosed changes that might enhance their embodied experiences of sexuality or mitigate his potentially off-putting obesity. Medication was a direct biological intervention that Renaldo hoped might have some positive effect, which would not require him to change his lifestyle or address the interpersonal and work problems that underpinned his chronic illness and erectile function change.

The Effects of Erectile Dysfunction Drugs Are Context Dependent
The men who believed that their erectile difficulties were caused by a range of factors were also cognizant of the possibility that physical, social, and structural situations might influence the physical effects of the

ED drugs. Although most decided on ED treatment as the most feasible way to address one of a set of life problems, they often noted that these same problems might hamper the function of the pharmaceuticals. Just as many of the participants who used ED drugs believed that the act of treatment itself might make them happier and thus facilitate erection, others told me that they feared that their sadness would overwhelm the effects of the drugs. As one element in composite masculinities that unhappy men were striving to reconfigure, their ED treatment experience was heavily influenced by other elements, such as job stress or relationship problems.

BENITO: DRUG EFFICACY CHANGES ACROSS TIME AND CONTEXT

This context dependence is illustrated by Benito's changing experience of ED drug treatment over time. As his life circumstances changed, Benito shifted from being one of the few happy patients attributing erectile difficulty to biological causes to a demoralized man who feared his sadness had hampered his ED treatment. A forty-year-old tollbooth attendant, Benito told me that although he closely subscribed to medical understandings of ED, he also believed that social and emotional problems exacerbated his condition to the point that the drug treatment failed. A trimly dressed man who read a self-help book in the waiting area, Benito talked a mile a minute from the moment our interview began. He was one of the only men I met who had come to the IMSS hospital explicitly for ED treatment. He reported, "I came for erectile dysfunction" and, echoing medical studies and marketing information about the condition, told me that today this was a common problem for many men worldwide. He said that he had had difficulty achieving erections for a decade, since he was thirty. Somewhat contradictorily, he saw this as both a medical condition for which one should not feel shame, because he said a person could not control his biology, and as a problem for his manhood.

He believed a range of physical and life problems caused his ED, attributing it to "bad diet and stress. My job was very stressful, physically, and with the schedule, I left very tired. It was also hard because the money wasn't enough." He was particularly stressed by constant fears of layoffs in the auto factory where he had worked because line workers were gradually being replaced with robots. Despite identifying the physical and the psychological consequences of his stressful job as the causes of his ED, Benito also saw this condition as a failing of masculinity, saying that "my erection would diminish; I wouldn't have as much as a man should have."

Before his divorce, when Benito's marital relationship was still strong, he said that he saw his ED as a treatable medical, and thus largely non-stigmatizing, condition. He repeated many times that one should not feel shame over medical problems, demonstrating that casting this bodily change as a medical issue was a key way that he dealt with the embarrassment it caused him. He said that even though he shouldn't feel shame over this physical issue, it did cause stress and negative emotion that compounded his erectile difficulty. He explained the etiology of his ED thusly: "With time came more problems; it didn't function the same. I also had less confidence that it would function. Because of that, I had less desire." After trying Viagra, which made him nauseous, he was prescribed Cialis with which "I was normal." He related this feeling of normalcy directly to the use of ED medications to regain his desired level of sexual function, saying, "As a man, to feel good, I even took a stronger pill that you've never heard of, imported from India, which lasts five days." At this point in his life, Benito felt that his erectile difficulty was a biological problem caused by stress, which generated further stress in a self-perpetuating cycle that needed to be broken with medication. By using this medication and reassuring himself that there was no need to feel shame over a medical problem, he said that he was able to recover his normal masculinity.

However, the drugs ceased to function when Benito's marriage failed and romantic problems were added to the set of stressful life problems he experienced. He said, "With my wife, when I was married, I took drugs and they worked well—no problem. Now, without a wife, the drugs don't work as well; it's a question of having trust with the person." For Benito, the severing of the trust-laden emotional connection that had supported his sexual performance in the face of stress-induced ED significantly exacerbated his condition. He reported that his divorce was particularly difficult because of the way in which his marriage dissolved: "The connection was lost. She lost her values. She didn't respect me; we split because it was affecting the kids. We were together for eighteen years. Today, there are many infidelities, and she had 'friends' she says." Although Benito used the term *connection* to describe the special relationship he had shared with his wife, this term also highlights the nature of this relationship as a key element of his composite masculinity. The way in which this connection was broken—her humiliating infidelity—also meant the loss of familial respect that the participants often saw as a key to good Mexican masculinity. Benito reported feeling shame at being cuckolded, telling me that he had lost the respect of his family. The losses of familial relationships and respect that had been key components of Benito's composite masculinity made him feel stress, sadness, and insecurity about his manliness that he believed further impeded his erectile function.

He said, "Now that I don't have a wife, it's harder. I'm failing more and more; it affects me as a person." He started dating someone, who he had since seen infrequently during a two-year relationship because she lived in Cuernavaca and he worked in Mexico City. He said that even his infrequent attempts at penetrative sex often failed. "It's frustrating; sometimes we get to the point of putting it in, and it goes to sleep." He said that he wanted to have sex with her, but sometimes could not, and that the medications worked less and less. "It's not that I don't want to, but I fail. Before, I would see her every fifteen days. I would take the pill before, and it was fine. Now I have to calculate." He was depressed by this situation, saying that, "One feels uncomfortable, deflated . . . But I also feel desire! This affects me." Benito thus reported that his inability to act out his desires deepened a depression that had ever-increasing bodily consequences.

Benito believed that his sexual problems were caused by interrelated factors: declining physical health, stress and negative emotions, and weak emotional relationships with sexual partners. In response, he continued to use medical ED treatment and also made various life changes to redress the different aspects of his condition. He sought out information on sexuality—and self-help literature more generally—as a way to control his stress. He told me that one should not feel shame about becoming educated about sexuality: "I seek out information so that I as a man feel better." Having this knowledge was particularly important to his sense of self because his parents were illiterate and "closed-minded" about sexuality, a state that through education "I am overcoming." Benito also changed jobs, leaving the stressful environment of the auto factory to work in a tollbooth. Unfortunately, his stress surrounding the need to earn enough money remained and directly affected his romantic relationships. For example, he said that he needed to save to buy a car because he believed that women did not like men without them. He also made lifestyle changes, trying to eat as well as he could on his low income, walking five kilometers a day, and lifting weights for exercise.

For Benito, as for many of the other treatment seekers, ED was a composite problem that required a range of solutions, and both his problems and the availability of solutions were shaped by his life situation. The nature of his erectile difficulty changed in concert with the new problems that confronted him. The failure of his marriage led to negative emotion that worsened his erectile function to the point that drug treatment failed. The context of work stress and financial difficulty further hampered his ability to form the sort of composite masculinity that he desired. Benito responded to this range of difficulties by incorporating self-help education into his treatment regimen, coupling it with pharmaceutical use to address both physiological and psychological problems. He hoped that by addressing a range of problems of masculinity that both caused and resulted from erectile difficulty, this new approach could make him feel better as a man. He also understood the success or failure of such attempts to be directly related to the other things going on in his life because these influenced his emotional state and, in turn, his biology. Overall, the range of elements available for inclusion in Benito's composite masculinity at different life points dramatically shaped his ability to live out particular kinds of manhood, as well as his success with ED drugs.

Social Effects of Erectile Dysfunction Treatment

When the study participants discussed their hopes for ED treatment, they focused on the new kinds of interpersonal interactions it could generate, not on simple physical changes. Just as the participants explained their reasons for having extramarital affairs more in terms of expressing particular kinds of selfhood than obtaining physical pleasure, men seeking ED drugs desired more than just the sensation of penetrative sex. The majority of the ED treatment seekers hoped that the drugs would enable them to physically express their desired kinds of relationships through sex. Some hoped to create, continue, or reignite loving relationships with romantic partners, whereas others sought to have sexual relationships that would demonstrate specific kinds of manliness.

EDUARDO: MEDICAL RELATIONSHIPS AS TREATMENT

The sociality of men's goals for a physiological treatment is exemplified by Eduardo's experience with ED treatment. Most of the participants saw having a sexual partner as a prerequisite for using ED drugs; in fact, some of the men who rejected the drugs were widowers who saw them as silly because they had no one to have sex with. However, Eduardo explicitly used the experience of medical treatment itself to try to reconfigure an undesirable composite masculinity, telling me that his physically unsuccessful ED treatments had significantly alleviated his emotional distress.

Eduardo, a fifty-nine-year-old, married, retired bus driver, suffered from several health problems that required frequent visits to the IMSS hospital. He told me that his worst conditions were diabetes, hypertension, and glaucoma; he had also had a prostate operation eight years ago. He said that he had not had an erection for four years but had been trying treatment after treatment with the personable Dr. Cárdenas. However, Eduardo reported that the treatments "did nothing." He said, "Injections—nothing. Viagra—nothing. Cialis—nothing. The science has run out." Both Eduardo and Dr. Cárdenas believed that his chronic diseases may have irreparably harmed his erectile function. Eduardo stated, "With my diabetes, it [ED] is a consequence of my body—diabetes and hypertension."

However, it was clear that Eduardo had come to see his medical encounters with the urologist as treatments in themselves. He characterized their interactions as some of the few moments of human connection in his "lonely" life. Eduardo seemed to desire his periodic medical appointments much more than the physical cure for erectile difficulty they might provide. For example, he rejected the doctor's suggestion that he use a penile vacuum pump on the grounds that it was too physically risky but nevertheless scheduled follow-up appointments to discuss possible future options. In the course of our long interview, Eduardo cast his IMSS interactions as sources of emotional support that made him feel better about the distance he felt from his wife and children.

Eduardo told me that he had had a difficult life, in which work, responsibility, and mistakes he had made "as a man" precluded emotional closeness with his family. Forced with his eleven siblings to cultivate the land in their small village, he said that he escaped by marrying "really young"—at age sixteen—and moving to Cuernavaca. In hindsight, he believed that he had been too immature for the "responsibility of a wife." He said that after they had six children, his first marriage ended because the "temptations of the city," including the availability of extramarital sex, made him unable to responsibly care for his family and led him to "abandon them." He remarried in 1976 and had nine children with his new wife. However, although he strove to be a more responsible father and husband by providing for them financially, he worked an ever-changing set of low-paid and physically taxing jobs. He said he was eventually forced to retire from his last job, which was driving a bus, when he was laid off by new management. He was bitter about the loss of this job and his subsequent fifteen-year period of unemployment because he was unable to find a new job as a result of poor health caused by diabetes. He told me that he had long felt trapped in the home, whereas his wife worked and his children "ignored" him.

This state of affairs hampered his sexual function. Eduardo believed that in addition to diabetes and aging, loneliness and depression made it impossible for him to achieve erections. He said that although they did not need her income, his fifty-four-year-old wife refused to retire from her job at a market food stall, stay home, and keep him company. He said, "That depresses me. I practically live alone because my wife works all day and my children are married . . . It's like God decreed that I be alone." He attributed this loneliness to his prior way of being a man, saying that "as a man" he did not develop the emotional closeness with his children that his wife did. He also reported feeling disconnected from his wife, both because of their different schedules and the fact that they did not share their emotions, leading to a distance that had frequently brought them "to the point of divorce." For Eduardo, this lack of emotional connection was exemplified by their lack of sex. He said, "I'm home all day; she's working. I believe that she doesn't have desire because of tiredness." He felt that his wife's refusal to stop working was an implicit rejection of increased temporal, emotional, and sexual closeness with him.

Eduardo felt this distance keenly as he tried to deal with his erectile function problems. He said that they had not discussed his sexual problems directly and had addressed the topic only during a consultation with a doctor. There, he said, she embarrassed him: "As a joke, she said, 'now he's worthless.' That hurt me." She was also unwilling to take the doctor's suggestion that they watch pornographic movies or do other things that might arouse him, saying she was too tired at the end of the workday. Eduardo saw her commitment to work as a rejection of not only his companionship but also their sex life. Furthermore, he feared that it highlighted his recent failure to perform the male role of provider and head of household.

Perhaps to rehabilitate one aspect of his composite masculinity, Eduardo said he wanted to continue having marital sex despite his marital and health problems, even though he no longer felt sexual desire or the need to procreate. He saw his erectile difficulty, health problems, and emotional distance from his family as combining into a composite failure of manhood. He believed that these problems might be divine punishment for past gendered mistakes because these aspects of his life felt as if they were curses from God. He asked, "Why is God punishing me this way? It's like I drank a forbidden drink, and these are the consequences. My kids don't pay attention to me; I don't have erections." Although he saw these sexual and social failings as related, he characterized his quest for ED treatment as a symptom of his underlying solitude: "It's not the lack of erection that depresses me; it's the loneliness." He felt this pain especially keenly as it signified a failure to enact the masculinity that he still wanted to perform, by caring for and controlling his family and body. He said, "It's hard continuing to be a man until you die." He also felt cheated, in that he believed he had performed his manly duty to provide for his second family, but the children from this marriage "ignored" him. He complained, "I gave them education, a home, food, and a place to play; now it's their turn to be responsible." In part, he felt hurt because their coldness made him feel as if he failed to teach them good manners, saying, "Sometimes there's depression; why are they acting badly?" He told me that he sometimes fantasized about showing them his "list of illnesses" to guilt them into paying more attention to him.

Rather than understanding ED treatment as a strictly biological intervention, Eduardo used it largely as a source of emotional support—as a way to experience the emotional intimacy he lacked with his family. He said that the IMSS doctors "reenergize the sick person [and] give you more will to live." He was not particularly happy with the medical interventions themselves; he complained that the ED treatments had no effect, probably as a result of untreatable changes that come with age. Furthermore, he said that "I'm now really tired of so many medicines." However, he did make some healthful lifestyle changes, including curtailing heavy drinking, based on the advice he received at the IMSS hospital. Overall, he characterized the IMSS hospital as a source of not only medical treatments and information but also, most importantly, emotional support. He said, "If you [health-care professionals] don't support me, who will support me? If you don't help me, who will help me?"

Eduardo's ED treatment created emotional connections that became crucial elements of his composite masculinity. Although his manliness was threatened by emotional distance from his family, he felt that relationships with the IMSS doctors provided a bit of this missing intimacy.

For this reason, although Eduardo characterized his "real problem" as loneliness, not a lack of erections, and reported that he no longer felt sexual desire, he persistently sought ED treatment. Eduardo's ED was an embodied composite of loneliness, failed social relationships, work disappointments, and perhaps even divine punishment for failure to be a good man during his first marriage. Although medical treatment offered him no physical change, it provided new emotional connections that enabled him to slightly revise his sense of self, from a lonely, forsaken person to one at least supported by caring doctors. Furthermore, the thought that ED treatment might someday produce erections enabled Eduardo to imagine future closeness with his wife. In sum, rather than providing erections, Eduardo's ED treatments offered social relationships that he could incorporate into his composite masculinity to partially fill the gaps left by unsatisfactory familial relationships.

Erectile Dysfunction Drugs in Private Practice

Just as ED treatment involved social interactions that might become important parts of patients' composite masculinities, clinical interactions also shaped the nature of ED diagnosis and drug prescription. The final section of this chapter contextualizes the IMSS patients' experiences by describing some of the other kinds of ED treatment in Cuernavaca, which encouraged different understandings of the nature of erectile difficulty. The biomedical actors treating ED in Cuernavaca ranged widely and included family-practice physicians, urologists, and clinics dedicated to sexual dysfunction. This section compares the treatment practices of two family-practice physicians who I interviewed and observed at work, as well as a sexual health clinic known widely by reputation in Cuernavaca.

When I observed consultations between private family physicians and male patients demographically similar to the IMSS study participants, I found that the private-practice patients discussed sexual health issues with their doctors in qualitatively different ways than IMSS patients did. Private doctors and patients usually had long-standing relationships and referred to past histories of illness, treatment, and life experience, when discussing current ailments. These patients appeared to feel the *confianza* with their private doctors that the IMSS study participants said was necessary, but often lacking, to discuss sex. They seemed to speak freely about both the embodied and social experiences of sexual difficulty and drug treatment. Because I attended, at the doctors' invitations, only those consultations that were likely to address the topic of ED, I cannot definitively say whether private-practice patients on the whole were more likely to broach this subject than IMSS patients. However, private-practice physicians' reports about the frequency with which they treated ED, and the IMSS survey finding that most of the men who used ED drugs sought them through private-practice consultations, suggest that ED is treated much more frequently in private practice than in IMSS practice.

It is likely that the more intimate doctor-patient interactions possible in private-practice settings may encourage both parties to understand non–life-threatening ailments, including erection problems, as medical concerns because the doctor has the time and the inclination to classify them as such. Although medical interactions in the IMSS hospital were brief and focused on a few key problems reported by the patient or the referring physician, the private-practice doctors I spoke with reported asking their patients questions about their health and lives in general, seeking to elicit a broader picture of their patient's health and pick up on unreported issues. They described needing to understand the full picture of a patient's life to provide appropriate treatment. Although this holistic clinical style was grounded in the physicians' beliefs about what constituted quality health care, it is important to note that these interactions were shaped by a different structural context than the IMSS appointments. Private-practice doctors had financial incentives to diagnose and provide ongoing treatment for diseases, which surely encouraged them to diagnose ED in the same way that limited resources discouraged the IMSS doctors from medicalizing erectile difficulty.

Yet although they appeared more likely to diagnose ED, some private-practice doctors espoused composite understandings of sexual difficulty similar to those held by the IMSS study participants. Dr. Peralta, whose suggestions that her patient Ernesto take ED drugs and have an affair are described in chapter 2, exemplifies this approach. Dr. Peralta has treated patients from her home office in a working-class neighborhood of Cuernavaca for over twenty years, during which she says she has won the "trust of the community." No doubt influenced by her sister, the local Cialis sales representative, Dr. Peralta leaves ED pamphlets in her waiting area so that patients can broach the topic simply by bringing the brochure into the consulting room. She says that although this topic can be sensitive, patients talk to her about it because she has known them and their families for years, and they feel that they can unburden themselves to her without shame, seeing her like a priest.

Offering treatment and advice with her patients' life stories in mind, Dr. Peralta not only prescribed ED drugs to her patients who were unhappy with their erectile function but also told them how to use the drugs socially. She told me that, often, her patients live in one room with their entire family. So, she would recommend that they send their family out, to the movie or even into the street, so that they could have private time to engage in sex with their partners. She also suggested that they could try nonpenetrative acts, such as oral sex or manual stimulation. She reported that her patients were frequently shocked to receive this advice but often tried it and sometimes returned to happily tell her about their progress. Dr. Peralta depended on these long-term, trusting relationships to provide her with clients, and thus she had financial and personal incentives to provide what she called "good advice" that might or might not include pharmaceutical treatments. Although quick to diagnose and medically treat ED, Dr. Peralta did so as part of a composite solution combining life advice with pharmaceutical aid.

In contrast, other private-practice doctors that had close relationships with their patients espoused largely biomedical understandings of erectile difficulty. For example, Dr. Ramírez, an elderly physician who treated private, middle-class patients from an office in Cuernavaca's city center, told me that he often asked about his patients' sexual health and encouraged them to use ED drugs. He explained that he had long known many of his patients and often used stories from his own life to explain medical concepts and make them feel more comfortable. For example, he said that for men he diagnosed with ED, "I tell them, 'don't be caught like Dr. Ramírez, on a vacation to Cuba without enough Cialis!'" Such interactions were worlds apart from the quick and formal medical appointments at the IMSS hospital.

These interactions were also shaped by Dr. Ramírez's close relationship with the Cialis representative, who, in fact, introduced us. He depended on her for free samples, educational materials for his patients, and access to promotional dinners and events that conferred social status in the local medical community. Although Dr. Ramírez told me that he believed that prescribing ED drugs in cases of decreased erectile function would enhance his patients' well-being, the structural context in which he worked likely influenced these beliefs. He also had a strong financial incentive to focus on drug treatments when addressing sexual health issues, to ensure follow-up medical visits and maintain good relationships with drug company representatives.

FIGURE 5.
A Boston Medical Group newspaper ad.

Although interactions among family doctors and patients were often informal and warm, appointments in specialized private-practice settings seemed far more focused. In clinics devoted to sexual dysfunction treatment, the patients often expected purely biomedical treatments, and the clinicians had structural and financial incentives to prescribe them. For example, many such clinics run clinical trials of ED drugs, enabling them to provide drug treatment to their patients but making them structurally invested in promoting the notion that impotence should be considered ED (Wentzell 2006). For-profit sexual health clinics have a clear incentive to provide medical ED treatment while minimizing the time-consuming discussion of nonphysiological aspects of decreased erectile function. The best known of these is the Boston Medical Group, an international chain of clinics that has a location in Mexico City and frequently advertises that their medical staff will visit Cuernavaca "for one day only!" Their ads, which ran semimonthly in the local paper during my research, feature an image of a male torso in the style of Michelangelo's *David* and promise men that they will "improve your sex life!" offering confidential medical help for impotence, premature ejaculation, and "achieving or maintaining an erection."

This clinical franchise is quite secretive, never specifying exactly what medical treatments they offer; they refused my repeated requests for interviews and information. However, the IMSS urologists said that they had heard from colleagues working there that they simply provide penile injections of papaverine, the pharmaceutical treatment that predated Viagra. A study participant who had received a Boston clinic consultation told me that for $6,900 pesos (about $550 USD), a huge cost by IMSS patients' standards, he was offered a series of thirty injections that he understood would "clear the veins in my penis." Thus, although the Boston Medical Group's marketing generates business by framing ED as a distressing but treatable problem of masculinity, it is structured to sell purely biomedical solutions to this social problem.

Overall, men's access to and beliefs about the need for medical ED treatment were co-constructed in ways that were constrained but not determined by structural context. Men who were demographically similar to the IMSS patients but chose to use scarce resources to seek private health care when experiencing erectile difficulty were likely to be diagnosed with ED, in contexts that may or may not have promoted multifaceted understandings of sexual health. Men who used cost-free IMSS care entered a situation where scarce resources encouraged the doctors to overlook erectile function change and where composite understandings of this change as simultaneously biological, social, and emotional were promoted. Such men were unlikely to regard their decreased erectile function as ED because busy clinicians for whom medicalizing various bodily changes would create an increased workload did not challenge their multifaceted understandings of health. In this medical silence, other voices and viewpoints came to the fore, and men were likely to listen to the suggestions of wives and other family members that they understand decreased erectile function as a normal part of aging. Men's responses to erectile difficulty were thus composite, composed of interrelated health beliefs, embodied experiences, and financial constraints.

Conclusion

Decreased Erectile Function in Context

This book has shown how men respond to illness, aging, social problems, structural inequalities, and the erectile difficulty that these experiences may cause. It has traced the ways in which the individual study participants drew from an array of culturally intelligible ways of understanding these experiences to revise their composite masculinities in attempts to incorporate often undesired changes into enactments of desired ways of being men. My aim has been to analyze the study participants' accounts of embodied and life experiences surrounding erectile difficulty and discern how they revised their ways of being men in relationship to these changes and the possibility of medical intervention. I have also sought to illuminate the ways that men's life contexts, especially economic hardships and relationships with wives and physicians, influenced their interpretations of and responses to erectile function change. The participants' experiences demonstrate how it is possible, in a country where penetrative sex is a famed marker of masculinity (to the point that the study participants often cast the abstract Mexican man as being sex obsessed) and ED drugs are heavily publicized and widely purchased, that men in particular social and structural positions might reject or complicate medicalization of erectile difficulty and make positive social use of decreased erectile function.

Although the life experiences of each participant differed, common patterns emerged as they drew from a shared cultural pool of ideas about health, aging, and male sexuality when responding to similar bodily changes. Despite the frequent occurrence of decreased erectile function among this group of aging and often chronically ill men, most of the study participants rejected medical fixes for erectile difficulty. Instead, they incorporated notions of age-appropriate male sexuality into their composite masculinities. Rather than seeking to continue youthful sexual practices with pharmaceutical aids, these men saw decreased erectile function as the embodiment of a shift to respectable older age, making responsible maturation one of their key ways of being men. They often did so at the behest of wives and family members, sometimes by adopting the idea that ED drugs were socially inappropriate for older men and thus potentially harmful physically. The participants were also encouraged to develop this view of erectile difficulty by the structural disincentives against ED diagnosis and treatment inherent in the IMSS system. Finally, men's holistic definitions of health supported their understandings of decreased erectile function as a simultaneously physical and social issue. Although a few of the study participants did seek ED treatment, wishing to alter undesired composite masculinities by incorporating penetrative sex and successful romantic relationships, they tended to share these multifaceted ideas of health. Thus most of the ED drug users in the IMSS hospital saw the treatments not as simple fixes for a bodily pathology but as remedies for one aspect of a complex set of social, emotional, and bodily problems that combined into nonideal masculinities.

The responses to decreased erectile function reported in this book represent men's individual reactions to bodily change in a specific social and structural context. The range of extant cultural notions about gender and health, existing medical technology, the structure of health-care access, and the economic climate are always in flux. Describing how men developed responses to erectile difficulty that seemed possible and sensical, this book demonstrates the context dependence of men's reactions to socially significant bodily changes. Yet rather than simply providing a static snapshot of men's responses to erectile difficulty at a certain place and time, this book aims to use these data in the service of illuminating the mechanics of change in the enactment of gender. Using erectile difficulty as a starting point for understanding gender as a dynamic composite, I have sought to demonstrate how men coordinate changing sets of elements into attempts to be particular kinds of men, through a range of narrative, embodied, and interpersonal practices. This book is intended to reveal the often purposeful, ever-changing ways in which men revised their composite masculinities in response to ongoing changes in their bodies, social worlds, and structural settings.

Ongoing shifts in Mexican cultural understandings of gender and health, as well as the continuing development and marketing of sexual health technologies, mean that the specific ways of incorporating erectile difficulty into composite masculinities described here are also likely to change. Although the previous chapters focused on using the composite approach to understanding individual gendered change in context, this concluding chapter uses this perspective to investigate macrolevel cultural changes in patterns of relating to decreased erectile function. After using the composite approach to shed light on how the study participants incorporated medicalization, a social trend often seen as totalizing, into broader composite masculinities, this chapter analyzes how these varying uses of medical perspectives are reflected in current ED drug marketing. It then identifies trends and probable long-term changes in the ways Mexican men demographically similar to the study participants might incorporate erectile difficulty and ED drug use into their ways of being men and concludes by discussing the utility of the composite perspective for understanding this phenomenon, as well as self-making and social changes more broadly.

Medicalization in Composite Masculinities

Medicalization, the widely noted and heavily critiqued trend of understanding problems and ills through the lens of biomedicine, is occurring worldwide as biomedical treatments are globally sold and marketed (Conrad and Leiter 2004). This phenomenon is sometimes seen as supplanting preexisting cultural understandings of health and bodily difference (Illich 1974), and it fundamentally alters the range of ways in which it becomes possible to understand bodily change and deviance from norms in a given society. However, researchers have noted that people can also deploy medicalization selectively or strategically when using medical means of embodying particular social norms (Nye 2003). The composite perspective is ideal for understanding the ways that people may relate complexly to new biomedical ways of understanding and treating conditions that were once seen as social, psychological, or natural. As the ED treatment seekers' narratives show, using or fantasizing about using medical treatments for socially problematic bodily changes can be one of a set of activities that unhappy people use to revise selves they find wanting.

This approach also sheds light on the concrete ways that people incorporate these medical interventions into multifaceted attempts to change their bodies and selves. Based on the view of decreased erectile function as a symptom of a composite problem of masculinity, some of the participants deployed drug treatment as a way to tackle what they saw as this issue's most treatable aspect. Although they saw their problems as more than medical, they used ED drugs to create physical changes they hoped would lead to a range of changes in other life areas. For them, defining and treating erectile difficulty as ED was a way to revise one element of an undesirable composite masculinity, in hopes of generating new sexual and social experiences for inclusion in a reconfigured way of being a man. Their varied experiences show how people might weave a single medical technology into very different gendered selfhoods; defining their erectile difficulty as ED provided not only a new, biological way of understanding their problems but also a new element to be included in varied and multifaceted ways of being men.

Men's accounts of seeking ED treatment at the IMSS hospital and other sites show that the public health-care context encouraged a partial rather than a wholesale adoption of medical perspectives. As demonstrated by the differences in ED prescription rates among demographically similar men receiving public versus private medical care, both the accessibility of and doctors' propensity to prescribe ED drugs influence men's use of these treatments and their understandings of the nature of decreased erectile function. Working with limited resources, IMSS urologists encountering patients who requested ED treatment but maintained multifaceted understandings of ED etiology did not feel the need to promote strictly biomedical explanations. Instead, these doctors drew on composite understandings of the condition that incorporated local cultural explanations, ranging from the psychological to the physiological, as well as their own experiences as men.

In this clinical setting, both patients and doctors generally saw medical diagnoses and treatments as applicable to only certain instances of erectile difficulty, which they viewed as symptoms of broader, more complex problems. This state of affairs left room for the doctors and the patients to consider the ways that different aspects of life came together to hamper erectile function, even in cases where the drugs seemed to be a good option for helping men "feel better." Ironically, the less-than-ideal standard of biomedical care that the IMSS patients received left social room for the development and the maintenance of holistic notions of health care that are sometimes seen as the cutting edge of luxury biomedicine. Because of its context, ED treatment at the IMSS hospital was a space where patients and doctors together constructed composite understandings of gendered illness.

Differences in Erectile Dysfunction Drug Marketing

Even ED pharmaceutical marketing, which is designed to sell biomedical understandings of erectile difficulty, reflects the differing ways that people may draw from culturally intelligible ways of understanding health and gender as they incorporate decreased erectile function into their composite masculinities. ED drug advertising in Cuernavaca reflects the multiplicity of cultural understandings of masculinity, love, sex, and health from which potential consumers crafted composite gendered selves and explanations of bodily changes. For example, this marketing incorporates a range of very different characterizations of the Mexican man.

Some of the ads rely on ideas about natural Mexican *machismo* and male hotness, claiming to facilitate a traditionally manly style of penetration-oriented sexuality. Viagra marketing often takes this approach, focusing on male rather than marital sexuality and promising to restore youthful sexual function. A typical Viagra ad shows a happily sleeping man, who looks middle aged yet muscular and healthy. He is face down, revealing a back covered in postcoital back scratches, with a note on his pillow that reads, "Thanks, you were incredible! You acted like you were 20." This image of a man alone suggests that obtaining virility, not specific kinds of romantic relationships, is the object of taking Viagra.

This ad presents the drug as an agent of bodily change that will enable the enactment of the kind of sexuality that the study participants often described as natural to young men. It sells the ability to satisfy women sexually, thus satisfying the social role stereotypically assigned to *el Mexicano*. Other marketing strategies developed by Pfizer, the maker of Viagra, also assume a macho user population, consisting of men likely to be unfaithful and who fear that admitting erectile difficulty will compromise their virile image. For example, a Pfizer sales representative told me that the company also sells Viagra's active ingredient in a drug called Patrex, which functions identically to Viagra but is marketed to—and thus only available from—physicians. This approach was intended to make Patrex a stealth alternative to Viagra, which urologists could prescribe to men who wanted to keep ED drugs in the house but conceal their use from wives because of either shame or their use to

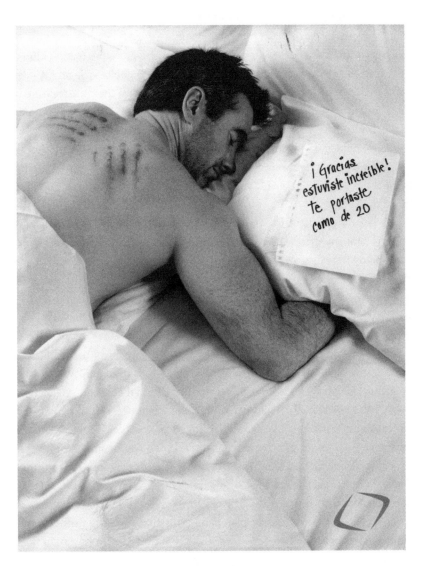

FIGURE 6.
Viagra ad.

facilitate extramarital sex. The representative said that the name *Patrex* was chosen because it could be easily confused with that of a common antibiotic.

Yet just as frequently, ED drug advertising positions the drugs as products that help men to resist *machismo*. For every ad that casts drug treatment as a way to recover lost youth through the act of penetration alone, one frames ED medication as a savior of companionate marriage. A Cialis sales representative told me that her company frames their ED treatment as a "quality of life drug" and seeks to show that ED "is a sickness, not a problem with your manliness." Showing me the photos of happy male-female couples in the Cialis marketing materials, she critiqued Viagra advertising for encouraging men to try to be "sexual superheroes," saying that the maker of Cialis, Lilly-ICOS, instead "focused on what's good for the family."

In keeping with this marketing strategy, a 2008 Cialis campaign claims that the drug will help men "rediscover intimacy with your partner." Showing neck-up images of smiling couples rubbing noses, such ads highlight emotional, rather than physical, engagement. Unlike the boudoir setting of the Viagra ad, the couples pictured wear formal attire, suggesting that they are on a romantic date. Positive relationships, not simple penetrative sex, appear to be on sale here.

Along these lines, although clinics such as the Boston Medical Group sold ED treatments based on phallocentric notions of sexuality and what the study participants would have called traditional characterizations of Mexican male sexuality, many doctors and sales representatives involved in ED drug marketing explicitly positioned taking the drugs as an anti-macho act. These marketing pitches highlighted responsibility, not virility, as a key element of manliness, arguing that it was men's *unwilling-ness* to admit that they needed the drugs that represented true *machismo*. Elena, the Cuernavaca Cialis sales representative, defined *machismo* as men's belief that ED could never happen to them, and she often organized educational lectures that conveyed this message. At one such talk, given by an urologist to a group of white-collar workers at a local transportation company, the speaker stressed that macho closed-mindedness and pride led men to fail to seek beneficial medical knowledge and treatment. In his presentation, this doctor cast seeking medical ED treatment as a progressive strike against backward, *machista* understandings of sexuality and health. He stated, "There's a lot of *machismo* here, which

FIGURE 7.
Cialis ad.

prevents us from getting treatment, from getting education." He also described men's reluctance to talk to their doctors about sexual problems
as a form of *machismo*, figuring educational activities akin to the talk as
a way of engaging in a more modern and healthy masculinity. Thus the
rhetoric surrounding ED drug use often positioned it as a way *not* to be
macho. The diversity of ED drug marketing strategies in Mexico suggests
that medicalizing erectile difficulty could become an element of a wide
array of different composite masculinities—an element assigned varying
meanings and used to multiple ends.

Patterns of Change over Time

This diversity in ED drug marketing highlights the widely different ways
of understanding sexuality, love, and gender with which Mexican men
may align themselves. Men's choices about which understandings of
these issues they will include in their composite masculinities profoundly
shape their responses to erectile difficulty, as well as their actions more
broadly. Their decisions about which views to take are also powerfully
constrained by factors including their relationships and historical life
experiences. Although men may incorporate a range of attitudes and
ideas into their ways of being men, those who have had similar experiences are likely to do so in similar ways. On the population level, generational differences in men's ways of being men occur as new gender norms
become standard or ideal; the study participants' stories demonstrate

both individual diversity and trends among age cohorts in responding to erectile difficulty. This section describes these differences, contextualizing the patterns of masculinity-making presented in the previous chapters and discussing the ways today's younger IMSS patients appear likely to incorporate future erectile difficulty into their ways of being men.

Although the study participants ranged widely in age, most self-identified as being "older" men. Thus this book has focused on these men's incorporations of shared cultural, structural, and embodied experiences into individual composite masculinities. Although unique, these ways of being men were shaped by the cultural norms regarding gender, sexuality, and relationships that were prevalent throughout their lives. Because local ideals regarding gender have radically changed over the course of older men's lives, from the idealization of hierarchically related separate spheres for men and women to the valorization of more egalitarian relationships, many of these participants' composite masculinities have incorporated such changes over time.

For example, many of the older participants told me that although they grew to love their spouses, they did not marry primarily for love. Instead, they saw marriage as an expected social step toward adulthood, and they sought wives who would be helpful, supportive, and industrious in the home and in child rearing. Although most saw tender marital relations as ideal, the participants often reported making "mistakes" in this area, remaining emotionally distant from their wives during youths focused on work, friends, and mistresses. Only in rare cases did older study participants, male or female, expect male marital fidelity. Instead, they saw discretion and uninterrupted financial support as the hallmarks of being a responsible husband.

However, such ideals have been challenged by the more recent cultural valorization of companionate marriage and emotionally fulfilling marital sex. Most of the study participants related this new ideal into their composite masculinities in some way, although many also drew on discourses of *machismo* and also noted that their romantic lives frequently fell short of their ideals. Many of the older men reported valuing emotionally close marriage later in life, likely because it was at this point in their histories that this ideal of marriage had become culturally dominant. Many told me that as they matured, ceasing to focus so much on work and affairs, they strove to forge new, more emotionally intimate relationships with their wives and families that they often characterized as emotionally rewarding. As discussed in chapters 1 and 2, these older participants often incorporated elements of the current ideal of companionate marriage, particularly emotional closeness, into their marriages as youthful sexuality fell by the wayside and became unavailable for inclusion in their composite masculinities. For example, a seventy-seven-year-old retiree explained that sexual passion "is like a flower. It has a beautiful moment but fades with the passage of time." He told me that "sexual love" changes over time into a deeper form of affection "less based on sexual contact."

MEN STRIVING TO BE DIFFERENT FROM THEIR FATHERS

Although many of the participants incorporated histories of youthful carousing as well as later-life companionate marriage as positive aspects of the composite masculinities they presented in our interviews, the chronologically younger study participants often held a very different view of older men's youths. In our interviews, they frequently recounted childhoods marred by neglectful or macho fathers. Many of the younger study participants told me that their parents' relationships were oppressive or problematically unequal, and they were angry that their fathers had mistreated their mothers. They often acted on these feelings, for instance, seeking to redress their mothers' suffering. This response was demonstrated by the adult children of the artisanal gelatin maker discussed in chapter 2, who told their mother that she had "suffered enough" at their father's hands and provided financial support for her move into her own home.

Similarly, other men said that they wanted to avoid putting their own wives through the pain that they had seen their mothers experience, especially in terms of neglect or domestic violence. For example, one participant explained, "It fell to me to see my dad hit my mom. I never hit my wife or my children. Those punches come to nothing; they're actually the problem." In these ways, many of the younger study participants used their parents' marriages as models for what not to do and strove to build more companionate and egalitarian relationships that would enable them to incorporate actions and beliefs they saw as modern into their composite masculinities.

Ethnographic studies of Mexican men in their twenties and thirties from different walks of life have shown that many explicitly seek to be "different" from their parents (Jiménez Guzman 2003; Ramirez 2009;

Salguero Velásquez 2007). This attitude was quite common among the younger study participants, who frequently made such difference a key element of their composite masculinities. Frequently, they described being a good man as doing whatever their own father had not done. When I asked them to tell me about what they did to be a good husband or parent, they often responded, "Be different than my father!" For instance, a thirty-year-old office worker said that his parents had married young, and his father was a macho Mexican who ordered his family around. In his own life, this participant told me that he did not want a situation where "you're the macho, you give the orders" because as a society, "we've opened our eyes a little." Many of the younger participants said that "because of what [we] have lived" as their fathers' children, "young people think in a different way."

Thus the younger study participants frequently critiqued the pattern of manly life course change in which physical passion dominates one's youthful love life and gives way to emotional tenderness with age, as antithetical to their ideals of passionate and affective marriage. Many came of age in a cultural context featuring disjunctive models of marriage; they consumed media (such as *telenovelas* and American romantic comedies) that promoted companionate marriage and often witnessed emotionally distant or adversarial relations between their own parents. Frequently judging their fathers negatively as harsh and too "traditional," the younger study participants usually judged their fathers' later life "softening" in accordance with the Mexican classic narrative as being too little, too late. Seeking to be different, they frequently told me that they felt they had to mature when they got married, which entailed being emotionally present for their wives and children. To this end, all of the younger study participants had married or hoped to marry women that they loved and saw maintaining romantic passion as crucial to maintaining a happy marriage. Although some said that their fathers saw these different choices as unmanly, others received support from "ex-*machista*" fathers who believed that younger men needed to be different, more modern kinds of husbands than they themselves had been.

Such attempts extended to their enactions of marital fidelity or infidelity. A much higher percentage of the participants who described themselves as younger rather than as older reported being faithful to their wives after marriage. Furthermore, those younger men who did cheat tended not to explain their actions as older men usually did—as an expression of their innate manliness or Mexicanness—but instead saw affairs as emotional entanglements prompted by interpersonal failings in companionate marriages. For example, the unemployed television executive discussed in chapter 1 said that emotional distance in his prior marriage led his wife to cheat, and he responded in kind to get revenge. He stressed to me that "I'm not a macho" and that his infidelity was thus not borne of *machismo* but of "the terrible mistake of acting out of vengeance."

The few younger women whom I interviewed often reported similar beliefs and actions. Although the older women I spoke with never reported infidelity and rarely described themselves as highly interested in sex, younger women were often unfaithful for the same kinds of reasons as their male counterparts. An IMSS physician in her early forties told me that although she loved her husband, she cheated when her marriage fell on hard times following his job loss. During this difficult time, she fell in love with another man who fulfilled different emotional and physical needs than her spouse and said that "there was a lot of emotional involvement" with her lover. Eventually, she became "disillusioned" with this other man because he did not provide the emotional support she had hoped for and was able to reconcile with her husband because "He's no macho" and was thus willing to talk through their problems. Overall, men and women who saw themselves as younger often strove to enact modernity by attempting to link sex and emotion, as well as being different in love and sex than their parents.

Context-Dependent Ideals for Marital Sex

The kind of sex that the participants had with their spouses also varied in ways that often related to their ideas about the point of marriage. Younger men embarking on what they hoped would be companionate marriages often engaged in oral and manual stimulation with their wives, seeking to "keep sex exciting" so that they would not be tempted to stray. Similarly, after refocusing on her marriage, the doctor quoted earlier began to practice tantric sex with her husband to "develop a new way of communicating." She said that by sharing a rewarding sex life, as well as other activities such as cooking classes and joint household chores, "we've become a team."

The participants also held widely varying ideas about which sexual acts were desirable. These ideas related to the notions about gender, relationships, and sexuality that individuals incorporated into their composite masculinities, and these often mapped onto generational differences. Both my findings and survey research have shown that younger Mexicans view a wider range of sexual practices as acceptable compared with their elders (De la Peña and Toledo 1991). Across generations, some of the study participants saw practices such as oral or anal sex as normal, although all who did understood such acts to be supplementary to penile-vaginal intercourse. Yet the older participants, especially women, were more likely to say that they found oral or anal sex distasteful. In contrast, many younger women reported enjoying a wider range of sexual practices. Highlighting the generational differences among women, the college-age daughter of an IMSS staff member told me that although her mother believed she was a virgin and was opposed to premarital sex, she had been engaging in vaginal and oral sex with a range of partners. Although she knew that her mother would see this behavior as incompatible with respectable womanhood, she said she saw it as the normal way for a college student to behave and as a healthy form of "experimentation" on the path to finding love. Age-related differences in people's understandings of acceptable sexual practice varied most widely in the case of anal sex. Most of the older participants seemed somewhat horrified by the practice, reporting that even heterosexual anal sex carried the stigma of male homosexuality. A sixty-year-old patient, refusing a digital rectal exam, cried, "That's homosexual! I don't even touch my wife there because that area is homosexual!" Many of the younger participants were also reticent about this practice, but none stated that anal sex with a woman cast doubt on a man's heterosexuality.

Broadening the category of acceptable sexual behavior made sense for the mostly younger study participants who viewed sex as a key emotional engine of their marriages. For instance, a thirty-year-old husband said that communication is crucial for his marriage, both in and out of the bedroom, and trying new things sexually "so that it doesn't get monotonous" is important for providing a strong "base for the marriage." Similarly, when the thirty-six-year-old taxi driver discussed in chapter 2 decided to become faithful and more emotionally present in his marriage, he began to perform "exciting" acts, such as oral and manual sex, that he had previously done only with mistresses, in the context of marital sex. In this way, he sought to forge a more intimate sexual bond that would mirror his and his wife's growing emotional closeness. Similar to many of the men who sought to have self-consciously modern relationships, he was also moving away from the common idea that sex acts other than penile-vaginal penetration were acceptable during extramarital sex but inappropriate for good women and the mothers of one's children (Szasz 1998). Overall, the individuals who sought to incorporate what they saw as modern sexuality and gender norms into their composite masculinities were less likely to see sex acts as situation specific, whereas men foregrounding natural *machismo* tended to have vaginal sex with wives and reserve other activities for extramarital liaisons.

Generationally Specific Consequences of Erectile Difficulty

These different ways of relating sexual practice into one's composite masculinity led to diversity in men's responses to erectile difficulty. Because younger men frequently saw affective and passionate sex as a crucial element of companionate marriage, they perceived decreasing erectile function as having very different consequences than for men who viewed it as an opportunity to mature. As discussed in chapter 2, the older women whom I interviewed reported disinterest in sex and tended to encourage their husbands, when faced with decreased erectile function, to respectably age out of active sexuality rather than seek alternatives to vaginal penetration. Even chronologically older couples who did want to continue having sex often adhered to norms of sexuality that made the nonpenetrative options available to them feel impossible. For example, many of the older men and women reported that they did not see oral sex as an acceptable alternative if erectile difficulty made vaginal penetration impossible. They often cited religious concerns. When I asked a fifty-five-year-old woman, who cried during our interview about the fact that she and her husband had been unable to have sex for twenty years, if they had tried oral sex, she replied, "No because God doesn't want us to."

Conversely, even younger people I spoke with who described themselves as religious said that they believed they would try a range of acts if faced with erectile difficulty. Although this problem was rare among the younger men I spoke with, some reported trying various solutions for other sexual problems, such as premature ejaculation. For example, a twenty-five-year-old department store clerk had been living with his girlfriend for a year and said that she was very supportive about helping him with the rapid ejaculation that he had always experienced. He said that although he felt ashamed of his quick ejaculation, with her "there is the support I need to get over it . . . We can talk about it. The first time, she said it wasn't a big deal, maybe something passing; it could change." They have tried various solutions, including focusing on oral sex, and although he had not been able to prolong his time to ejaculation, he reported that "she's still supportive; we decided together that I should go to the doctor [and] seek professional help." The doctor prescribed Prozac, a common off-label treatment for premature ejaculation, and the study participant reported that he was looking forward to trying it with his partner. Couples such as this one who see sex as an important part of their emotional connection and value emotional closeness seem willing to seek a range of solutions to sexual problems that may include medical treatment.

Men of this younger generation thus seem more likely than their elders to seek medical ED treatment when faced with erectile function change that threatens the sexual passion they consider key to marital happiness. Although the older study participants were able to use decreasing erectile function as a way to forge new emotional bonds with their wives, today's younger men are likely to understand this bodily change as a threat to the emotional core of their relationships. As this latter group ages, ED drugs may become an attractive way for them to continue performing the penetrative sex and related emotional intimacy that form important aspects of their marriages and composite masculinities. For them, taking ED drugs may become a practice that demonstrates marital responsibility and also becomes an important component of their ways of being good men.

This shift is likely to be facilitated by increasing acceptance of pharmaceutical treatments as a healthy option because younger men may hold more firmly biomedical ideas of bodily function than their elders. When discussing medical treatments for a range of illnesses, the older study participants were more concerned with avoiding the dangerous side effects of the drugs and maintaining bodily balance, whereas the younger participants focused more on obtaining biomedical diagnoses for their illnesses and treating particular symptoms, not overall bodily well-being. The younger study participants more readily accepted pharmaceutical treatments for different problems, including erectile function change. A generational shift toward accepting biomedical ED treatment seems to be already occurring among working-class men in private practices. Dr. Peralta reported that her older patients seeking help for erectile difficulty generally ask for "vitamins" and frame their problem as one of general body vitality and balance, whereas younger men tell her that they have "erectile dysfunction" and ask for ED drugs by brand name.

However, just as the men in chapter 1 who considered themselves younger had chronological ages ranging into the nineties, an important caveat to this prediction is that categories such as age and generation are broad glosses for group tendencies that do not determine individual attitudes. Not all members of a generation or a group share the goals and ideals commonly attributed to that category, and even those that do may be unable to realize them. For example, although most of the older study participants saw male infidelity as a natural part of being a man, some men of this generation rejected this notion. Thus some younger men held what they characterized as traditional beliefs about marriage and manliness, whereas some chronologically older men held more companionate ideals. For example, a sixty-eight-year-old retired businessman told me that he loved his wife of forty years and had always been faithful because "when you have it at home, you're happy; you don't want to risk it, seek out problems." He said that his peers mocked him, attributing his faithfulness to "cowardliness, spinelessness." However, he believed that his fidelity strengthened the foundations of his marriage, explaining, "If you have love but not trust and respect, the love has an unstable foundation. There's danger. You need a base of trust and respect."

Thus, although this concluding chapter presents broad trends in the study participants' ways of understanding the role sex plays in marriage, which are shaped by the cultural contexts to which different generations of men have been exposed, it is important to note the great individual variation within these broad groups, as well as the fact that many men's attitudes change radically over time. While analyzing narratives such as those presented in this book can uncover patterns within people's responses to a particular experience, the composite approach reveals that these patterns are composed of unique incorporations of similar themes integrated into composite selves. The following case demonstrates the interaction of both perceived generational differences and individual change over time in a self-identified younger woman's unhappy marriage to an older man.

ANA: GENERATIONAL DIFFERENCES WITHIN A MARRIAGE

Ana's story demonstrates the way that different understandings of marriage, ideal masculinity, and the role of sex in love and manhood can occur—even within one couple. As a thirty-three-year-old former IMSS nurse who frequently returned to visit friends in the hospital, Ana told me that she and her husband's different notions of what their relationship should be, and how they should act as spouses and parents, had led to severe marital problems. A pretty and vivacious woman, Ana described herself as someone with strong feelings who felt trapped by the choices she had made and the life in which she found herself. Her discussion of the conflicts in her relationship revealed that she sought to include what she called "modern" gender roles, as well as participation in a companionate relationship, into her composite selfhood. She felt thwarted in these efforts by a husband who she characterized as enacting a "traditional" masculinity, marriage, and parenting style. She told me that she desired an egalitarian and sexually passionate relationship; she was frustrated by her husband's emotionally distant, patriarchal behavior, which she said led him to try to instill traditional understandings of gender in their children and seek sexual satisfaction outside the marriage.

Twelve years before our interview, when she was twenty-one years old, Ana married a fifty-three-year-old large animal veterinarian who had already fathered five children with three different women. In hindsight, she told me that she believed she had done so largely to escape from her controlling and abusive mother. Caught up in her feelings of love and desirous of the freedom of establishing her own household, she said that she ignored her and her husband's problematic differences, such as their discrepant beliefs about child rearing and her husband's unwillingness to participate in the activities she enjoyed. However, she said that these incompatibilities had become increasingly troubling and painful. It was clear that her and her husband's desires to incorporate very different styles of gender and marriage into their own composite selfhoods had left her feeling unable to be the kind of person she hoped to be.

Their different parental styles epitomized these differences. They had three children together—two girls who were eleven and twelve at the time of our interview and a six-year-old boy—and Ana said that she had long been upset about her husband's way of parenting them and his other children. For example, although she said that she tried to emotionally support his troubled sixteen-year-old son from a previous relationship, she believed that her husband "is authoritarian with him," to the point that he has developed psychological problems. As a self-described "open-minded" woman with many gay male friends, she was deeply troubled by her husband's insistence "that his sons have a strong manliness"; for example, when he saw his teenage son's ear piercing he yelled, "You look like a faggot!" She explicitly tried to "break this boundary," letting her young son wear pink shirts if he wanted to and encouraging him to express his emotions.

Ana said that she was also disturbed by the way her husband treated women, including herself, as "objects," not people with needs and emotions. She described having to constantly challenge his framings of women in ways she found undesirable. For example, she said that when he attempted to control his daughters, she told them, "We're in the twenty-first century, not the *Porfiriato*.[1] He doesn't understand that a woman can be self-sufficient, autonomous." She also counseled them to someday seek out husbands who are different from their own father, telling them to find "an intelligent man to get ahead in life with; even if he's ugly, look past that for a good man who's smart and treats you well. If I had to do it again, I wouldn't marry your father. He can't appreciate me." She told me that her husband expected her to focus on housework as a "traditional" wife would, although she was more interested in developing her and her children's minds through classes and outings, as well as having a satisfying career.

Although she no longer loved her husband, she told me that she felt that she had to stay with him for the sake of their children. Crying, she said that when she discussed the possibility of divorce with her children, they asked her to stay married, so she decided, "If the happiness of the children depends on him, I'll stay with him." She asked him if they could at least "live separate lives," which would allow her to date other men without feeling ethically compromised, a solution she felt he should accept because she knows he sleeps with other women. However, "as a selfish man," he refused. Feeling bereft over her failure to achieve the companionate marriage she desired, she decided to seek emotional closeness elsewhere. She told me, "You get tired of the lack of attention and care. You start to find what's missing with friends, colleagues, the closeness you don't get from him . . . I find love in sharing a coffee, in talking with my friends." Unable to have the kinds of interactions that she wanted to include in a modern femininity with her husband, she sought to create them elsewhere. However, to continue including living out her idea of good motherhood in her composite selfhood, she remained in her unhappy marriage.

1 The period from 1876 to 1911 during which the conservative dictator Porfirio Díaz ruled Mexico, which was ended by the Mexican revolution.

Despite her distaste for her spouse's way of being a husband, father, and man, Ana said that she continued to try to improve the marriage she was "stuck" in, striving to move it toward her companionate ideal both emotionally and sexually. Ana told me that her marital sex life had never been fulfilling because she desired emotion-laden sex and an exciting variety of sex acts, whereas her husband was "very monotonous" in bed. She said that he always wanted the same, limited sex life, but she tried to initiate new things; "I said, 'Learn my body, touch me, so that I also feel pleasure.'" She told me that she likes oral and anal sex, but for these to be enjoyable, one's partner needed to have patience and, for the latter, use lubrication. However, he was not willing to do use these techniques because "he was not interested in giving me pleasure." Nevertheless, Ana said that because she had to stay with him, she kept trying to "rediscover love—to find something new in him"—by forging deeper sexual intimacy. She has tried to "seek sensuality, passion, craziness. I'll say let's do it in the car at night or in a hotel. He says, 'No, that's why we have a house.'" Despite her dislike for her husband, Ana still sought to include companionate sexuality into her composite femininity. The kind of marital sexuality she sought unfortunately clashed with her husband's desire to include adherence to a historically older sexual double standard, in which men have "respectable" sex with wives and adventurous sex extramaritally, in his composite masculinity.

Her attempts to improve their sex life and relationship have included suggesting a range of ED treatments. For a long time, she said, "the physical contact hasn't been so much" between her and her husband because he had difficulty achieving erections. She attributed this problem to his hypertension and work stress and sought advice from one of the IMSS urologists. Eventually, drawing authority from her work as a nurse, she told her husband both to relax and take a multivitamin, arranging a vacation during which he could recover from the pressures of his job. She said that these interventions did make it easier for him to attain erections. Unfortunately, Ana and her husband still had very different ideas about how these erections should be used and what their sex life and marriage should be. Thus she said that their sex life had not really improved, despite his use of measures to increase his erectile function.

The incompatibility among the styles of gender, marriage, sexuality, and parenting through which, according to Ana, each partner sought to be a particular kind of person demonstrates the centrality of relationships to both forming and constraining one's composite gendered selfhood. The differences in Ana's marriage exemplified the different attitudes about marriage, manliness, and sex common among the study participants. Her story also shows how ED treatment may be important to people who see marital sex as a site for forging emotional intimacy, although the use, function, and outcome of such treatment is profoundly context dependent.

Advantages of the Composite Approach

Ana's story demonstrates the pain that can arise when people in a relationship have different ideas about how men and women, parents, sex, and marriage should be. Throughout this book, many study participants voiced similar pain. This sometimes stemmed from their inability to be the kind of men they wanted or felt that others wanted them to be, because they did not have the bodies, resources, or relationships needed to link together into composite selves they hoped to create. Their experiences show that although men themselves construct their composite masculinities, they do so from the hands they were dealt. Men striving to be particular kinds of husbands, fathers, and lovers attempt to link acts, attitudes, and experiences constrained by their bodies, social worlds, and structural settings into these ways of being men. Depending on the gulf between their desires and constraints, some felt successful, whereas others believed that they were failing to be the kinds of men they wanted to be. Such failures not only caused great social suffering but also became inescapable elements of their composite masculinities, influencing their future ways of being men and their perceived ability to incorporate new elements into their composite selfhoods. Furthermore, the study participants often crafted composite masculinities that diverged from the ideals held by their loved ones, as demonstrated by Johnny and Mayra's unceasing argument over how he should be a man after his penectomy. These disjunctions led to marital, familial, and social strife.

By answering calls from gender studies and anthropology to highlight relationality and change within masculinity, not only among men and on the societal level but also within individual men's lived enactments of gender over time (Connell and Messerschmidt 2005; Inhorn and Wentzell 2011), the composite approach sheds light on this pain and the ways people seek to avoid it. This final section describes the key ways in which the composite perspective enables the study of men's concrete ways of being men and their changes over time and in context. It discusses how using this approach sheds light on the relationship of agency and constraint in gendered self-making, the social deployment of notions of gender as natural, the ways that people can reconcile seemingly incompatible aspects of their ways of being men, and the interplay between gender and other elements of individual selves. Finally, it discusses the political utility of this approach, which can be applied by people seeking to alter composite gendered selves that cause social suffering.

By offering a way to track the changing elements that comprise individual ways of being men and their shifting relationships, the composite approach enables an analysis of how men's lived experiences of social, structural, and physical constraint influenced their ability to craft desired composite masculinities. In their descriptions of experiences with erectile difficulty, aging, and illness, the study participants described feeling that the possible ways in which they could be men were limited by factors ranging from bodily weakness to economic deprivation to innate Mexican *machismo*. They constructed composite masculinities from the elements that they experienced as available and often felt forced to include unwanted but inescapable elements, such as sickness. By revealing the range of ways in which individuals feel able or required to be men, the composite approach sheds light on the agentive ways that men craft gendered selves within the constraints that they experience.

This perspective also highlights the different ways that men related to beliefs about natural bodily desires and urges over time. Even men who felt constitutionally predisposed to enact macho behaviors by their Mexican bodies "gave in to" or "resisted" these impulses at various life points, depending on the other elements they were incorporating into their composite masculinities. Men often reported living out *machismo* when they were seeking to construct masculinities foregrounding youth, health, and virility but later incorporated cessation of these traits into masculinities centered on maturity, through which they incorporated aging and illness into their ways of being men. Conversely, men incorporating modernity into their composite masculinities often also included rejection of the notion of *machismo* as innate. The participants responded to changing bodies and social worlds by incorporating different culturally intelligible practices of manliness into their composite masculinities and found varying practices possible, desirable, and appropriate at specific life points. The composite approach is thus helpful for evaluating how people deploy notions of the natural in the service of enacting particular forms of gendered selfhood and coping with the forces that constrain them.

Along these lines, this approach also provides a nonreductive way to understand how men may simultaneously resist and enact specific cultural archetypes of masculinity. Many of the study participants reported concurrent and often conflicting beliefs that their manly actions and impulses were natural, appropriate, and socially negative. For example, the same men who believed their innate *machismo* caused their frequent youthful infidelity argued that younger generations of men would have to enact different, more modern gender practices. Viewing men's own beliefs about the nature of masculinity as composite makes this seeming contradiction—that their bad behavior is natural whereas younger men's is learned—make sense. The narratives presented here demonstrate that either over time or all at once, men may incorporate a range of different and conflicting beliefs about and embodiments of manliness into their composite masculinities. By offering a way to map and understand this lived disjunction, the composite perspective builds on earlier models of masculinity that account for power-laden differences among men enacting different styles of masculinity, to highlight inconsistency, disjunction, and change within individual men's gendered selfhoods.

The composite approach is also a useful way for studying personhood more broadly, including aspects of self not directly related to gender or health. This book has shown that other key aspects of selfhood, such as people's understandings of health and the body, can also be fruitfully understood as composites. For example, it showed that the study participants frequently rejected ED drugs, although they used biomedical treatments for other ailments, because they saw them as inappropriate for their complex bodies and social situations. The composite perspective sheds light on the ways that individual men weave biomedical, emotional, and humoral understandings of illness causation into their illness experiences, in ways that make social sense. Furthermore, it is useful for understanding the simultaneous contributions of bodily predisposition, individual action, and structural constraint to incidences of chronic illness, as well as for understanding the logic behind men's treatment choices. As with the study participants' complex understandings of masculinity as simultaneously biological and social, innate and deliberate, composite understandings of their illness experiences shed light on their treatment choices. This approach illuminates men's attempts to choose appropriate treatments for situations they saw as simultaneously physical and social, making sense of their simultaneous rejection and adoption of various biomedical interventions.

Overall, in its applicability to multiple areas of life, the composite perspective can shed light on people's holistic practices of self-making. It is useful at different levels of analysis, from composite masculinities and illness experiences to the composite selves that integrate illness and gender. Although they focus on particular elements of life in particular contexts, people constantly integrate and interrelate changing ranges of acts, attitudes, and experiences into their senses of who they are. Applied to observational or narrative data, the composite perspective enables an analysis of specific ways that individuals do selfhood. It reveals how people construct and revise the relationships among the very different elements that make them who they are as they inhabit changing bodies, move through shifting social contexts, and encounter new structural constraints. In short, a composite approach to personhood is one that uncovers specific intersections of relationality, embodiment, and practice at a particular time and place.

This book has focused on the concrete mechanics of masculinity, detailing how men incorporated decreased erectile function and related changes into their revisions of their ways of being men. However, it ends with a reminder that neither the social suffering that stems from both men's inability to achieve desired masculinities nor their achievement of ways of being men that hurt others are inevitable. Just as decreased erectile function does not necessarily need to be interpreted as the medical pathology ED, and doing so requires a host of deliberate practices on multiple societal levels, the participants' definitions of the right ways to be men overall depended on a range of practices and experiences.

When presenting the notion of disease conditions as composite objects, Annemarie Mol wrote, "If reality is multiple, it is also political" (2002, 7). This statement suggests that the process of tracing the social work involved in making a seemingly natural and singular entity "be" can also uncover the power dynamics and cultural contingency involved in the very existence of things. My aim in emphasizing the multiplicity inherent in a class of things that have great, daily life consequences for the way people see themselves and treat each other—gendered selfhoods, sexual health diagnoses, relationships, and health beliefs—is to show how people do and might change these things over time. Tracing how seemingly straightforward things are made to seem coherent through practice opens them to the possibility of reconfiguration through different practices.

My hope is that this book provides a clear way to assess the sources, interaction, and consequences of different elements of individuals' composite gendered selfhoods. This analytic can be useful for the academic analysis of how people do gender and how and why their ways of doing so change over time. However, it may also have an applied use, facilitating change in men's ways of being men that cause social suffering. By asserting that masculinities can be conceived of as composite in nature, this book shows that even in the face of sets of similar constraints and experiences, people can forge very different masculine selfhoods, which shape their and their loved ones' daily lives for better or worse. The composite approach thus holds the promise of moving denaturalization arguments beyond the abstract to the concrete, enabling scholars and activists to trace how and why people might link certain elements into certain ways of being men, and how they could do so differently.

Bibliography

Adler Lomnitz, Larissa, and Rodrigo Salazar. "Cultural Elements in the Practice of Law in Mexico: Informal Networks in a Formal System." In *Global Prescriptions: The Production, Exportation, and Importation of a New Legal Orthodoxy*, edited by Yves Dezalay and Bryant G. Garth, 209–248. Ann Arbor: University of Michigan Press, 2002.

Aguilar-Salinas, Carlos A., Rosalba Rojas, Francisco J. Gomez-Perez, Victoria Valles, Juan M. Ríos-Torres, Aurora Franco, Gustavo Olaiz, Juan A. Rull, and Jaime Sepúlveda. "High Prevalence of Metabolic Syndrome in Mexico." *Archives of Medical Research* 35, no. 1 (2004): 76–81.

Alcoholicos Anónimos. "Central Mexicana de Servicios Generales de Alcohólicos Anónimos, A.C." Copyright 2012. http://www.aamexico.org.mx.

Amuchástegui, Ana. "Partner Violence, Technologies of the Self, and Masculinity in Mexico." *Culture, Society and Masculinities* 1, no. 2 (2009): 155.

Amuchástegui, Ana, and Peter Aggleton. "'I Had a Guilty Conscience Because I Wasn't Going to Marry Her': Ethical Dilemmas for Mexican Men in Their Sexual Relationships with Women." *Sexualities* 10, no. 1 (2007): 61–81.

Amuchástegui, Ana, and Ivonne Szasz, eds. *Sucede que me Canso de ser Hombre: Relatos y Reflexiones sobre Hombres y Masculinidades en México*. Mexico City: El Colegio de México, 2007.

Anderson, E. N., Jr. "Why Is Humoral Medicine So Popular?" *Social Science and Medicine* 25, no. 4 (1987): 331–337.

Baca Zinn, Maxine. "Chicano Men and Masculinity." *Journal of Ethnic Studies* 10, no. 2 (1982): 29–44.

Baer, Roberta D., Susan C. Weller, Javier G. De alba Garcia, Mark Glaser, Robert Trotter, Lee Pachter, and Robert E. Klein. "A Cross-Cultural Approach to the Study of the Folk Illness Nervios." *Culture, Medicine and Psychiatry* 27 (2003): 315–337.

Baglia, Jay. *The Viagra Ad Venture: Masculinity, Media, and the Performance of Sexual Health*. New York: Peter Lang Publishing, 2005.

Barroso-Aguirre, Javier, Fernando Ugarte y Romano, and Diana Pimentel-Nieto. "Prevalencia de Disfunción Eréctil en Hombres de 18 a 40 Años en México y

Factores de Riesgo Asociados." *Perinatol Reproducción Humana* 15 (2001): 254–261.

Becker, Gay. *Disrupted Lives: How People Create Meaning in a Chaotic World.* Berkeley: University of California Press, 1997.

Berg, Mark, and Annemarie Mol, eds. *Differences in Medicine: Unraveling Practices, Techniques, and Bodies.* Durham, NC: Duke University Press, 1998.

Bledsoe, Caroline H. *Contingent Lives: Fertility, Time, and Aging in West Africa.* Chicago: University of Chicago Press, 2002.

Bliss, Katherine. "Paternity Tests: Fatherhood on Trial in Mexico's Revolution of the Family." *Journal of Family History* 24, no. 3 (1999): 330–350.

Bolton, Ralph. "Coming Home: The Journey of a Gay Ethnographer in the Years of the Plague." In *Out in the Field: Reflections of Lesbian and Gay Anthropologists,* edited by Ellen Lewin and William Leap, 147–199. Urbana-Champaign: University of Illinois Press, 1996.

Brandes, Stanley. *Staying Sober in Mexico City.* Austin: University of Texas Press, 2002.

———. "Drink, Abstinence, and Male Identity in Mexico City." In *Changing Men and Masculinities in Latin America,* edited by Matthew C. Gutmann, 153–178. Durham, NC: Duke University Press, 2003.

Brusco, Elizabeth. "The Reformation of Masculinity: Asceticism and Masculinity among Colombian Evangelicals." In *Rethinking Protestantism in Latin America,* edited by V. Garrard-Burnett and D. Stoll, 143–158. Philadelphia: Temple University Press, 1993.

Carillo, Héctor. *The Night Is Young: Sexuality in Mexico in the Time of AIDS.* Chicago: University of Chicago Press, 2002.

———. "Imagining Modernity: Sexuality, Policy, and Social Change in Mexico." *Sexuality Research and Social Policy: Journal of NSRC* 4, no. 3 (2007): 74–91.

Carpenter, Laura M., and John D. DeLamater. "Studying Gendered Sexualities over the Life Course: A Conceptual Framework." In *Sex for Life: From Virginity to Viagra, How Sexuality Changes throughout Our Lives,* edited by Laura M. Carpenter and John D. DeLamater, 23–44. New York: New York University Press, 2012.

Carrier, Joseph. *De Los Otros: Intimacy and Homosexuality among Mexican Men.* New York: Columbia University Press, 1995.

———. "Reflections on Ethical Problems Encountered in Field Research on Mexican Male Homosexuality: 1968 to Present." *Culture, Health and Sexuality* 1, no. 3 (1999): 207–221.

Clarke, Adele E. *Situational Analysis: Grounded Theory after the Postmodern Turn.* Thousand Oaks, CA: SAGE Publications, 2005.

Clarke, Adele E., Janet K. Shim, Laura Mamo, Jennifer R. Fosket, and Jennifer R. Fishman. "Biomedicalization: Technoscientific Transformations of Health,

Illness, and U.S. Biomedicine." *American Sociological Review* 68, no. 2 (2003): 161–194.

CNN. "Elderly Men to Get Free Viagra in Mexico City." Last modified November 14, 2008. http://edition.cnn.com/2008/WORLD/americas/11/14/mexico.city.viagra/.

CNN Expansión. "El Salario Mínimo Aumenta 4% en 2008." Last modified December 21, 2007. http://www.cnnexpansion.com/actualidad/2007/12/21/salario-minimo-aumenta-4-en-2008.

Coca-Cola Company. "Per Capita Consumption of Company Beverage Products." Last modified 2008. http://www.thecoca-colacompany.com/ourcompany/ar/pdf/perCapitaConsumption2007.pdf.

Comisión Interinstitucional del Cuadro Básico de Insumos del Sector Salud. *Cuadro Básico y Catálogo de Medicamentos.* Mexico City: Consejo de Salubridad General, 2009.

Congress, E. P. "Cultural Differences in Health Beliefs: Implications for Social Work Practice in Health Care Settings." *Social Work in Health Care* 17 (1992): 81–96.

Connell, R. W., and James W. Messerschmidt. "Hegemonic Masculinity: Rethinking the Concept." *Gender and Society* 19, no. 6 (2005): 829–859.

Conrad, Peter, and Valerie Leiter. "Medicalization, Markets and Consumers." *Journal of Health and Social Behavior* 45 (2004): 158–176.

De la Peña, Ricardo, and Rosario Toledo. "Vida ¿en Pareja? El Sexo en México. Primer Informe. (Part 3)." *El Nacional Dominical,* June 9, 1991.

Demetriou, Demetrakis Z. "Connell's Concept of Hegemonic Masculinity: A Critique." *Theory and Society* 30 (2001): 337–361.

Dirección General de Información y Evaluación del Desempeño, Secretaria de Salud. "Estadísticas de Mortalidad en México: Muertes Registradas en el Año 2001." *Salud Pública de México* 44 (2003): 565–576.

Dow, James W. "The Expansion of Protestantism in Mexico: An Anthropological View." *Anthropological Quarterly* 78, no. 4 (2005): 827–850.

El Economista.mx. "Cuelgan Cadáveres de Cuatro Hombres en Cuernavaca." *El Economista,* August 22, 2010. http://eleconomista.com.mx/seguridad-publica/2010/08/22/cuelgan-cadaveres-cuatro-hombres-cuernavaca.

Ewing, Katherine P. "The Illusion of Wholeness: Culture, Self, and the Experience of Inconsistency." *Ethos* 18, no. 3 (1990): 251–278.

Fausto-Sterling, Anne. "The Bare Bones of Sex: Part 1—Sex and Gender." *Signs* 30, no. 2 (2005): 1491–1527.

Finkler, Kaja. *Physicians at Work, Patients in Pain: Biomedical Practice and Patient Response in Mexico.* Boulder, CO: Westview Press, 1991.

———. *Women in Pain: Gender and Morbidity in Mexico.* Philadelphia: University of Pennslyania Press, 1994.

Foster, George M. *Hippocrates' Latin American Legacy: Humoral Medicine in the New World*. Langhorne, PA: Gordon and Breach, 1994.

Frenk, Julio, Jaime Sepúlveda, Octavio Gómez-Dantés, and Felicia Knaul. "Evidence-Based Health Policy: Three Generations of Reform in Mexico." *Lancet* 362, no. 9396 (2005): 1667–1671.

García, Brígida, and Orlandina de Oliveira. "El Ejercicio de la Paternidad en el México Urbano." In *Imágenes de la Familia en el Cambio de Siglo*, edited by Marina Ariza and Orlandina de Oliveira, 283–320. Coyoacan, México City: Instituto de Investigaciones Sociales, Universidad Nacional Autónoma de México, 2004.

Garda, Roberto. "'I Want to Recover Those Things I Damaged': The Experience of Men's Groups Working to Stop Violence in Mexico." *Development* 44, no. 3 (2001): 104–106.

González-López, Gloria. *Erotic Journeys: Mexican Immigrants and Their Sex Lives*. Berkeley: University of California Press, 2005.

Guarnaccia, Peter J., Melissa Rivera, Felipe Franco, and Charlie Neighbors. "The Experiences of Ataques de Nervios: Towards an Anthropology of Emotions in Puerto Rico." *Culture, Medicine and Psychiatry* 20 (1996): 343–367.

Gutiérrez Arriola, Angelina. *México Dentro de la Reformas a los Sistemas de Salud y Seguridad Social de América Latina*. Mexico City: UNAM Instituto de Investigaciones Económicas, 2002.

Gutmann, Matthew C. *The Meanings of Macho: Being a Man in Mexico City*. Berkeley: University of California Press, 1996.

———. "Trafficking in Men: The Anthropology of Masculinity." *Annual Review of Anthropology* 26 (1997): 385–409.

———. *Fixing Men: Sex, Birth Control, and AIDS in Mexico*. Berkeley: University of California Press, 2007.

———. "The Missing Gamete? Ten Common Mistakes or Lies about Men's Sexual Destiny." In *Reconceiving the Second Sex: Men, Masculinity and Reproduction*, edited by Marcia C. Inhorn, Tine Tjornhoj-Thomsen, Helene Goldberg, and Maruska la Cour Mosegaard, 21–45. New York: Berghahn Books, 2009.

Hearn, Jeff. "From Older Men to Boys: Masculinity Theory and the Life Course(s). *Norma: Nordic Journal for Masculinity Studies* 2, no. 1 (2007): 79–84.

Herdt, Gilbert, and Shirley Lindenbaum. *The Time of AIDS: Social Analysis, Theory, and Method*. Thousand Oaks, CA: SAGE Publications, 1992.

Hirsch, Jennifer. *A Courtship after Marriage: Sexuality and Love in Mexican Transnational Families*. Berkeley: University of California Press, 2003.

Hirsch, Jennifer, and Sergio Meneses Navarro. "'Que Gusto Estar de Vuelta en mi Tierra': The Sexual Geography of Transnational Migration." In *Mobility,*

Sexuality and AIDS, edited by Felicity Thomas, Mary Haour Knipe, and Peter Aggleton, 131–142. New York: Routledge, 2009.

Huerta Rojas, Fernando. "El Cuerpo Masculino como Escenario de la Vasectomía: Una Experiencia con un Grupo de Hombres de las Ciudades de México y Puebla." In *Sucede que me Canso de ser Hombre: Relatos y Reflexiones sobre Hombres y Masculinidades en México*, edited by Ana Amuchástegui and Ivonne Szasz, 479–518. Mexico City: El Colegio de México, 2007.

Illich, Ivan. "Medical Nemesis." *Lancet* 11, no. 1 (1974): 918–921.

INEGI. *Delimitación de las Zonas Metropolitanas de México 2005*. Mexico City: Instituto Nacional de Estadística, Geografía e Informática, 2007.

———. *Mujeres y Hombres en México 2009*. Mexico City: Instituto Nacional de Estadística, Geografía e Informática, 2009.

———. "Censo de Población y Vivienda 2010." http://www.censo2010.org.mx/.

Inhorn, Marcia C. "Middle Eastern Masculinities in the Age of New Reproductive Technologies." *Medical Anthropology Quarterly* 18, no. 2 (2004): 162–182.

———. *The New Arab Man: Emergent Masculinities and Islam in the Middle East*. Princeton, NJ: Princeton University Press, 2012.

Inhorn, Marcia C., and Emily Wentzell. "Embodying Emergent Masculinities: Reproductive and Sexual Health Technologies in the Middle East and Mexico." *American Ethnologist* 38, no. 4 (2011): 801–815.

Jackson, Michael. *Minima Ethnographica: Intersubjectivity and the Anthropological Project*. Chicago: University of Chicago Press, 1998.

Jaspersen-Gastelum, J., J. A. Rodríguez, F. J. Espinosa de los Monteros, L. Beas-Sandoval, José Guzmán-Esquivel, D. D. Calvo, and T. Gutiérrez. "Prostatic Profile, Premature Ejaculation, Erectile Function and Andropause in an At-Risk Mexican Population." *International Urology and Nephrology* 41, no. 2 (2008): 303–312.

Jiménez Guzman, Lucero. *Dando Voz a Los Varones: Sexualidad, Reproducción y Paternidad de Algunos Mexicanos*. Cuernavaca, Morelos: Universidad Nacional Autónoma de México, Centro Regional de Investigaciones Multidisciplinarias, 2003.

Katz, Stephen, and Barbara Marshall. "New Sex for Old: Lifestyle, Consumerism, and the Ethics of Aging Well." *Journal of Aging Studies* 17, no. 1 (2002): 3–16.

King, H., R. E. Aubert, and W. H. Herman. "Global Burden of Diabetes, 1995–2025: Prevalence, Numerical Estimates, and Projections." *Diabetes Care* 21 (1998): 1414–1431.

Kirkland, Anna, and Jonathan Metzl, eds. *Against Health: How Health Became the New Morality*. New York: New York University Press, 2010.

Kleinman, Arthur. *The Illness Narratives*. New York: Basic Books, 1988.

Kubin, M., G. Wagner, and A. Fugl-Meyer. "Epidemiology of Erectile Dysfunction." *International Journal of Impotence Research* 15 (2003): 63–71.

Latour, Bruno. *Science in Action: How to Follow Scientists and Engineers through Society.* Cambridge, MA: Harvard University Press, 1987.

Lerman, I. G., A. R. Villa, C. L. Martinez, L. Cervantes Turrubiatez, C. A. Aguilar Salinas, B. Wong, F. J. Goméz Pérez, and L. M. Gutierrez Robledo. "The Prevalence of Diabetes and Associated Coronary Risk Factors in Urban and Rural Older Mexican Populations." *Journal of the American Geriatrics Society* 46, no. 11 (1998): 1387–1395.

Lizza, E. F., and R. C. Rosen. "Definition and Classification of Erectile Dysfunction: Report of the Nomenclature Committee of the International Society of Impotence Research." *International Journal of Impotence Research* 11 (1999): 141–143.

Loe, Meika. "The Viagra Blues: Embracing or Resisting the Viagra Body." In *Medicalized Masculinities*, edited by Dana Rosenfeld and Christopher A. Faircloth, 21–44. Philadelphia: Temple University Press, 2006.

Lumsden, Ian. *Homosexuality, Society and the State in Mexico.* Toronto: Canadian Gay Archives, 1991.

Mamo, L., and J. Fishman. "Potency in All the Right Places: Viagra as a Technology of the Gendered Body." *Body and Society* 7, no. 4 (2001): 13–35.

Manderson, Lenore. "Hot-Cold Food and Medical Theories: Overview and Introduction." *Social Science and Medicine* 25, no. 4 (1987): 329–330.

Manderson, Lenore, and Carolyn Smith-Morris, eds. *Chronic Conditions, Fluid States: Chronicity and the Anthropology of Illness.* New Brunswick, NJ: Rutgers University Press, 2010.

McKee Irwin, Robert. *Mexican Masculinities.* Minneapolis: University of Minnesota Press, 2003.

McKinnon, Susan, and Sydel Silverman. *Complexities: Beyond Nature and Nurture.* Chicago: University of Chicago Press, 2005.

McLaren, Angus. *Impotence: A Cultural History.* Chicago: University of Chicago Press, 2007.

McMurray, Christine, and Roy Smith. *Diseases of Globalization: Socioeconomic Transitions and Health.* London: Earthscan Publications, 2001.

Melhuus, Marit. "Configuring Gender: Male and Female in Mexican Heterosexual and Homosexual Relations." *Ethnos* 63, no. 3 (1998): 353–382.

Melhuus, Marit, and Kristi Anne Stolen. "Introduction." In *Machos, Mistresses, Madonnas: Contesting the Power of Latin American Gender Imagery*, edited by Marit Melhuus and Kristi Anne Stolen, 1–33. London: Verso, 1996.

Melman, Arnold, and J. Clive Gingell. "The Epidemiology and Pathophysiology of Erectile Dysfunction." *Journal of Urology* 16, no. 1 (1999): 5–11.

Messner, Ellen. "The Hot and Cold in Mesoamerican Indigenous and Hispanicized Thought." *Social Science and Medicine* 25, no. 4 (1987): 339–346.

Mintz, Sidney W., and Christine M. Du Bois. "The Anthropology of Food and Eating." *Annual Review of Anthropology* 31 (2002): 99–119.

Mol, Annemarie. *The Body Multiple: Ontology in Medical Practice*. Durham, NC: Duke University Press, 2002.

Moreno, Pedro, Silvia Tamez, and Claudia Ortiz. "Social Security in Mexico." In *State of Working in México, 2003*, edited by Enrique de la Garza and Carlos Salas, http://www.solidaritycenter.org/files/WorkingMexicoChapter10.pdf. Washington, DC: Solidarity Center, 2003.

National Diabetes Information Clearinghouse. "Diabetes." Last modified August 20, 2012. http://diabetes.niddk.nih.gov.

National Institute of Diabetes and Digestive and Kidney Diseases. "Erectile Dysfunction." Last modified March 28, 2012. http://kidney.niddk.nih.gov /kudiseases/pubs/impotence/.

National Institutes of Health. "Prostrate Cancer." Last modified June 2011. http://nihseniorhealth.gov/prostatecancer/symptomsanddiagnosis/01.html.

National Kidney and Urologic Diseases Information Clearinghouse. "Prostate Enlargement: Benign Prostatic Hyperplasia." Last modified March 23, 2012. http://kidney.niddk.nih.gov/kudiseases/pubs/prostateenlargement/.

National Library of Medicine. "Enlarged Prostate." Last modified September 19, 2011. http://www.nlm.nih.gov/medlineplus/ency/article/000381.htm.

Nichter, Mark, and Nancy Vuckovic. "Agenda for an Anthropology of Pharmaceutical Practice." *Social Science and Medicine* 39, no. 11 (1994): 1509–1525.

Núñez Noriega, Guillermo. "Vínculo de Pareja y Hombría: 'Atender y Mantener' en Adultos Mayores del Río Sonora, México." In *Sucede que me Canso de ser Hombre: Relatos y Reflexiones sobre Hombres y Masculinidades en México*, edited by Ana Amuchástegui and Ivonne Szasz, 141–184. Mexico City: El Colegio de México, 2007.

Nye, Robert A. "The Evolution of the Concept of Medicalization in the Late Twentieth Century." *Journal of History of the Behavioral Sciences* 39, no. 2 (2003): 115–129.

Ochs, Elinor, and Lisa Capps. "Narrating the Self." *Annual Review of Anthropology* 25 (1996): 19–43.

Oliffe, John. "Constructions of Masculinity Following Prostatectomy-Induced Impotence." *Social Science and Medicine* 60 (2005): 2249–2259.

Olsson, A. M., M. J. Speakman, W. W. Dinsmore, F. Giuliano, C. Gingell, M. Maytom, M. D. Smith, I. Osterloh, and Sildenafil Multicentre Study Group. "Sildenafil Citrate (Viagra) Is Effective and Well Tolerated for Treating Erectile Dysfunction of Psychogenic or Mixed Aetiology. *International Journal of Clinical Practice* 54, no. 9 (2000): 561–566.

Omran, Abdel R. "The Epidemiologic Transition: A Theory of the Epidemiology of Population Change." *Milbank Memorial Fund Quarterly* 49, no. 4 (1971): 509–538.

Padilla, Mark B. "From Sex Workers to Tourism Workers: A Structural Approach to Male Sexual Labor in Dominican Tourism Areas." In *Globalization,*

Reproduction and the State, edited by Carole H. Browner and Carolyn F. Sargent, 159–174. Durham, NC: Duke University Press, 2011.

Parédes, Americo. "Estados Unidos, México y el Machismo." *Journal of Inter-American Studies* 9 (1967): 65–84.

Parker, Richard G. *Bodies, Pleasures, and Passions: Sexual Culture in Contemporary Brazil.* Boston: Beacon Press, 1991.

Paz, Octavio. *The Labyrinth of Solitude and Other Writings.* Translated in 1961 by L. Kemp. New York: Grove Weidenfeld, 1985.

Penson, David F., and June M. Chan. "Prostate Cancer." Accessed January 12, 2009. http://kidney.niddk.nih.gov/statistics/uda/Prostate_Cancer-Chapter03 .pdf.

Petryna, Adriana, and Arthur Kleinman. "The Pharmaceutical Nexus." In *Global Pharmaceuticals: Ethics, Markets, Practices*, edited by Adriana Petryna, Andrew Lakoff, and Arthur Kleinman, 1–32. Durham, NC: Duke University Press, 2006.

Phillips, M., and J. Salmerón. "Diabetes in Mexico: A Serious and Growing Problem." *World Health Statistics Quarterly* 45, no. 4 (1992): 338–346.

Potts, Annie, Victoria Grace, Nicola Gavey, and Tiina Vares. "Viagra Stories: Challenging 'Erectile Dysfunction.'" *Social Science and Medicine* 59 (2004): 489–499.

———. "'Sex for Life'? Men's Counter-Stories on 'Erectile Dysfunction,' Male Sexuality and Ageing." *Sociology of Health and Illness* 28, no. 3 (2006): 306–329.

Prieur, Annick. "Domination and Desire: Male Homosexuality and the Construction of Masculinity in Mexico." In *Machos, Mistresses, Madonnas: Contesting the Power of Latin American Gender Imagery*, edited by Marit Melhuus and Kristi Anne Stolen, 83–107. London: Verso, 1996.

———. *Mema's House, Mexico City: On Transvestites, Queens, and Machos.* Chicago: University of Chicago Press, 1998.

Ramirez, Josué. *Against Machismo: Young Adult Voices in Mexico City.* New York: Berghahn Books, 2009.

Rasmussen, Susan. "Dymanic Processes and the Anthropology of Emotions in the Life Course and Aging: Late-Life Love Sentiments and Household Dynamics in Tuareg Psycho-Biographies." In *Dynamic Process Methodology in the Social and Developmental Sciences*, edited by Jean Valsiner, Peter C. M. Molenaar, Maria C. D. P. Lyra, and Nandita Chaudhary, 541–566. New York: Springer, 2009.

Ratsch, Christian. *Plants of Love: Aphrodisiacs in Myth, History, and the Present.* Berkeley, CA: Ten Speed Press, 1997.

Rebhun, L. A. "Nerves and Emotional Play in Northeast Brazil." *Medical Anthropology Quarterly* 7, no. 2 (1993): 131–151.

————. *The Heart Is Unknown Country: Love in the Changing Economy of Northeast Brazil*. Stanford, CA: Stanford University Press, 1999.

Romero, Rolando, and Amanda Nolacea Harris, eds. *Feminism, Nation and Myth: La Malinche*. Houston, TX: Arte Publico Press, 2005.

Rosen, Raymond C. "Psychogenic Erectile Dysfunction: Classification and Management." *Urologic Clinics of North America* 28, no. 2 (2001): 269–278.

Rubel, Arthur J., Carl W. O'Nell, and Rolando Collado-Ardón. *Susto: A Folk Illness*. Berkeley: University of California Press, 1985.

Rubin, Gayle. "The Traffic in Women." In *Toward an Anthropology of Women*, edited by Rayna R. Reiter, 157–210. New York: Monthly Review Press, 1975.

Salguero Velásquez, Ma. Alejandra. "Preguntarse cómo ser Padre es También Preguntarse cómo ser Hombre: Reflexiones sobre Algunos Varones." In *Sucede que me Canso de ser Hombre: Relatos y Reflexiones sobre Hombres y Masculinidades en México*, edited by Ana Amuchástegui and Ivonne Szasz, 563–602. Mexico City: El Colegio de México, 2007.

Sato, Kanji. "Formation of La Raza and the Anti-Chinese Movement in Mexico." *Transforming Anthropology* 14, no. 2 (2006): 181–186.

Scheper-Hughes, Nancy, and Margaret M. Lock. "The Mindful Body: A Prolegomenon to Future Work in Medical Anthropology." *Medical Anthropology Quarterly* 1, no. 1 (1987): 6–41.

Steigenga, Timothy J., and Edward L. Cleary, eds. *Conversion of a Continent: Contemporary Religious Change in Latin America*. New Brunswick, NJ: Rutgers University Press, 2007.

Stern, Alexandra. "From Mestizophilia to Biotypology: Racialization and Science in Mexico, 1920–1960." In *Race and Nation in Modern Latin America*, edited by Nancy P. Appelbaum, Anne S. and Karin A. Macpherson, Rosemblatt, 187–210. Chapel Hill: University of North Carolina Press, 2003.

Szasz, Ivonne. "Masculine Identity and the Meanings of Sexuality: A Review of Research in Mexico." *Reproductive Health Matters* 6, no. 12 (1998): 97–104.

Tarrant, Anna. "'Maturing' a Sub-discipline: The Intersectional Geographies of Masculinities and Old Age." *Geography Compass* 4, no. 10 (2010): 1580–1591.

Thompson, Charis. *Making Parents: The Ontological Choreography of Reproductive Technologies*. Cambridge, MA: MIT Press, 2007.

Tiefer, Leonore. "The Medicalization of Impotence: Normalizing Phallocentrism." *Gender and Society* 8, no. 3 (1994): 363–377.

————. "The Viagra Phenomenon." *Sexualities* 9, no. 3 (2006): 273–294.

Torres, Alberto. "Marcha por la Paz inicia en Cuernavaca, Morelos." *El Universal*, May 5, 2011. http://www.eluniversal.com.mx/notas/763477.html.

Tovar-Guzmán, Víctor, Carlos Hernández-Girón, Olga López-Rios, and Eduardo C. Lazcano-Ponce. "Prostate Cancer Mortality Trends in Mexico, 1980–1995." *Prostate* 39, no. 1 (1999): 23–27.

van der Geest, Sjaak. "'No Strength': Sex and Old Age in a Rural Town in Ghana." *Social Science and Medicine* 53, no. 10 (2001): 1383–1396.

van Wolputte, Steven. "Hang On to Your Self: Of Bodies, Embodiment, and Selves." *Annual Review of Anthropology* 33 (2004): 251–269.

Varley, Ann, and Maribel Blasco. "Exiled to the Home: Masculinity and Ageing in Urban Mexico." *European Journal of Development Research* 12, no. 2 (2000): 115–138.

Vasconcelos, José. *The Cosmic Race: A Bilingual Edition.* Translated by Didier T. Jaén. Baltimore, MD: Johns Hopkins University Press, 1997.

Walsh, Patrick C., and Pieter J. Donker. "Impotence Following Radical Prostatectomy: Insight into Etiology and Prevention." *Journal of Urology* 167, no. 2 (2002): 1005–1010.

Walter, Nicholas, Philippe Bourgois, and H. Margarita Loinaz. "Masculinity and Undocumented Labor Migration: Injured Latino Day Laborers in San Francisco." *Social Science and Medicine* 59 (2004): 1159–1168.

Weinhardt, Lance S., Andrew D. Forsyth, Michael P. Carey, Beth C. Jaworski, and Lauren E. Durant. "Reliability and Validity of Self-Report Measures of HIV-Related Sexual Behavior: Progress Since 1990 and Recommendations for Research and Practice." *Archives of Sexual Behavior* 27, no. 2 (1998): 155–180.

Wentzell, Emily. "Mexico: Viagra and Changing Masculinities." In *Men of the Global South: A Reader,* edited by Adam Jones, 43–46. London: Zed Books, 2006.

——. "Imagining Impotence in America: From Men's Deeds to Men's Minds to Viagra." *Michigan Discussions in Anthropology* 25 (2008): 153–178.

Wentzell, Emily, and Jorge Salmerón. "Prevalence of Erectile Dysfunction and Its Treatment in a Mexican Population: Distinguishing between Erectile Function Change and Dysfunction." *Journal of Men's Health* 6, no. 1 (2009a): 56–62.

——. "You'll 'Get Viagraed': Mexican Men's Preference for Alternative Erectile Dysfunction Treatment." *Social Science and Medicine* 68, no. 10 (2009b): 1759–1765.

Williams, Simon J. "Chronic Illness as Biographical Disruption or Biographical Disruption as Chronic Illness? Reflections on a Core Concept." *Sociology of Health and Illness* 22, no. 1 (2000): 40–67.

Wilson, Duff. "As Generics Near, Makers Tweak Erectile Drugs." *New York Times,* April 13, 2011.

Wilson, Peter W. F., Ralph B. D'Agostino, Daniel Levy, Albert M. Belanger, Halit Silbershatz, and William B. Kannel. "Prediction of Coronary Heart Disease Using Risk Factor Categories." *Circulation* 97 (1998): 1837–1847.

Index

105–6, 108; social issues and, 87, 89, 93, 96–97, 101–2, 104, 106–8; stress and, 86–88, 91–94, 97, 99–100, 102, 105; structural causes of, 98–101; symptoms and, 81, 86–97, 101–3, 124–25, 127, 130, 135, 138–39, 142–48, 156, 165, 176; treatments and, 101–4; wives and, 90–97, 104, 106, 117, 119. *See also* Specific type

Cialis (tadalafil): advertising of, 168, 169f; erectile dysfunction treatment and, 5, 7, 69, 138, 151, 154, 158–59, 168, 169f; Lilly-ICOS and, 168, 169f

Clarke, Adele E., 25, 136

Cleary, Edward L., 77

Clinics: changing bodies and, 12, 15, 21; chronic illnesses and, 105; erectile dysfunction treatments and, 157, 160–61, 165, 168; family medicine and, 15, 18, 94, 112

Clinton, Bill, 56n3

Coca-Cola, 12, 99–101, 149

Collado-Ardón, Rolando, 87

Colostomy, 106–7

Communication: *confianza* (trust) and, 18–21, 114–15, 157; importance of, 174; marriage and, 11, 40, 57–58, 71–73, 75, 141, 173–74; open, 71–72; status and, 17

Composite masculinities: advantages of composite approach and, 181–85; chronic illnesses and, 87–88, 100, 104–9; concept of, 26–33; cultural issues and, 162–66, 169–72, 175–76, 180–84; erectile dysfunction treatment and, 111–12, 121–22, 134, 136–37, 146, 150–57, 162–66, 169–72, 175–76, 180–84; Johnny and, 29–32; medicalization and, 164–66; Mexicanness and, 36–40, 43, 46, 48, 51, 53, 55–59; relationships and, 60–67, 71–72, 74, 77–81, 84–85

Confianza (trust), 18–21, 114–15, 157

Congress, E. P., 93

Connell, R. W., 25, 181

Conquistadors, 3, 42, 45

Conrad, Peter, 164

Contraception, 11

Criminals, 35

Crohn's disease, 106–7

Cuernavaca, Mexico, 1, 7, 9, 152, 154; drug advertising in 166, 168; growth of, 82; hospital field site and, 11–15; IMSS health care and, 112, 114–15, 157; Peralta and, 69; private practice and, 157–60; resettlement and, 12; urbanization of, 12, 131; as vacation site, 11–12, 15; wages in 63

Cultural issues: advantages of composite approach and, 181–85; advertising and, 166–69; aging and, 33, 175–79 (*see also* Aging); American comedies and, 172; ancestral rape and, 3; anthropology and, 11, 19–25, 28, 42, 87, 136, 181; barriers to discussing sexual issues and, 12, 17–18, 22; being a good provider and, 38, 49, 156; changes over time and, 162–85; changing bodies and, 3–7, 10–11, 19, 24–25, 27, 32–33; changing ideals in, 10–11, 162–85; children and, 178; chronic illnesses and, 94, 96, 108; context-dependent ideals for marital sex and, 173–75; emotions and, 163, 168, 170–83; erectile dysfunction treatments and, 114, 130–34, 139; failure and, 38–39, 44, 64, 71, 81, 104–5, 107, 137, 139–43, 146–47, 150, 152–53, 155–57, 181; food and, 101; gender roles and, 23, 31–33, 38, 43, 59, 68, 164, 178; good providers and, 37, 60, 62–63, 66, 83–84, 139, 155; homosexuality and, 16, 47, 126, 174; husbands and, 170, 172–81; identity and, 27, 36, 41–43, 45, 59, 172; *Instituto Mexicano del Seguro Social (IMSS)* and, 162–65, 170, 173–74, 177, 180; *machismo* and, 3, 6, 10, 23, 28, 33, 36, 41–43, 46–51, 58–60, 85, 166, 168–70, 173, 175, 182–83; *machistas* and, 33, 45–46, 48, 121, 168, 172; macho behavior and, 6, 10, 19, 35–51, 59–60, 77, 79, 166, 168–73, 182; marriage and, 10–11, 168–81; masculinities and, 3 (*see also* Masculinities);

Cultural issues (continued)
  Mexicanness and, 35–36 (*see also*
    Mexicanness); open secrets and, 12;
    paternal differences and, 171–73;
    patterns of change over time, 169–73;
    penis and, 3–4, 29; psychological issues
    and, 164–65, 178; purity and, 35; *la raza*
    and, 42; relationships and, 61, 63, 68, 70,
    77; retirement and, 13–14, 35, 37–46,
    53–56, 64, 68–69, 71–72, 74, 77, 79,
    90–95, 98–105, 117–31, 138, 140, 149,
    154–55, 171, 177; social issues and,
    162–66, 170, 181–85; status and, 1–2, 5,
    17, 30–31, 47–48, 67, 116, 143, 146, 159;
    stereotypes and, 19–20, 60; *telenovelas*
    and, 172; wives and, 162–80
Cysts, 118

Death: body acceleration drugs and,
    119–21; cancer and, 86; cardiovascular
    disease and, 10, 90; chronic illnesses
    and, 86, 89–90, 119; diabetes and, 10, 89;
    relationships and, 78; thinking of, 1;
    Viagra and, 119–20
DeLamater, John D., 3
De la Peña, Ricardo, 11, 174
Demetriou, Demetrakis Z., 25
De Oliveira, Orlandina, 43
Depression: changing bodies and, 1–2, 31;
    chronic illnesses and, 94–95, 105;
    erectile function treatments and, 142,
    152, 155–56; relationships and, 62, 65
Diabetes: alcohol and, 104–5; amputation
    and, 89; biomedical understandings of,
    89–92; blindness and, 89; blood sugar
    and, 89, 102–3, 123, 128, 131, 147; bodily
    changes and, 29, 90, 102, 105, 138; as
    cancer, 102–3; cardiovascular disease
    and, 88–90, 125; coma and, 89;
    composite perspective on, 86, 88–95,
    97–105; death and, 10, 89; diet and,
    98–99; as disease of development, 92;
    emotions and, 93–95, 97, 104, 155; as
    epidemic, 10, 89; erectile dysfunction
    and, 56, 89, 100, 102, 119, 122–30, 134,

138, 143, 145, 147–49, 154–55; food and,
    99, 103–6, 127–28, 149; genetics and, 97,
    101; headaches and, 102; heart attacks
    and, 125; infections and, 105; infidelities
    and, 67; insulin and, 89–90, 100;
    kidneys and, 89–92, 102; lifestyle and,
    90, 97–100, 103–5, 122, 127–28, 149;
    medicine and, 83, 99, 103–4, 123, 134;
    National Diabetes Information
    Clearinghouse and, 89; National
    Institute of Diabetes and Digestive and
    Kidney Diseases and, 89–90, 92;
    persistent wounds and, 89; poor health
    care and, 148; relationships and, 66–67,
    82–83, 119; sex and, 56, 66–67; tobacco
    and, 98; type 2, 18, 82, 86, 89–93, 123,
    147; urban men and, 89; vascular system
    damage and, 88
Diarrhea, 106
Díaz, Porfirio, 179n1
Diet. *See* Food
Dionísio, 77–78
Divorce, 72–73, 82, 132, 151, 155, 179
Donker, Pieter J., 88
Dow, James W., 77
Drugs: advertising of, 9–10, 79, 80f, 160,
    166–69; alternative treatments and, 124,
    128–29; choosing right treatment and,
    126–33; chronic illnesses and, 90, 97;
    Cialis, 5, 7, 69, 138, 151, 154, 158–59, 168,
    169f; complexity of human body and,
    110, 123–26, 129, 164, 183; composite
    masculinities and, 164–66; context-
    dependent effects of, 149–53; danger of,
    117–22, 130; economic issues and, 5, 7,
    134, 139, 145, 161; fear of, 110–35; federal
    law and, 115; free, 7, 115; herbal
    treatments and, 7–9, 113, 127–31, 135;
    hypertension and, 126, 130; IMSS
    patient population and, 112–14;
    inappropriateness of, 111, 117–22;
    Levitra, 5, 7, 120, 127; marijuana, 35;
    marketing differences and, 166–69;
    narcos and, 15; naturopathic remedies
    and, 7, 103; as oversimplistic solutions,

122–26; pain, 127; Patrex, 166–68; pharmacies and, 5, 7–9, 23, 115, 129; private practice and, 157–61; Prozac, 176; regulation of, 6; rejection of erectile dysfunction treatments and, 110–35; relationships and, 65, 67, 69, 77, 81; side effects and, 9, 65, 113, 120, 129, 145, 176; stimulants and, 58, 132; structural disencentives for using, 114–16; trafficking of, 15; treatment context and, 136–40, 142, 144–47, 149–54, 157–61; truck drivers and, 58; Viagra, 5–7, 9f, 10, 67, 69, 79, 80f, 83, 110–12, 119–21, 124, 128–29, 135, 138, 144, 146, 151, 154, 166–68; youth and, 77

Drug violence, 15

Drunkenness, 35, 49, 78, 105

Economic issues: advertising and, 9–10, 79, 80f, 160, 166–69; children and, 141; chronic illnesses and, 98–99; drugs and, 7, 134, 139, 145, 161; erectile dysfunction treatment and, 7, 113, 134, 139, 145, 161; federal law and, 115; fiscal solvency and, 38, 55; food and, 38, 99; global crisis and, 15; good providers and, 37, 60, 62–63, 66, 83–84, 139, 155; herbal treatments and, 9; inequality and, 7; injections and, 161; *Instituto Mexicano del Seguro Social (IMSS)* and, 13–14, 115; masculinities and, 55, 137, 146–47, 162–63, 182; medical treatment and, 124; Mexico and, 115; monetary gifts and, 62–63; peso value and, 7; poor providers and, 30; prostitution and, 63; status and, 1–2, 5, 17, 30–31, 47–48, 67, 116, 143, 146, 159; stress and, 141; unemployment and, 48, 142, 155, 173; upheavals and, 14–15; women and, 11, 62–63; worker wages and, 77

Education, 17; lack of, 48; pharmaceutical companies and, 159; providers and, 38, 49, 156; school and, 14, 56n3, 130, 141, 179; self-help, 153; sexuality and, 152, 168–69; status and, 48; traditional

gender roles and, 178; treatment regimes and, 156; women and, 11, 14

Ejaculation: premature, 62, 160, 175–76; rapid, 82, 175; retrograde, 92, 126

Emotions: aging and, 54–56; anger, 46–47, 93–95, 102, 105, 125, 127; anxiety, 63, 97; arguments and, 2, 10, 30–31, 49, 76, 82, 181; children and, 154–56; chronic illnesses and, 67, 87–105, 108; *confianza* (trust) and, 18–21, 114–55, 127; cultural issues and, 163, 168, 170–83; depression, 1–2, 31, 62, 65, 94–95, 105, 142, 152, 155–56; diabetes and, 93–95, 97, 104, 155; distant children and, 154–56; erectile dysfunction and, 110–11, 112n1, 116, 121, 123, 126, 130–32, 134, 137–57, 161, 163, 168, 170–83; fear, 2, 16, 19, 29–31 (*see also* Fear); happiness, 22–23, 31 (*see also* Happiness); hot tempers and, 97, 105, 119, 125; hypertension and, 94–95, 104; loneliness and, 154–57; *machismo* and, 3 (*see also* Machismo); masculinities and, 3–4, 7, 19, 26–29, 32, 38, 40–42, 44–45, 51, 54–59; maturity and, 54–56; negative, 63–64, 67, 87–88, 93, 95, 98, 100, 103, 116, 123, 138, 142–43, 148, 151–53; nerves and, 24, 88, 92–95, 97, 138, 140–41, 145; pain and, 93; passion and, 43, 171–72, 175–76, 178, 180; positive, 137; psychological issues and, 164–65, 178 (*see also* Psychological issues); rage, 93–95; relationships and, 61–79, 82–84; sadness, 50–51, 65, 68, 71, 94–95, 102, 105, 142, 146, 148, 150, 152, 159, 164, 177, 179; self esteem and, 83–84, 143; shame, 18, 42, 47, 53, 87–88, 92, 106–7, 114, 141, 150–52, 158, 166, 175; stress and, 4 (*see also* Stress); women and, 31, 179

Enfermedad (sickness), 92

Erectile dysfunction: advertising and, 9–10, 79, 80f, 160, 166–69; alternative treatments and, 124, 128–29; anthropology and, 11, 19–25, 28, 42, 87, 136, 181; assessment of as composite object,

Heart disease. *See* Cardiovascular disease

Herbal treatments, 7–9, 113, 128–31, 135

Herdt, Gilbert, 20

Herman, W. H., 10

Himcaps, 7, 113

Holistic medicine: chronic illnesses and, 103, 108; erectile dysfunction treatments and, 115–16, 133–34, 137, 142–44, 158, 163, 165, 184; status and, 116

Homosexuals, 16, 47, 126, 174, 178

Hospitals: brief appointments and, 18; *Centro Medico Nacional la Raza* and, 42; checkups and, 35, 48, 55, 75; choosing right treatment and, 126–33; chronic illnesses and, 89, 98–100, 106; clinics and, 12, 15, 21, 105, 157, 160–61, 165, 168; composite masculinities and, 26, 32, 42, 48, 55, 64–65, 69; *confianza* (trust) and, 18–21, 114; Cuernavaca and, 1, 7, 9, 11–15, 63, 69, 82, 112, 114–15, 131, 152, 154, 157–60, 166, 168; erectile dysfunction treatments and, 112–17, 131, 134, 143–45, 148, 150, 154, 156, 158–59, 163, 165, 177; family medicine and, 15, 18, 94, 112; government-run, 2, 7; high patient load and, 16, 18; IMSS and, 12 (*see also Instituto Mexicano del Seguro Social (IMSS)*; long waits at, 13, 16, 18; Mexicanness and, 42, 48, 55; nurses and, 2, 15, 24–25, 30–31, 112n1, 177, 180; physicians and, 9, 13, 15–21, 23–25, 28–30, 33, 45, 53, 61, 64, 69, 75, 78–79; private practice and, 15, 17–18, 81, 113, 116, 131, 157–61, 176; referral-based services and, 13; resources and, 13; specialization and, 15; standard of care in, 17; study ethics and, 23–24; urology department and, 1–2, 12 (*see also* Urology); waiting rooms and, 10, 13, 16, 18

Hotness (*caliente*): emotional, 97, 105, 119, 125; humoral notion of, 44n2, 88, 96–97; sexual, 9, 43–46, 64, 97, 119, 166

Housework, 38, 179

Huerta Rojas, Fernando, 3

Hugo, 47, 57–58

Humoral notions: balance and, 88, 96–98, 108, 123, 125–27, 129–30, 133–34, 176; chronic illnesses and, 88, 95–98, 108, 110, 123–26, 130, 134, 142, 183; erectile dysfunction treatment and, 110, 123–26, 130, 134, 142, 183; hotness and, 44n2, 88, 96–97

Husbands: arguments and, 2, 10, 30–31, 49, 76, 82, 181; bad, 2, 20, 30, 53, 67; chronic illnesses and, 93, 97; communication and, 40, 57–58, 71–73, 75, 141, 173–74; cultural issues and, 170, 172–81; erectile dysfunction treatment and, 127, 138, 155, 170, 172–81; good, 40, 67, 84, 172; masculinities and, 35, 37, 40–41, 51, 53, 66–76, 79, 83–84; Mexicanness and, 35, 37, 40–41, 51, 53; as providers, 37–38, 49, 60, 62–63, 66, 83–84, 139, 155; relationships and, 66–76, 79, 83–84; responsibility and, 30, 37–41, 45–53, 59, 63, 66–67, 85, 105, 119, 122, 139–41, 154–56, 163, 168, 170, 176; unfaithfulness and, 28, 44–46, 51, 53, 56, 70, 81, 84, 93, 117, 166, 173; wives helping revive masculinities of, 71–76

Hygiene, 42, 119

Hypertension: cardiovascular disease and, 90–91; chronic illnesses and, 90–91, 94–95, 97; drugs for, 126, 130; emotions and, 94–95, 104; erectile dysfunction and, 119, 125–27, 130, 138, 140, 145, 154, 180; lifestyle and, 97; nerves and, 94; tranquility and, 104

Identity: bachelorhood and, 106–7; good providers and, 37, 60, 62–63, 66, 83–84, 139, 155; masculinities and, 2 (*see also* Masculinities); Mexicanness and, 27, 36, 41–43, 45, 59, 172; self esteem and, 83–84, 143; selfhood and, 21, 25–26, 28–29, 48, 50, 54–55, 87, 105–6, 108, 136, 140, 153, 165, 178–85; status and, 1–2, 5, 17, 30–31, 47–48, 67, 116, 143, 146, 159

Illich, Ivan, 164

marketing and, 161; relationships and, 64; semen and, 92, 126; urination difficulties and, 18, 29, 65, 72, 86, 89, 91–92, 148; vacuum pumps and, 62, 125, 154

Penson, David F., 92

Pepe, 65–68, 93

Peralta, Dr., 69, 81–84, 158–59, 176

Petryna, Adriana, 136

Pfizer, 79, 80f

Pharmaceuticals: advertising of, 9–10, 79, 80f, 160, 166–69; medicine and, 120, 123, 125. *See also* Drugs

Pharmacies, 5, 7–9, 23, 115, 129

Phillips, M., 89

Physical strength, 39, 51–52, 87, 95, 141–42

Physicians: brief appointments and, 18; checkups and, 35, 48, 55, 75; choosing right treatment and, 126–33; chronic illnesses and, 87, 94–97, 99, 102–3, 105, 107; clinics and, 12, 15, 21, 105, 157, 160–61, 165, 168; composite masculinities and, 28–30, 33, 45, 53, 61, 64, 69, 75, 78–79, 81–84; *confianza* (trust) and, 18–21, 114; discrepant test results and, 28; erectile dysfunction and, 112–18, 124–25, 130–34, 140–48, 154–62, 165–69, 173, 176; family medicine and, 15, 18, 94, 112; fear of questioning, 17; female, 16, 19; interviews of, 23; office brochures and, 9; patient load and, 16–18; private practice and, 15, 17–18, 81, 113, 116, 131, 157–61, 176; public consultations and, 23–24; referral-based services and, 13; specialization and, 15, 160

Pimentel-Nieto, Diana, 10

Potts, Annie, 6, 19

Powersex, 7, 8f

Pregnancy, 72

Prieur, Annick, 20

Private practice: drugs and, 157–61; erectile dysfunction treatment and, 157–61; physicians and, 15, 17–18, 81, 113, 116, 131, 157–61, 176

Prostate, 74, 102; cancer of, 18, 86, 89, 91–92, 114, 118, 138; checkups and, 35, 55, 75; enlargement of, 18, 57–58, 86, 89, 91–92, 94, 100, 114, 118, 125, 129, 148; exams of, 16, 55, 76; genital nerves and, 88; heat and, 96; high sexual activity and, 97; medicine and, 123; operations on, 2, 24, 46, 48, 53, 64–65, 92, 94, 97, 105, 119, 126, 138, 141, 143, 154; prevalence of ailments of, 91–96; retrograde ejaculation and, 126; urinary pain and, 18; vitamins and, 144; work stress and, 100

Prostitutes, 20, 50, 56n3, 60–66, 84, 107, 119

Protestantism, 14–15, 77

Providers, 37, 38, 49, 60, 62–63, 66, 83–84, 139, 155

Prozac, 176

Psychological issues, 9, 48, 64; chronic illnesses and, 90–94; cultural issues and, 164–65, 178; erectile dysfunction treatment and, 116, 118, 124, 142–47, 150, 153; nerves and, 24, 88, 92–95, 97, 138, 140–41, 145

Rage, 93–95

Ramirez, Dr., 159

Ramirez, Josué, 11, 43, 171

Rape, 3, 35, 42

Rasmussen, Susan, 5

Ratsch, Christian, 4

Rebhun, L. A., 93

Rectal exams, 16, 174

Relationships: advertising and, 166–69; aging and, 66–67, 69–70, 74–75; *amiguitas* and, 62, 66–68; arguments and, 2, 10, 30–31, 49, 76, 82, 181; bachelorhood and, 106–7; cars and, 152; children and, 65, 72–79, 82, 154–56, 170–72; communication and, 11, 40, 57–58, 71–73, 75, 141, 173–74; cultural issues and, 61, 63, 68, 70, 77; death and, 78; diabetes and, 66–67, 82–83, 119; drugs and, 65, 67, 69, 77, 81; emotions

and, 28; mature masculinities and, 71–75; Mexicanness and, 35–41, 44–59; narcos and, 15; relationships and, 60–77, 79, 81–83; responsibility and, 154; reviving husband's masculinities and, 71–76; unfaithfulness and, 28, 44–46, 51, 53, 56, 61, 70, 81, 84, 93, 117, 166, 173

Womanizers, 35, 54, 56

Womb, 31

Women: aging and, 173, 175; *amiguitas* and, 62, 66–68; attraction to, 1, 53, 140; autonomy and, 179; birth and, 30–31, 37n1, 49, 52, 54; cars and, 152; chronic illnesses and, 106; communication and, 11, 19, 22; contraception and, 11; domestic violence and, 46–47, 171; economic issues and, 62–63; education and, 11, 14; egalitarian views and, 170; emotions and, 31, 179; as equals, 48; extramarital affairs and, 40–41, 44, 49, 51, 54–55, 60–67, 79, 121, 153–54, 168, 175, 180; frigid, 64, 68–71, 149; hierarchical roles and, 11; housework and, 38, 179; increasing economic participation of, 11; lubrication and, 117, 180; marriage and, 11, 172 (*see also* Marriage); masculinities and, 27, 45, 48; menopause and, 68, 70, 119–20; mothers, 13, 19, 42, 46, 62–63, 66–67, 82, 101, 132, 171, 174–75, 178–79; nonsexual love and, 2, 54; as objects, 46–47, 179;

place of in home, 51; pregnancy and, 72; prostitutes and, 20, 50, 56n3, 60–66, 84, 107, 119; rape and, 3, 35, 42; relationships and, 33, 62–69, 73–74, 82, 170, 181; self-sufficient, 179; sex and, 2 (*see also* Sex); sleeping around with, 35, 43–45, 54–58, 62, 73, 117–18, 127, 132, 139, 166, 178–79; stated/imagined needs of, 68–71; subordination of, 42; survival strategies and, 62–63; unfaithful, 70–71, 173; work and, 38–39, 48, 66

Work: being a good provider and, 37, 60, 62–63, 66, 83–84, 139, 155; hard, 37–38, 48, 50, 55, 139; housework and, 38, 179; inability to, 1, 38, 105; migration and, 3, 32, 51, 107; obsession with, 51; pride in, 37; responsibility and, 30, 37–41, 45–53, 59, 63, 66–67, 85, 105, 119, 122, 139–41, 154–56, 163, 168, 170, 176; retirement and, 13–14, 35, 37–46, 53–56, 64, 68–69, 71–72, 74, 77, 79, 90–95, 98–105, 117–31, 138, 140, 149, 154–55, 171, 177; women and, 38–39, 48, 66

Youthful masculinities; looking back on, 98, 106, 111–12, 118–21, 126, 143, 163, 166, 168, 170–72, 182–83 (*see also* Aging); Mexicanness and, 33, 36, 50–59; relationships and, 60–61, 65–67, 71, 73, 77–79